Taxcafe.co.uk Tax Guides

Using a Property Company to Save Tax

By Carl Bayley BSc FCA

Important Legal Notices:

Taxcafe®
TAX GUIDE - 'Using a Property Company to Save Tax'

Published by:
Taxcafe UK Limited
67 Milton Road
Kirkcaldy
KY1 1TL
Tel: (01592) 560081
Email address: team@taxcafe.co.uk

Sixteenth Edition, December 2020
ISBN 978-1-911020-63-9

Disclaimer
Before reading or relying on the content of this Tax Guide please read the disclaimer.

Disclaimer

1. Please note that this publication is intended as **general guidance** only and does NOT constitute accountancy, tax, financial or other professional advice. The author and Taxcafe UK Limited make no representations or warranties with respect to the accuracy or completeness of the contents of this publication and cannot accept any responsibility for any liability, loss or risk, personal or otherwise, which may arise, directly or indirectly, from reliance on information contained in this publication.

2. Please note that tax legislation, the law and practices of government and regulatory authorities (e.g. HM Revenue and Customs) are constantly changing. Furthermore, your personal circumstances may vary from the general information contained in this tax guide which may not be suitable for your situation. We therefore recommend that for accountancy, tax, financial or other professional advice, you consult a suitably qualified accountant, tax specialist, independent financial adviser, or other professional adviser who will be able to provide specific advice based on your personal circumstances.

3. This guide covers UK taxation only and any references to 'tax' or 'taxation', unless the contrary is expressly stated, refer to UK taxation only. Please note that references to the 'UK' do not include the Channel Islands or the Isle of Man. Foreign tax implications are beyond the scope of this guide.

4. While in an effort to be helpful this tax guide may refer to general guidance on matters other than UK taxation, Taxcafe UK Limited and the author are not expert in these matters and do not accept any responsibility or liability for loss which may arise from reliance on such information contained in this guide.

5. Please note that Taxcafe UK Limited has relied wholly on the expertise of the author in the preparation of the content of this tax guide. The author is not an employee of Taxcafe UK Limited but has been selected by Taxcafe UK Limited using reasonable care and skill.

6. The views expressed in this publication are the author's own personal views and do not necessarily reflect the views of any organisation which he may represent.

About the Author

Carl Bayley is the author of a series of 'Plain English' tax guides designed specifically for the layman and the non-specialist. Carl's particular speciality is his ability to take the weird, complex and inexplicable world of taxation and set it out in the kind of clear, straightforward language taxpayers themselves can understand. As he often says himself, "My job is to translate 'tax' into English."

Carl enjoys his role as a tax author, as he explains, "Writing these guides gives me the opportunity to use the skills and knowledge learned over more than thirty years in the tax profession for the benefit of a wider audience. The most satisfying part of my success as an author is the chance to give the average person the same standard of advice as the 'big guys' at a price everyone can afford."

Carl takes the same approach when speaking on taxation, a role he frequently undertakes with great enthusiasm, including his highly acclaimed annual 'Budget Breakfast' for the Institute of Chartered Accountants.

In addition to being a recognised author and speaker, Carl has often spoken on taxation on radio and television, including the BBC's 'It's Your Money' programme and BBC Radio 2's Jeremy Vine Show.

Carl began his career as a Chartered Accountant in 1983 with one of the 'Big 4' accountancy firms. After qualifying as a double prize-winner, he immediately began specialising in tax. He worked for several major international firms until beginning the new millennium by launching his own practice, through which he provided advice on a wide variety of tax issues; especially property taxation, inheritance tax, and tax planning for small and medium-sized businesses, for twenty years, before deciding to focus exclusively on his favourite role as author and presenter.

Carl is a former Chairman of the Tax Faculty of the Institute of Chartered Accountants in England and Wales and a member of the Institute's governing Council. He is also a former President of ICAEW Scotland and member of the ICAEW Board. He has co-organised the annual Practical Tax Conference for the last eighteen years.

When he isn't working, Carl takes on the equally taxing challenges of hill walking and creative writing: his Munro tally is now 105 and he is currently waiting for someone to have the wisdom to publish his first novel, while he eagerly works on the next three.

Carl lives in the Scottish Borders, where he enjoys spending time with his partner, Linda. He has three children and his first grandchild is now on the way.

Dedication & Thanks

A Special Dedication

Normally, as regular readers will know, I like to dedicate my books to my family, past, present... and those who will brighten my future.

This time, however, I would like to dedicate this book to the heroes working for the NHS, in care homes all over the UK, and elsewhere on the front line helping to keep our country running, and to keep us all safe: you have my thanks, my eternal gratitude, and my deepest admiration.

As for my family, past, present and future, you are of course still in my thoughts.

Lastly, I could not close this dedication without mentioning my partner Linda, who is one of those heroes. Bless you princess, I'm so proud of you.

Thanks
Thanks to the Taxcafe team, past and present, for their help in making these books more successful than I could ever have dreamed.

I would like to thank my old friend and mentor, Peter Rayney, for his inspiration and for showing me that tax and humour can mix. Thanks also to Rebecca, Paul and David for taking me into the 'fold' at the Tax Faculty and for their fantastic support at our Practical Tax Conference over many years.

And last, but far from least, thanks to Nick for giving me the push!

C.B., Roxburghshire, December 2020

To Our Readers
At this difficult time, the author and Taxcafe would like to offer our very best wishes to all our readers and their families and friends.

Contents

Foreword

By the author

This sixteenth edition of *'Using a Property Company to Save Tax'* comes at a time of great difficulty, uncertainty, and stress to us all. At the time of writing, the coronavirus crisis is still at a critical stage. If you are reading this guide many months, or even years, from now, you may be puzzled by the odd comment written in the context of the current situation. Hopefully, from your point of view, it is all just a bad memory.

Naturally, this edition is fully updated for all the technical changes in property taxation, and company taxation, that have taken place, including temporary changes made in response to the coronavirus crisis and the 'window of opportunity' this may provide for those looking to transfer property into their own company in the near future. That 'window of opportunity' may be further enhanced by current market conditions, which could mean even greater savings are available in some cases. We will look at the impact of the current, hopefully temporary, reduction in some property values later in the guide.

However, this guide is also about long-term planning opportunities for property investors using a company. Hence, while we cannot ignore the fact the current situation is somewhat different to usual, when we come to look at long-term predictions, it makes sense to assume what we all hope: namely that the private rented sector, other property businesses, and property values, will all swiftly recover from this crisis and return to more normal patterns of growth, rental yield, etc, before very long.

Nonetheless, while we hope the commercial situation will return to a more normal position in the near future, it is also likely the tax environment will change significantly as a result of the coronavirus crisis. However, while it is highly likely significant tax changes will take place, it is impossible to predict exactly what those changes will be, or when they will happen. Hence, since there is now so much uncertainty about potential future tax changes, I have decided to take a two-pronged approach in this edition of the guide.

Firstly, for the majority of the guide, I have simply based my calculations on the current tax regime, assuming no future tax changes. While I am certain there **will** be significant changes in the future, using the current regime gives us a solid 'base' from which to make our analysis of the tax-saving potential of using a company.

Those potential tax savings arise not because of the company tax regime alone, in isolation, but because of the differences between the company tax regime and the personal tax regime. The Government is generally keen to maintain a balance between the personal and company tax regimes, so it is not unreasonable to suppose most future tax changes will

1

have a broadly similar impact on both regimes overall. Hence, the opportunity to save tax by using a property company should remain broadly the same.

Secondly, however, there are a few pointers about some of the future tax changes we may see, and it is worth taking a look at these and their potential impact on property companies. There is also the possibility some future tax changes may be specifically targeted at property companies, or small companies and their owners in general. For this edition, I have therefore added a new chapter to take a more detailed look at the potential consequences of some of the more likely future tax changes, including recommendations made by the Office for Tax Simplification (yes, there really is such a thing) regarding potential changes to Capital Gains Tax, in a report issued in November 2020.

Combining these two approaches should, I believe, give property investors as much guidance on the long-term implications of using a property company as it is possible to give.

People in the UK have invested in property for centuries, but substantial increases in personal wealth and disposable income over the last few decades, together with problems in other areas of investment, have made property investment an important area of personal financial planning. I personally believe the property investment sector as we know it today is here to stay. Naturally, the sector will have its ups and downs, as any business sector does, but the philosophy of property investment as a 'career move', or a 'pension plan', is now so well entrenched it is impossible to imagine it could ever disappear altogether.

In 2002, in response to the huge demand for advice on property taxation we had been experiencing at Taxcafe.co.uk, we published the first edition of *'How to Save Property Tax'*, the sister publication to this guide. In the following years, the demand for property taxation advice continued to grow at a phenomenal pace and is responsible for the fact our first guide is now in its twenty-fifth edition and this guide in its sixteenth.

But it isn't just the *quantity* of advice demanded we have seen increase, it is also the level or, if you like, the *quality* of advice.

We have also seen a huge broadening in the type of activities undertaken by the typical property 'investor', many of whom will now, at least partly, be classed as property developers, dealers, or managers. This guide, along with its sister publication, has evolved in line with our readership, and caters for the whole range of property businesses our readers undertake.

As I have already suggested, many people now enter the property investment business as a profession, or a means to save for retirement. This 'new breed' of property investor is entering the market with a much higher degree of sophistication and is prepared to devote substantial time and resources to the business. Almost every one of these 'professional investors' asks me the same question, "Should I use a company?" Very often, they are hoping for a nice, simple, single-word answer and, being the helpful chap I am, I give them one, "Maybe!"

Being an accountant, you may think my slightly evasive response is merely a ploy to enable me to earn more fees from consultancy work. However, you would be wrong, as 'maybe' is the only answer I could possibly give. This question is not an easy one to answer. There are a huge number of factors to be taken into account, not all of which relate to taxation, and it is therefore impossible (not to mention inadvisable) to simply give a straightforward 'yes' or 'no' answer. (And, in any case, I have retired from consultancy work now anyway!)

The first aim of this guide, though, *is* to answer that question, not in a single word, but in the many thousands of words that, in reality, the answer to this highly complex question actually requires. So, to provide you with a truly thorough answer to this crucial question, we will begin, in Chapters 1 and 2, by looking at the basic tax (and non-tax) implications of using a company.

The UK tax regime for companies is quite different to that applying to individuals, or indeed to partnerships, trusts or other potential investment vehicles. The company tax regime has a few quirks, which can prove to be costly traps for the unwary. It is therefore extremely important any property investor considering the company route understands what they are getting themselves into.

In Chapters 3 to 8, we will move on to a more detailed look at the taxation of UK property companies. Here we will discover there are several different types of property companies and each gives rise to a different set of tax implications that need to be considered carefully by the prospective corporate property investor.

Chapter 9 covers the crucial issue of how and when to extract funds from your company tax efficiently: something almost every property company owner will want to do sooner or later, and which has a profound impact on how beneficial your company will be.

Chapter 10 provides a summarised comparison of the tax position of companies and individuals. Following that, in Chapter 11, we take a detailed look at the factors involved in making the decision whether to use a company, and their implications for the property investor. This is illustrated throughout by several examples designed to highlight the key issues.

In Chapter 12 we will begin to apply what we have learned so far by focussing on one of the most important benefits of using a property company: interest relief.

As most readers will know, individual residential property investors are now subject to restrictions on the rate of relief available for interest and finance costs. These restrictions are covered in detail in the Taxcafe.co.uk guides *'How to Save Property Tax'* and *'The Big Landlord Tax Increase'*, although we will also take a brief look at them in Chapter 12 of this guide.

Companies are not subject to these restrictions: providing a major benefit to investors running a residential property letting business through a company. (A separate set of restrictions do apply to companies: but these only apply to annual interest costs in excess of £2m.)

Furthermore, on top of this, individual landlords can only set interest and finance costs against their rental income: often leading to rental losses or surplus unrelieved interest that can generally only be carried forward and cannot usually be set off against other income or even capital gains on the same property.

A further benefit for a property investor using a company is the ability to set interest on funds borrowed for a company's property investments against other income or capital gains within the company, or even the investor's own salary, personal rental profits, or other income.

In Chapter 12 we will see the difference this treatment of interest costs can make to a property investor over many years as the economic cycle produces both short-term losses and long-term gains.

Reaching a Conclusion

In the end, only **you** can decide whether a property company is appropriate for you: by undertaking a detailed examination of your individual position and weighing up all the factors involved.

My aim in this guide is to enable you to reach that unique individual conclusion and make a well-informed decision, armed with a strong understanding of the many issues you need to consider.

Whether you're one of those 'professional investors' I referred to earlier, or one of the many 'gifted amateurs' I frequently meet; whether you see your property business as your pension plan or just a good way to supplement your income; whether you're developing, dealing, managing or just renting out your properties; whether you've always had a master plan or you stumbled into property investment by accident; in fact, whatever your circumstances may be, this guide will help you understand the questions you need to ask yourself before you can make a truly informed decision about whether to use a property company or not.

And 'yes' or 'no' are not the only answers to the property company question you may come up with. Many property investors decide the answer for them is 'partly' or 'later'.

There is absolutely nothing to stop an investor running two property businesses in parallel: one as an individual and one through a company. Many investors also find the best route for them is to start with a small property business owned personally then start up a second property business in a company later on.

Operating Your Property Company

Once you've made the decision to operate some or all of your property business through a company, you will want to set up and run your company in the most beneficial way possible.

The second function of this guide is therefore to provide the tax-planning advice and warnings of potential pitfalls you need to know in order to minimise your tax burden as a property company owner.

A great deal of this advice is included in the early chapters of this guide where, in addition to providing an overall summary of the property company tax regime, we have already covered many potential planning opportunities and possible pitfalls. Nonetheless, the later chapters include many further tax-saving opportunities available to property investors setting up and running their own property company, supplementing the wealth of information already provided.

In Chapter 13, we will look at some of the practical issues you need to know when setting up and running a company. In addition to dealing with HMRC and satisfying the company's tax obligations, we will also cover accounting requirements, dealing with Companies House, and the question of whether you need an auditor (and how to choose one).

Chapter 14 examines the issue of putting an existing property business into a company. The stakes are high, with massive savings available in the right circumstances, but many costly traps awaiting the unwary. We look at how to avoid the traps, mitigate the costs and maximise the benefits; as well as alternative strategies you might want to pursue instead. This edition also includes illustrations of the substantial additional savings that may be available due to the 'window of opportunity' mentioned above.

Chapter 15 highlights some additional tax issues for property companies and their owners and Chapter 16 introduces some more specialised property company structures.

Finally, Chapter 17 summarises our findings, as well as looking at the possible future tax changes we may see over the next few years, and considering their potential impact on the question of whether using a property company will still save you tax in the years to come.

Tips and Warnings

Sprinkled throughout this guide, you will find many **'Tax Tips'** and **'Wealth Warnings'** designed to highlight key points where there are extra savings to be made or traps to catch the unwary. There are also a few **'Practical Pointers'** designed to make life easier. Watch out for all of these as you read the guide.

Scope of this Guide

This guide is aimed primarily at UK resident property investors considering or using a UK resident company to run their property business (although issues facing non-UK resident investors or non-UK resident companies are covered briefly in Section 15.5).

The guide covers investors resident anywhere in the UK investing in property anywhere in the UK. Readers should be aware there are current or proposed variations in the taxes applying in the nations outside England making up the rest of the UK. These variations are covered within this guide as follows:

i)   Income Tax rates applying to Scottish taxpayers: Section 15.8
ii)   Land and Buildings Transaction Tax on purchases of property in Scotland: Section 8.10
iii)   Land Transaction Tax on purchases of property in Wales: Section 8.11
iv)   Corporation Tax for companies operating in Northern Ireland: Section 2.3

The implications of these variations for investors using a property company are covered within the relevant sections listed above. In most cases, the variations make little difference to the question of whether it is advantageous for the investor to use a company or not. Hence, in order to avoid a lot of additional, and largely unnecessary, complexity, throughout the rest of this guide I will ignore the variations listed above unless specifically stated to the contrary.

In particular, I will refer only to Stamp Duty Land Tax on purchases of property. Readers should be aware that slightly different rates of tax apply on purchases of property in Scotland or Wales, and the name of the tax will be different, but this will generally make little difference: although the current Stamp Duty Land Tax 'holiday' does mean there are bigger differences than usual at present.

The reader must also bear in mind the general nature of this guide. Individual circumstances vary and the tax implications of an individual's actions will vary with them. For this reason, it is always vital to get professional advice before undertaking any tax planning or other transactions that may have tax implications. The author and Taxcafe UK Limited cannot accept any responsibility for any loss that may arise as a consequence of any action taken, or any decision to refrain from action taken, as a result of reading this guide.

Predicting the Future

In order to reinforce the issues discussed in this guide, I will demonstrate the tax implications of corporate property investment through the use of several worked examples.

In my examples, I have naturally had to make various assumptions about external factors beyond the control of the property investor, including:

- The growth of property values
- The future rate of inflation
- Interest rates
- The rates of return on property investment (market rental levels)
- Future changes to the UK tax system

I have made my assumptions as reasonable as possible, based on my experience of the property investment sector and the UK taxation regime.

As discussed above, for this edition, I have generally assumed market conditions will swiftly return to normal following the coronavirus crisis. Additionally, for the majority of the guide, I have assumed the UK tax regime will remain unchanged in the future except to the extent of any announcements already made at the time of publication.

However, if I can predict one thing with any certainty it is that the future will not be exactly as any of us may predict (a lesson we have surely all learned this year!) Hence, while I believe the conclusions I have drawn in this guide are validly based on sound principles, the reader must nevertheless bear in mind those conclusions are, to some extent, dependent on uncertain predictions about the future.

The tax rates and allowances for 2020/21 are included in Appendix A. For illustrative purposes, we will assume these rates continue to apply in future years, unless stated to the contrary.

Appendix A also includes estimated tax rates and allowances for 2021/22. These are based on the latest Government announcements (see Section 17.2 for details). However, these remain estimated figures and have therefore not been used for the purpose of any calculations in this guide.

In reality, we are bound to see more significant changes to the UK tax system in the future. While we have no idea exactly when such changes will take place, they will almost certainly occur within the timescale most long-term property investors are considering. Hence, in Chapter 17, at the end of the guide, I have analysed the potential impact of some of the changes we may see over the next few years.

Nevertheless, despite the ever-present possibility of changes to the tax regime, I remain firmly of the opinion there will always be a great many property investors for whom the use of a company vehicle to hold their investments will continue to be highly beneficial.

About the Examples

In addition to the points made above regarding the future of the UK tax regime, please note, unless specifically stated to the contrary, all persons described in the examples in this guide are:

i)   UK resident and domiciled for tax purposes
ii) Not subject to the High Income Child Benefit Charge
iii) Not claiming the marriage allowance
iv) Not Scottish taxpayers (i.e. pay Income Tax at normal UK rates)

See Section 15.8 regarding the Income Tax rates applying to Scottish taxpayers and the impact this has on the issues discussed in this guide.

All persons described in the examples in this guide are entirely fictional characters created specifically for the purposes of this guide. Any similarities to actual persons, living or dead, or to fictional characters created by any other author, are entirely coincidental.

Likewise, the companies described in the examples in this guide are similarly fictional corporations created specifically for the purposes of this guide and any similarities to actual companies, past or present, are again entirely coincidental.

Married Couples & Registered Civil Partnerships

Throughout this guide, you will see me refer to 'married couples', or 'spouses'. In each case, the treatment being outlined applies equally to married couples of all types and to civil partners.

References to 'married couples' should be taken to include registered civil partnerships; references to the taxpayer's 'spouse' will include their civil partner where relevant; and references to 'husbands' or 'wives' will include spouses of the same gender and civil partners.

However, it remains important to remember, unless specified to the contrary, the tax treatment being outlined applies to legally married couples and legally registered civil partners only. Unmarried couples are subject to entirely different rules.

Lastly, it is worth pointing out that, while marriage, or civil partnership, is generally advantageous for tax purposes, there are some important exceptions. It really is a case of 'for better or worse'!

Abbreviations and Terminology

Generally, at Taxcafe, we don't like using jargon because we want to keep our guides as simple as possible. To save some space, however, we have allowed ourselves a few abbreviations. We think they are fairly obvious ones, so they should not cause any confusion. We will explain each abbreviation the first time we use it and they are set out again in Appendix D for ease of reference.

- The word 'Limited' (as in 'Taxcafe UK Limited', for example) will be abbreviated to 'Ltd'.
- Large amounts, such as £1,000,000 or more, are abbreviated by use of the letter 'm'. For example, £2,500,000 will be written as '£2.5m'.
- Business asset disposal relief (mentioned several times in this guide) was formerly known as entrepreneurs' relief.

The Last Word

When it comes to tax, I believe you should never pay more than your fair share, and you have every right to undertake sensible planning measures to legitimately reduce, or delay, your tax bills. However, when all is said and done, the reason we pay tax is to fund vital public services, something that is now more important than ever. Tax is the hallmark of civilisation and, while I will help you pay no more than your fair share that is still something we should all remember.

Whatever type of property investor you are, and whatever decision you reach about the benefits of using a company, I would like to thank you for buying this guide and wish you every success with your investments.

Chapter 1

Why Use a Company?

1.1   INTRODUCTION

Many UK property investors are drawn towards the idea of holding their property investments through a limited company. Why is this?

Unlike most other types of business, it does not generally appear to be due to the protection afforded by a company's limited liability status.

No, this decision appears to be almost entirely tax-driven and is a direct result of the comparatively favourable Corporation Tax ('CT') regime.

In 2010, former Chancellor George Osborne announced a series of reductions in CT rates. These were later improved upon, with further reductions announced in subsequent Budgets, although, sadly, a recent U-turn announced by Boris Johnson means the CT rate has remained 19%. For the purposes of our calculations in this guide, we will assume it will remain 19% for the foreseeable future, although this is an issue we will return to in Chapter 17.

While CT rates have fallen over the last decade, Governments of all persuasions have put in place a series of personal tax increases for individuals. With personal tax rates looking set to remain high for the foreseeable future, the apparent attraction of running any type of business through a company has been significantly increased.

For property investors, the relatively beneficial CT regime looks extremely tempting. With the CT rate considerably lower than higher rate Income Tax at 40% or additional rate tax at 45%, many investors feel using a company must surely be the easiest way to save tax on their investments. Furthermore, the more beneficial interest relief regime enjoyed by investors using a property investment company (see Chapter 12) is often also an important factor.

With lower tax on profits and better relief for both interest and losses; using a property company does initially seem pretty attractive. But is it really that simple? Clearly, the fact we have published a whole guide dedicated to this question indicates it is not!

Yes, at first glance, the CT rate does look very attractive compared with higher or additional rate Income Tax. However, as we shall see, basing the decision to use a company on this one factor alone would be extremely short-sighted.

As we proceed to examine the issue in greater depth, we will see the CT benefits are not always as great as they may, at first, appear to be. The advantage gained through the lower CT rate is reduced or sometimes even eliminated by the problems surrounding the extraction of profits from the company.

Furthermore, with the range of CGT reliefs available to individual property investors, there is sometimes a danger the long-term position, taking capital growth and the eventual disposal of investment properties into account, may be significantly and detrimentally affected by the use of a company.

Nevertheless, despite these drawbacks, there are still many situations where using a company can prove advantageous to the long-term investor acquiring a portfolio of properties over time. Where the property portfolio is effectively regarded as a 'pension plan', for example, there may be substantial long-term benefits to be derived from using a company as an investment vehicle.

Furthermore, for those involved in property development, dealing or management, the way these businesses are treated for Income Tax and NI purposes means a company can be even more attractive in these cases.

1.2   NON-TAX REASONS FOR USING A COMPANY

Before we go on to examine the taxation considerations behind the use of a company for property businesses, it is first worth having a brief look at some of the non-taxation factors involved. There are many issues to be considered in the decision whether to use a company. Some of these are covered briefly below, although this list is far from exhaustive.

Limited Liability Protection
Although this does not appear to be the major reason behind most property investors' decision to incorporate, it is still, nevertheless, a factor to be considered. A company is a separate legal entity and, as such, is responsible for its own debts and other liabilities.

The usefulness of this, however, is often limited. Banks will often insist on personal guarantees from the directors or shareholders before they will lend money to the company. Furthermore, modern insolvency law passes a large part of the company's financial responsibilities to its directors, who may find themselves personally liable where the company has been used in an attempt to avoid the payment of liabilities arising in the normal course of its business.

Nevertheless, limited liability is useful when the business faces unexpected losses or legal liabilities. This can be particularly important when the economy takes a turn for the worse!

Note that limited liability status can also be obtained by using a Limited Liability Partnership ('LLP'). For property investors, however, LLPs suffer the major drawback that interest relief is not available for funds invested in an LLP engaged in property investment.

Flexibility of Ownership
Without the use of a company, it is difficult to involve many other people in the ownership of your property business. Joint ownership with your spouse or partner is easy enough to achieve but as the business grows you may wish to involve adult children or key employees. It is far easier to spread small parcels of ownership of the business through the medium of company shares.

Separation of Ownership & Management/Succession Planning
A company structure will also enable you to separate ownership and management. As your business grows and the years go by, you may eventually wish either to retire or move on to other ventures. However, you may still have a highly profitable business you do not yet wish to sell.

Using a company will enable you to retain ownership (as a shareholder) while passing management responsibility to others (the directors). A company structure also enables this business succession process to take place at a more controlled pace.

Tax Tip
A company is often a good vehicle for passing wealth to children (or other intended beneficiaries). The problem with a property investment or letting business is it does not qualify for business property relief for Inheritance Tax ('IHT') purposes. Hence, on the owner's death, the whole portfolio is exposed to IHT.

What a company can provide in this situation is a means to effectively allow the owner to pass on small parcels of ownership over a number of years. A sophisticated share structure may also enable you to keep control of your company while passing on a significant proportion of the underlying value to your children. See the Taxcafe.co.uk guide *'How to Save Inheritance Tax'* for further details.

Wealth Warning
Conversely, a property company may prove disadvantageous on the owner's death: see Section 15.7.

Finance
Many investors wishing to hold properties through the medium of a company find it difficult or expensive to obtain the finance they require. This problem seems to most affect those who are just starting their property business, or who only have one or two investment properties.

Conversely, for larger portfolios, corporate status seems to become a positive factor in the eyes of many lenders.

Some advisers suggest a 'Deed of Trust' could be used to get around the difficulties of raising finance for a property company. We will look at how this type of arrangement might work in Section 12.7.

Legal Rights

If you run your business through a company, you personally will no longer own property. Instead, you will own company shares. Legally, these are an entirely different kind of asset, giving rise to different legal rights. What kind of difference this will make to your affairs will depend on your personal circumstances, as well as what part of the UK (or other country) you and your properties are located in.

As I am not a lawyer, I will not attempt to advise property investors on these issues. The advice I **will** give is you should get legal advice on the implications of owning your properties through a company.

Company Law

If you use a UK-registered company, you will be subject to the requirements of UK company law. This, for example, may restrict your ability to utilise funds from your business for private purposes.

Audit and Other Statutory Requirements

Larger companies require a statutory annual audit of their accounts. Even the smallest companies must file annual accounts and certain other documentation with Companies House. We will take a closer look at these requirements in Chapter 13.

Costs

Inevitably, the additional statutory requirements involved in running a company will lead to increases in accountancy and other professional costs. These additional costs must be weighed against the tax and other benefits incorporation brings.

1.3   OVERVIEW OF COMPANY TAX PROS AND CONS

We now turn to the tax implications of running a property business through a company. As a broad overview, in general terms, it is reasonable to say **a company often produces a better result on income BUT personal ownership can sometimes produce a better result on capital growth**.

To illustrate this further, let's take a look at some of the main taxation pros and cons of investing through a limited company.

Using a Company: The Pros

- Companies pay CT at just 19% on any level of annual profits, including capital gains
- Companies are not subject to the horrendous restrictions on relief for interest and finance costs that apply to individuals
- You may choose any year-end accounting date for your company
- A company may claim relief for interest and finance costs on rental properties against any income or capital gains arising in the same period or, in many cases, against income or capital gains of future periods. (But see Section 4.9 regarding furnished holiday lets)
- A company may also claim relief for other losses arising from a UK property letting business against other income or capital gains it has for the same period or, in most cases, a later one. (This does not apply to losses on furnished holiday lets)
- An investor may claim relief for interest costs on funds borrowed to invest in a property company against any other income, including salary, self-employment income, or their own personal rental income. (Although this relief is subject to some limitations: see Section 12.11)

Using a Company: The Cons

- Companies do not get a personal allowance
- Companies do not get an annual exemption for capital gains purposes
- Companies are not eligible for business asset disposal relief (see Section 7.3)
- Any personal use of properties owned by the company, by the investor or their close relatives, may have severe tax consequences
- Personal tax liabilities usually arise when extracting trading or rental profits, or property sale proceeds, from the company
- It may sometimes be more difficult to obtain tax relief for certain administrative expenses, such as 'use of home as office', when investing via a company
- Companies cannot have a private residence, and hence are unable to claim principal private residence relief, or rent-a-room relief
- Companies cannot calculate taxable profits on a 'cash basis'

Despite some of these 'cons', the benefit of the lower CT rate is highly significant, especially when combined with the more generous regime for relieving interest costs when using a company. As we shall see later in the guide, these benefits will often be large enough to ensure the company route remains preferable overall.

The biggest problem, however, is the additional tax arising when rental profits or property sales proceeds are extracted from the company. What this, and the other 'cons' above, mean is that using a company is an extremely complex decision requiring very careful consideration.

Chapter 2

A Plain English Guide to Corporation Tax

2.1 WHAT TAXES DO COMPANIES PAY?

In this chapter, we will take a detailed look at how CT is calculated: sticking, as far as possible, to plain English. First, however, it is worth summarising the taxes companies pay.

Income and Capital Gains
A UK resident company pays CT on its total profits, made up of its worldwide income, profits and capital gains. It does not pay Income Tax or CGT (see Section 15.6 for exceptions occasionally applying to gains realised before 6th April 2019).

Occasionally, a company may suffer a deduction of Income Tax at source on part of its income, but this can be deducted from its CT liability for the same period.

Stamp Duty and Stamp Duty Land Tax
Companies generally pay Stamp Duty and SDLT on their purchases at exactly the same rates as an individual; with the exception of some purchases of residential property for a consideration in excess of £500,000 or the first purchase of any residential property. These taxes are covered further in Chapter 8.

Inheritance Tax
Companies are only liable for IHT in the most exceptional of circumstances and, even then, the tax only arises as a result of external factors involving the company's shareholders. A company does not die, so IHT does not arise. Instead, companies are wound up and we will come to the implications of this later in the guide.

None of this alters the fact that, when a shareholder dies, the value of their property company shares must be taken into account as part of their estate for IHT purposes.

VAT
Broadly speaking, a company is liable for VAT in the same way as an individual.

National Insurance

If you employ anyone to help you in your corporate property business, the company will be liable for secondary Class 1 NI, at the rate of 13.8%, in its capacity as an employer (subject to the £4,000 employment allowance and other exemptions covered in Section 9.2).

The company is also liable for Class 1A NI on any benefits in kind provided to employees and Class 1B NI on any voluntary settlements negotiated with HM Revenue and Customs ('HMRC') (e.g. on the cost of sandwiches provided at lunchtime business meetings).

Furthermore, like any other employer, the company has to deduct primary Class 1 NI from its employees' pay and account for this through the PAYE system.

All of this is exactly the same as when you employ someone to help you in your sole trader or partnership business. The key difference, however, comes from the fact that NI will also be due if you pay yourself a salary out of the company's profits, or provide yourself with any benefits in kind (such as a company car). We will look further at the implications of this in Section 9.2.

Apart from Class 1, 1A and 1B, a company cannot be liable for any other Class of NI. Unlike a sole trader or partnership, this remains the case regardless of what type of property business you have and there can never be any question of Class 2 or Class 4 NI being payable.

The Annual Tax on Enveloped Dwellings ('ATED')

ATED applies to companies owning UK residential properties worth in excess of £500,000, which are not in 'business use'. We will look at this charge in more detail in Section 15.6.

2.2   INTRODUCTION TO CORPORATION TAX

All of a company's income and capital gains for an accounting period are added together and treated as a single total sum of profits chargeable to CT (apart from some gains arising prior to 6th April 2019 that are subject to CGT: see Section 15.6).

The starting point for establishing the company's taxable profits is its statutory accounts for the relevant accounting period (see Section 13.6). Further, more detailed, accounts may also need to be prepared where the company has more than one type of income for CT purposes.

Fundamentally, capital gains, rental profits and trading profits within a company are all calculated in much the same way as for individuals. However, differences arise in the way the income and gains are taxed; the way interest and finance costs are relieved (see Section 4.9); the reliefs and exemptions available; and the rates of tax applying.

We will return to the differences between the corporate and personal tax regimes in Chapters 10 to 12, where we will be taking a detailed look at their impact on the property investor.

Financial Years
CT operates by reference to 'Financial Years'. Just to make life even more confusing than it already undoubtedly is, the Financial Year is slightly different to the tax year ending on 5th April that applies to income received by individuals.

A Financial Year is the year ending on 31st March in any calendar year, but is officially described by reference to the calendar year in which it began. Hence, for example, the 2020 Financial Year is the year commencing 1st April 2020 and ending 31st March 2021. It is important to be aware of this official terminology, as this is what is used on the CT Return.

Periods Spanning Two Financial Years
Where your company's accounting period does not end on 31st March, it will generally span two Financial Years. The profits of the accounting period are then split across the two Financial Years on a pro rata basis. For example, a profit of £100,000 for a twelve month accounting period ending 31st December 2020 would be split as follows:

2019 Financial Year: £100,000 x 91/366   £24,863
2020 Financial Year: £100,000 x 275/366 £75,137

2.3   CORPORATION TAX RATES

Since 2015, there has been one single CT rate applying to companies of all sizes and profit levels (except companies operating in the oil and gas sector). The past, current, and confirmed future levels of this single CT rate are as follows:

1st April 2015 to 31st March 2017:   20%
1st April 2017 to 31st March 2022:   19%

The position beyond March 2022 is currently unknown but, for the remainder of this guide, we will assume the rate will remain at 19% for the foreseeable future. This is effectively now our best forecast for the long term and we will be basing our calculations on this rate when we come to make our long-term predictions regarding the benefits of a property company later in the guide.

Northern Ireland

Different rates are to apply to companies trading in Northern Ireland at some point in the future. The rate is likely to match the rate used in the Irish Republic. That rate is currently 12.5% but, like everything else, it may, of course, change in the future. Furthermore, the date of introduction for the special rate for Northern Ireland remains uncertain.

Nonetheless, if and when the proposals for a separate CT rate for Northern Ireland come to fruition, taxpayers investing in property in the province may be able to save an additional 6.5% of rental or trading profits derived from Northern Irish property by using a company.

2.4 PAYING CORPORATION TAX

For most companies, CT is due in one single lump sum payable within nine months and one day after the end of the accounting period. For example, the CT for the year ending 31st December 2020 is due by 1st October 2021. All CT liabilities must be paid online and, as usual, interest is charged on late payments. Unlike Income Tax, interest on overdue CT is a deductible expense.

Larger companies with annual profits in excess of £1.5m must pay their tax in quarterly instalments. Very large companies or groups with profits in excess of £20m are subject to even earlier payment dates: such companies are now required to pay all their CT 'in-year'.

2.5 CASHFLOW BENEFITS OF USING A COMPANY

The timing of a company's CT payment is totally dependent on its accounting year-end date. This is quite different to individuals and partnerships, where tax is always due on the same dates under the Self Assessment system (i.e. instalments on 31st January during the tax year and 31st July following the tax year, with a balancing payment, or repayment, the following 31st January).

For stable and profitable property businesses, there is a huge cashflow advantage to using a company. This is quite independent of any tax savings that might be involved. Let's look at an example by way of explanation:

Example
Gordon has a thriving property letting business. His Income Tax liability has remained at the same level for a number of years (pretty rare in practice, but this is just an example, after all) and hence he has to pay half his tax on 31st January within the tax year and half on the following 31st July. If we 'averaged out' these two payments, this would be equivalent, for cashflow purposes, to a single payment on 1st May.

18

*Remember that, like any other individual with property letting income, Gordon MUST pay tax based on his profits for the year ending 5th April. Hence, on average, he effectively has to pay his tax just **26 days** after the end of his accounting period!*

If we contrast this 26-day 'average' payment period with the nine months and a day available to most companies, we can see what a large cashflow advantage the companies have: over eight months!

Wouldn't you rather keep your money for an extra eight months? Think what you could do with it in that time, especially in the rapidly moving property investment sector!

What if Profit isn't Stable?

The example above is perhaps not entirely typical, as it is based on a stable annual profit. In practice, profits tend to fluctuate, which can sometimes mean the company cashflow advantage is not quite so great. Nevertheless, in the vast majority of cases, the 'average' payment date for an individual investor (or partnership) would still fall within three months of the end of the accounting period, meaning a company would usually produce at least six months of cashflow advantage.

> #### Wealth Warning
> If the company is making large enough profits to be under the quarterly instalment system (see Section 2.4), its 'average' payment date is actually about a month **before** the end of its accounting period. In this case, the company produces a cashflow *disadvantage* (although, by the time profits have reached this level, other considerations are likely to be more important).

> #### Tax Tip
> As already explained, a company may choose any accounting year-end date, whereas an individual property investor is effectively forced to stick with 5th April (accounts can be drawn up for any period but the tax liability will always be based on profits for the year to 5th April). In the corporate regime this can sometimes provide scope to delay tax on profits that do not arise regularly over the year. This is particularly relevant to holiday lets or student accommodation.

Example

Laura lets out a number of student flats through Laura's Lettings Ltd. Generally, they are let from October to June, but are often vacant during the summer. Hence, all of Laura's profit arises during the nine months to June. If the company were to draw up accounts to 30th June, its CT liability would be due on 1st April the following year. Instead, Laura arranges for Laura's Lettings Ltd's accounting year-end to be 30th September. The company's CT is therefore not due until 1st July the following year. This simple step gives Laura an extra three-month cashflow saving every year!

2.6 COMPANY TAX RETURNS

Companies fall under a self-assessment system referred to as Corporation Tax Self Assessment or 'CTSA' for short. Under CTSA, the company is generally required to submit a tax return within twelve months of its accounting date.

The CTSA return document is called a CT600. With its CTSA return, the company is also required to submit its accounts; a CT computation (a calculation of the amount of profits and gains chargeable to CT for the accounting period); and a CT self-assessment (a calculation of the amount of CT due). The last two items can generally be prepared as a single combined calculation and there is plenty of accountancy software available to produce this.

Online filing of CT Returns and supporting documentation is compulsory. Electronic versions of the supporting documents outlined above need to be submitted in 'iXBRL' format.

Making Tax Digital
As many readers will be aware, the Government is planning to introduce a new quarterly reporting system, known as 'Making Tax Digital', or 'MTD' for short. At present, the system is only mandatory for some businesses and only for VAT purposes. The Government is, however, planning to make the system mandatory for most businesses for Income Tax purposes from April 2023 (see the Taxcafe.co.uk guide *'How to Save Property Tax'* for further details).

Current plans for the introduction of MTD for CT purposes include a voluntary pilot due to start in 2024, with the introduction of mandatory MTD for CT in 2026, or possibly later.

Chapter 3

Different Types of Property Company

3.1   INTRODUCTION

In Chapter 2 we looked at the basic principles of how a company is taxed in the UK. We will now begin looking in more detail at the UK taxation issues relating specifically to *property* companies.

While it would be possible to come up with a very long list of different 'types' of property companies, I would tend to regard the following four categories as the definitive list as far as UK taxation treatment is concerned:

a) Property investment (or letting) companies
b) Property development companies
c) Property trading (or dealing) companies
d) Property management companies

Before we go on to look at the detailed tax treatment of these different types of property companies, it is perhaps worth spending a little time to explain exactly what these different terms mean in a taxation context.

I should also point out at this stage that there is nothing different about the way these different types of companies are formed, nor usually in their constitutions (see Section 13.2). No, it is the nature of the property business itself that determines what type of company we are looking at.

It is also important to understand these different types of property business are not exclusive to companies and these different categorisations may also be applied to an individual property investor, a partnership, or any other property investment vehicle.

Over the course of the next five chapters, we will examine the CT consequences of having a company that falls into each of the four categories outlined above, as well as the implications for the owner of the company. SDLT and VAT will be considered in Chapter 8 and Section 15.1 respectively. NI payable by companies was covered in Section 2.1 and will be unaffected by the type of property business involved.

A company can, of course, carry on more than one type of property business, which would result in a mixture of tax treatments. I will spend a little time on the possible consequences of this in Section 3.6.

Why Does It Matter?

As we will discover over the next few chapters, the type of property business carried on by the company has only a relatively minor effect on the way the company itself is taxed.

The impact on the owner of the company is more significant however, as several important CGT and IHT reliefs are dependent on the type of company you have.

Even more important is the fact that individuals who are not using a company are taxed very differently on different types of property business. This means the contrast between an individual investor's tax position and a company investor's tax position is significantly affected by the type of property business involved.

Hence, it is absolutely crucial to understand what type of property business you have in order to determine whether a company is appropriate for you.

We will return to take a detailed look at the contrast between individual and company investors with different types of property business in Chapters 10 to 12 when we have finished looking at how the various types of property companies and their owners are taxed.

3.2   PROPERTY INVESTMENT COMPANIES (AKA PROPERTY LETTING COMPANIES)

These are companies that predominantly hold properties as long-term investments. The properties are the company's fixed assets, which are held to produce income in the form of rental profit.

While capital growth will be anticipated and will form part of the company's business plan, short-term property disposals should usually only take place where there is a strong commercial reason, such as an anticipated decline in value in that particular geographical location or a need to realise funds for other investments.

Example
All Blacks Ltd purchases three properties 'off-plan'. On completion of the properties, the company sells one of them in order to provide funds for continued expansion. The other two properties are rented out for a number of years. Although All Blacks Ltd sold one of the properties very quickly, there was a good commercial reason for doing so. Hence, the company may still be regarded as a property investment company.

In general, therefore, most properties will usually be held for a long period and rapid sales for short-term gain will be exceptional. Having said that, where exceptional opportunities for short-term gains do arise it would be unreasonable to suggest that the company, like any other investor, should not take advantage of those opportunities.

In some cases, the investors themselves will have a minimal level of involvement in the day-to-day running of the business, but there are also many property letting businesses that are much more 'hands on'.

As long as the company meets the overall long-term investment criterion outlined above, it remains a property investment company for all tax purposes, regardless of the level of the investor's own personal involvement on a day-to-day basis.

Managing your company's own properties would not, in itself, mean you had a property management company.

Tax Treatment
A property investment company is **not** regarded as a trading company. This has some unfortunate consequences for the company owner:

- The shares in the company are not eligible for business asset disposal relief or holdover relief for CGT purposes (see Chapter 7)
- The shares in the company are not eligible for business property relief for IHT purposes, meaning the full value of the company would be included in the investor's estate on his or her death when calculating the IHT due

> **Tax Tip**
> Furnished holiday lets (see Section 4.8) enjoy a special status for tax purposes. While companies whose income is derived predominantly from these lettings continue to be regarded as property investment companies for a number of purposes, shares in such companies remain eligible for business asset disposal relief and holdover relief. Shares in such companies may occasionally also be eligible for business property relief for IHT purposes, although this is rare.

How Are Property Investment Companies Taxed?
A property investment company must account for its rental profits under the specific rules applying to property income (see Chapter 4).

Interest and finance costs are not treated as part of the company's rental business, but are regarded as a general overhead of the company, with some very generous rules applying to the way these costs are relieved for CT purposes. We will cover those rules in Section 4.9.

Different rules apply to interest costs relating to furnished holiday lets. We will again examine these in Section 4.9.

Property disposals are dealt with as capital gains (see Chapter 6).

Is there any advantage to having a property investment company rather than any other type of property company?

Very little! For a company, the only advantage in having a property investment business rather than any other type of property business was the availability of indexation relief when investment properties were sold. Unfortunately, indexation relief has now been frozen and is limited to the increase in the retail prices index from the date of purchase until the earlier of date of sale or December 2017 (see Section 6.4 for further details).

Individuals (as well as partnerships, trusts, etc.), however, *do* enjoy a number of advantages if regarded as having a property investment business, rather than another type of property business.

It is therefore essential to understand what type of property business you have, or will have, before deciding whether you want to operate it within a company.

> **Wealth Warning**
> Although there is little advantage to this type of tax treatment for a company, it is nevertheless important to appreciate it is the way you carry on your business that determines the tax treatment: you cannot choose how your company is taxed!

The vast majority of landlords and 'buy-to-let' investors are carrying on a property investment business and hence, if they form a company, they will have a property investment company.

This is, perhaps, unfortunate, since it is in the case of property investment businesses that we see most uncertainty over whether the use of a company is beneficial or not. The subject therefore warrants a great deal of further detailed examination and we will return to this issue in Chapters 10 and 11.

For other types of property business, it is often far more clear-cut that a company would be beneficial.

3.3   PROPERTY DEVELOPMENT COMPANIES

These are companies that predominantly acquire properties or land and carry out building or renovation work with a view to selling developed properties for profit.

The term covers a broad spectrum of activities, from major building companies that acquire vacant land and construct vast new property developments, to small owner-managed companies that acquire the occasional 'run-down' property to 'do up' for onward sale at a profit.

No one would doubt the former are correctly categorised as property development companies, but not everyone realises the latter type of activity may also lead to the company being regarded as a property development company.

Generally speaking, a property will be disposed of as soon as possible after building or renovation work has been completed.

It is the profit derived from this work that produces the company's income and it does not usually look to rent properties out other than as a matter of short-term expediency.

Example
All Whites Ltd purchases three old barns in August 2020 and converts them into residential property. The work is completed in February 2021 and the company sells two of the properties immediately.

The third property, unfortunately, proves difficult to sell. In order to generate some income from the property, All Whites Ltd lets it out on a short six-month lease. The property is never taken off the market during the period of the lease and a buyer is found in July 2021, with completion taking place in September.

Although All Whites Ltd let one of the properties out for a short period, its main business activity remained property development. This was reinforced by the fact the property remained on the market throughout the lease. All Whites Ltd is therefore a property development company.

Tax Treatment
A property development company is regarded as a *trading company*. Shares in the company are eligible for both business asset disposal relief and holdover relief for CGT purposes (see Chapter 7).

It is important to stress we are talking here about the shares in the company rather than the properties owned by the company. Companies cannot qualify for business asset disposal relief or holdover relief on the properties they own (nor, indeed, any other assets).

Shares in a property development company are also eligible for business property relief for IHT purposes.

The company's profits from its property development activities, i.e. the profits arising from development property sales, are taxed as trading profits. We will look at the taxation of trading profits in more detail in Chapter 5.

Interest and finance costs relating to the company's property development activities are simply treated as part of its normal trading expenses and do not require the special treatment set out in Section 4.9.

Capital gains treatment applies to any disposals of the company's long-term fixed assets, such as its own offices. However, with indexation relief now only covering the period from date of purchase until December 2017, capital gains treatment will become less beneficial over time.

Where, as in the example above, there is some incidental short-term rental income it should, strictly speaking, be dealt with under the specific rules applying to property income. In practice, however, it has sometimes been known for this to be accepted as incidental trading income. This is very important, since this treatment ensures the company's trading status is not affected.

Property developers utilising the services of subcontractors for any building work, including plumbing, decorating and electrical work, are required to operate the Construction Industry Scheme for tax purposes. This may involve having to deduct tax, at a special rate particular to the Construction Industry Scheme, from payments made to subcontractors, and account for it to HMRC, rather like PAYE.

The current rate for the mandatory deductions under the Construction Industry Scheme is either 20% or 30%, depending on whether the subcontractor is registered under the scheme.

3.4   PROPERTY TRADING COMPANIES

Property trading companies generally only hold properties for short-term gain. Properties are bought and sold frequently and are held as trading stock. Properties will not usually be rented out, except in the interests of short-term financial expediency. Such companies are sometimes also known as property dealing companies.

The company's income is derived from making a profit on the properties it sells. These companies differ from property development companies in that no actual development takes place on the properties. Profits are made simply by ensuring a good margin between buying and selling price.

Example
All Greys Ltd has bought 20 different properties 'off-plan' over the last few years. In each case, it has sold the properties immediately on completion of the development.

Since All Greys Ltd has neither developed the properties, nor held on to them as investments for any length of time, it is clearly a property trading company.

Tax Treatment

A property trading company's profits should be taxed as trading income (see Chapter 5). Interest and finance costs relating to the company's property trading activities will represent trading expenses.

Any incidental letting income that does arise should be dealt with under the specific rules applying to property income.

Shares in such a company are specifically not eligible for business property relief for IHT purposes.

As for CGT, the theory is that a property trading company is still a 'trading company' and hence the shares in such a company should be eligible for both business asset disposal relief and holdover relief (see Chapter 7).

In practice, however, I fear there is a strong danger that some resistance will be encountered, with HMRC contending the company is, in fact, a property investment company, so that its shares do not qualify for these reliefs. This is very much a 'grey area' and HMRC can be expected to examine borderline cases carefully and argue for the treatment that produces the most tax.

Conversely, new legislation applying since 2016 enables HMRC to ***deem*** the profit arising on disposal of UK land and property to be a trading profit under certain circumstances. We will take a closer look at that legislation in Section 3.7.

3.5   PROPERTY MANAGEMENT COMPANIES

These companies do not generally own properties at all. Instead, they provide management services to property owners. If you have a property letting agent taking care of the day-to-day running of your properties, the chances are your agent is probably a property management company.

A property management company's income is derived from the management or service charges that it charges to the actual owners of the property.

Tax Treatment

A property management company is a trading company for all tax purposes. Hence, shares in such a company are usually eligible for business asset disposal relief and holdover relief for CGT purposes (see Chapter 7) and business property relief for IHT purposes.

The company's profits from its property management activities will be treated as trading profits. Interest and finance costs incurred in relation to property management activities will be treated as trading expenses.

Capital gains treatment will apply to any disposals of the company's long-term fixed assets, such as its own offices, for example.

Any incidental letting income should, as usual, be dealt with under the specific rules applying to property income.

The interesting point is that, under the right circumstances, you may be able to set up your own property management company. The possible use of such a company for tax-planning purposes is examined in Section 16.1.

3.6   COMPANIES WITH A 'MIXED' PROPERTY BUSINESS

"What if my company doesn't happen to fit neatly into one of these four categories?" you may be asking.

If the company has a 'mixed' property business, involving more than one of the four types of business described above, then each business type will need to be dealt with separately. It may even be necessary to draw up separate accounts for the different elements of the business.

The impact on the owner of the company will depend on which types of property business are involved and in what proportions.

Capital Gains Tax

For CGT purposes, the company will only be considered a trading company, with its shares eligible for both business asset disposal relief and holdover relief (see Chapter 7), if its activities do not include any 'substantial' element of non-trading. For this purpose, property investment and property letting are deemed to be non-trading activities (except furnished holiday lets).

HMRC has told us it regards 'substantial' as meaning 'more than 20%'. "More than 20% of what?" you ask. Here, it has attempted to retain more control over the situation since, depending on the facts of the case, it may apply this '20% rule' to any of the following:

- Turnover (i.e. gross income)
- Profit
- Expenditure
- Time spent by directors and employees
- Asset values

HMRC's view of the meaning of 'substantial' is not, however, the law; it is merely its interpretation of the law. In particular, most experts suggest it should only be necessary to keep non-trading activities under the 20% level according to some of the measures set out above, rather than all of them; and the position should be decided by looking at the overall picture formed by the company's activities.

Furthermore, in a recent case, the tribunal judges pointed out that HMRC's '20% rule' had no basis in law and could not be relied upon. They went on to state that "substantial should be taken to mean of material or real importance in the context of the activities of the company as a whole."

Nevertheless, HMRC's 20% guideline is still generally regarded as a good 'rule of thumb', albeit with the important proviso that it remains essential to look at the overall picture rather than focus on any single factor alone. Hence, to ensure both business asset disposal relief and holdover relief are available on the shares in a company carrying on a mixed property business, it remains important to keep the company's non-trading activities down to a level not exceeding 20% of the majority of the measures set out above; preferably all of them, if possible.

Tax Tip
As we shall see in Chapter 7, whether your company qualifies as a trading company for CGT purposes can make an enormous difference to the amount of tax you will pay on a sale of your shares, or a winding up of your company. For a couple owning a company together, the potential tax saving generated by preserving the company's trading status could be up to £200,000.

To preserve the trading status of the company, it will often be worth keeping 'non-trading' activities, such as property letting, separate from activities accepted as trading by HMRC. This can be done either by keeping the 'non-trading' activities out of the company, or by putting them into a different company.

Impact on Business Property Relief for Inheritance Tax
The test for whether shares in a company with a 'mixed' property business qualify for business property relief is considerably less stringent than the CGT test set out above and it is only necessary to ensure the company's business does not consist wholly or mainly of property investment, property letting, or dealing in property.

'Mainly' is defined as over 50%, meaning a property company's shares will generally remain eligible for business property relief if over half its business comes from property development or property management.

To maximise the available business property relief, it is also important to ensure all the company's activities are an integral part of the same business and not run separately.

For further details on the benefits of business property relief, see the Taxcafe.co.uk guide 'How to Save Inheritance Tax'.

3.7   INVESTMENT OR TRADING?

It makes little difference to a UK company's CT liabilities whether its property disposals are treated as trading profits or capital gains. However, this issue is hugely important to:

i)   The CGT and IHT treatment of the owner's shares,
ii)   Non-resident companies selling properties held before April 2019 (see Section 15.5), and
iii)   Individual property investors

Point (iii), in turn, impacts on the question of whether using a company will be beneficial for those investors. All three points make it important for us to examine this critical issue in detail.

In general terms, it is usually beneficial for individuals if their property disposals are treated as capital gains. Historically, this has also been the case for non-resident companies, and still will be in many cases, but the position is changing and we will look at this in more detail in Section 15.5.

It generally makes little difference to UK resident companies themselves, but it is usually beneficial for their owners if the company's activities give rise to trading profits.

So, in very broad terms, trading works better in a company; long-term investment is better for individuals. However, as we shall see in later chapters, none of that means a company will not be beneficial for long-term investments in some cases.

In the meantime let's take a look at the 'investment or trading' issue.

The Boundary between Investment and Trading
Until fairly recently, a property disposal was generally treated as a capital gain unless the *sole or main purpose* behind the acquisition of the property was to realise a profit on disposal.

Legislation applying from July 2016, however, states that the profit on disposal of UK property will be *treated* as a trading profit whenever the main purpose, or *one of the main purposes*, behind its acquisition was to realise a profit on disposal.

This broadens the scope of what might be considered to be a trading profit quite considerably. It does not, however, alter the basic principles that determine when a trade actually exists. In other words, a middle ground has been created where there is no actual trade, but where profits are simply treated as trading profits.

The situation can therefore be summarised as follows:

1. **Where the sole or main purpose behind the acquisition was to make a profit on disposal:** a property trade exists and the profit on disposal is trading income.
2. **Where one of the main purposes behind the acquisition (but not the only, or dominant, purpose) was to make a profit on disposal:** the profit on disposal will be treated as trading income but, for all other purposes, the business will be treated as a property investment business.
3. **Where making a profit on disposal was not a main purpose behind the acquisition:** the profit on disposal will be a capital gain and, if a business does exist, it will be a property investment business.

The principles used in determining whether a business falls under Category 1 are well established and have been discussed earlier in this chapter, but the dividing line between Categories 2 and 3 is perhaps less clear. The problem lies in understanding what '**a** main purpose' is. It is far easier to identify '**the** main purpose'!

When the legislation was first published, many commentators feared almost all property disposals would be treated as giving rise to a trading profit since almost every time anyone buys a property they hope to realise a gain on its disposal.

However, in contrast to the rather broad scope of the legislation, HMRC guidance issued in December 2016 suggests very few disposals will fall into Category 2. The guidance states the legislation should not apply to "Transactions such as buying or repairing a property for the purpose of earning rental income or as an investment to generate rental income and enjoy capital appreciation", or "Straightforward long-term investment where the economic benefit arising to the owner is the result of market movement from holding that asset ..."

The guidance also states that long-term capital appreciation may be a reasonable expectation without it necessarily forming a main purpose of the acquisition.

The general thrust of the guidance seems to suggest it is only where a profit can already be anticipated due to the property's current value, or where a profit is anticipated due to some action to be carried out by the owner (typically developing the property), that the deemed trading provisions can apply. Even then, the profit on disposal will need to be a 'main purpose' behind the acquisition.

The mere hope of a long-term gain does not make this a main purpose behind the acquisition. There would need to be a more concrete strategy involving the realisation of a gain before this can be regarded as one of the main purposes behind the acquisition. Nonetheless, it is clear the 'goalposts' have been moved and investors need to be careful about documenting their intentions when acquiring property.

It is impossible to give a definitive answer to explain exactly when investment becomes trading, but some useful guidelines are set out below. (Those marked * are included within the HMRC guidance on the issue)

Renovation and Conversion Work*
Activity such as building, conversion or renovation work may sometimes be indicative that there is a trading motive behind the purchase of land or property. However, the mere fact that this work takes place does not, in itself, necessarily make it a property development trade.

If the property is held for several years after completion of the building work, it is likely that it is still an investment property.

On the other hand, however, if the property is sold immediately after completing the work, a trade is likely to exist unless the investor's original intention had been to keep the property and rent it out, but some change in circumstances led them to change their mind.

Frequency of Transactions
If an investor only sells a property once every few years, they are likely to be carrying on a property investment business. If they make several sales every year, representing a high proportion of their portfolio, they may be a property trader or developer.

Number of Transactions
As well as their frequency, the number of property transactions which the investor has carried out can be a factor in deciding whether they are trading.

Finance Arrangements*
Long-term finance arrangements, such as mortgages or longer term loans are generally indicative of an investment activity. Financing a purchase through short-term arrangements, such as bank overdrafts will be more indicative of a development or dealing trade. Short-term finance tends to indicate short-term assets.

Length of Ownership*
There is no definitive rule as to how long a property must be held for it to be an investment rather than trading stock. Like everything else, length of ownership is just one factor to consider. For example, many property developers hold land stocks for many years before commencing development (known as a 'land bank') but this does not alter the trading nature of their activities.

Where there is no obvious trading activity, I have heard it suggested an ownership period of three years or more is generally regarded as being indicative of a property investment business: although there is no legal basis for this. This is not to say ownership for any lesser period cannot represent an investment where the facts of the case otherwise support it.

In practice, the longer properties are held for, the more likely they are to be accepted as investments.

Renting the Properties Out*
Renting properties out provides a pretty good indication that they are being held as investments and not part of a property trade. Like everything else on this list though, it may not be conclusive on its own.

Living in a Property*
Living in the property is another useful way to evidence an intention to hold it as a long-term asset. Once again though, this may not be enough if the other facts of the case prove to be contrary to this idea.

This will generally only be relevant to properties held by individuals: see Section 15.3 regarding the dangers of making personal use of a property held by your own company.

'Hands On' Involvement
Being actively involved in the renovation or development of a property makes the owner look like a property developer. Contracting all of the work out looks more like property investment.

Existing Trade*
Where an investor already has an existing property trade, such as property development or property dealing, then it is more likely that other property investments will also be trading assets.

In Summary
Remember each of the points examined above is just one factor in determining what kind of property business an investor has. Ultimately, it is the overall picture formed by the investor's intentions, their behaviour, and their investment pattern, that will eventually decide whether they have a property investment business, a property trade, or both.

In many cases, this 'overall picture' will point to a fairly clear answer and the correct treatment of the business will be obvious. In some cases, however, the position may be more borderline and the correct treatment will not be clear. This could create a risk the investor might fall into the second of the three categories described at the beginning of this section.

In these cases, it may sometimes be beneficial to adapt your behaviour a little, bearing the guidelines set out above in mind, in order to produce a clearer picture of the nature of the business.

Changes of Intention

An existing investment property may become a trading asset where there is a change of intention. In this case, the profit arising after the change will be a trading profit, but any increase in value arising prior to that point will remain a capital gain.

Example

BOD Ltd buys a block of ten flats for £1m in 2020. It rents out the flats until 2023, at which time the property is worth £1.2m. The company then redevelops the property into four luxury apartments at a cost of £250,000 and sells all the apartments for £500,000 each.

As usual, the treatment of the development gain will depend on a number of factors: the most important being BOD Ltd's intentions at the time the redevelopment work commenced.

However, if it is clear the redevelopment was carried out with a main purpose of realising an additional profit on the disposal of the property then the development gain of £550,000 will be a trading profit. (4 x £500,000 = £2m – £1.2m – £250,000 = £550,000)

The gain of £200,000 (£1.2m – £1m) arising prior to the start of the development work will continue to be a capital gain. However, because no indexation relief can be claimed (see Section 6.4), there is unlikely to be any benefit in having the amount treated as a capital gain rather than trading profit.

Chapter 4

Property Rental Income and Expenses

4.1   CORPORATION TAX ON RENTAL PROFITS

In this chapter, we will look at how rental income and other property investment income received by a company are taxed. In the next chapter, we will move on to the tax treatment of companies with property businesses classed as trades.

The first point to note is that interest and finance costs incurred by the company in connection with most investment or letting properties are not treated as expenses of the letting business, but as general overheads instead. We will look at the treatment of these costs, and how the company obtains CT relief for them, in Section 4.9.

Subject to this rather peculiar quirk, property letting is treated like any other business from a purely accounting point of view. The company has to draw up accounts, usually once a year, which detail all its rental income, as well as all relevant expenses.

If the company is letting a number of UK properties on a commercial basis, these will usually be treated as a single UK property business. Landlords operating through companies may, of course, draw up separate sets of management accounts for any individual property, or group of properties, if they wish.

Some types of letting must, however, be accounted for separately for CT purposes, as they are subject to different tax rules. In these cases, a separate set of accounts will be required in support of the company's CT calculations.

Separate letting accounts are required in the following cases:

- Furnished holiday lets in the UK
- Furnished holiday lets in the European Economic Area
- Other overseas lettings
- Non-commercial lettings

Special rules apply to furnished holiday lets in the UK or European Economic Area. The qualifying criteria for furnished holiday lets are set out in Section 4.8 and their different treatment for CT purposes is covered as appropriate throughout this chapter.

'Non-commercial lettings' refers to cases where less than full market rent is charged for a property due to some special relationship between the landlord and the tenant. Generally, as we will see later in the guide, I would advise strongly against holding such properties through a company.

Company accounts must be drawn up in accordance with either UK 'Generally Accepted Accounting Principles' ('GAAP') or International Financial Reporting Standards ('IFRS'). Most UK companies draw accounts up under GAAP, as IFRS is only mandatory for large companies.

The most important aspect of GAAP is that accounts must be drawn up on an 'accruals' basis. This means income and expenditure is recognised when it arises, or is incurred, rather than when it is received or paid (the latter being the 'cash basis', which is not permitted for CT purposes).

Example
Jake, Sandy and Tilly own a small property company, JST Properties Ltd, which draws up accounts to 30th November each year. JST Properties Ltd acquires a new property on Kirkcaldy High Street in October 2020 and rents it out for the first time on 29th November at a monthly rent of £1,000 payable in advance.

At 30th November 2020, JST Properties Ltd will have received one monthly rental of £1,000. However, under the 'accruals' basis, the company is only required to account for two days' rent. This amounts to just £66 (£1,000 x 12 x 2/365 = £66). This simple (and correct) adjustment reduces JST Properties Ltd's CT bill due on 1st September 2021 by £177.

Tax Tip
Expenses should similarly be recognised as they are incurred. The timing of allowable expenditure is therefore critical in planning your CT affairs and it is the date expenses are *incurred* (i.e. when work takes place, or goods are purchased) that is important, not when they are invoiced or paid for.

Example
MYB Ltd has an accounting date of 31st March, and has some roof repairs carried out on one of its rented properties in March 2021. The roofer does not get around to invoicing the company until May and it pays the invoice in July.

Despite the fact MYB Ltd does not pay for the repairs until July, it may nevertheless still deduct the cost in its accounts for the year ending 31st March 2021.

4.2 CALCULATING RENT RECEIVABLE

A company is subject to CT on its rental **profits**, rather than its gross rental **income**. It is tempting to think, therefore, that it does not matter whether rental expenses are shown separately in the accounts, or just deducted from rental income, as long as the net rental profit is correct. This is not the case however, as the correct calculation of gross rental income is important for a number of reasons, including:

- Accounting disclosure requirements (Section 13.6)
- The VAT registration threshold (Section 15.1)
- The audit threshold (Section 13.6)

Gross rental income is derived from rent receivable and therefore includes any amounts of rent due but unpaid (i.e. bad debts). Any agent's commission deducted from rents received must also be added back for these purposes and shown separately as an expense.

Tenant's deposits should not be included within rental income unless and until the landlord has cause to retain them (or part of them), usually at the end of a lease.

4.3 EXPENSES YOU CAN CLAIM

The rules on what types of expenditure may be claimed by the company as deductions are generally much the same as for property-letting businesses run by individuals or partnerships. Some of the main deductions include:

- Property maintenance and repair costs
- Heating and lighting costs, if borne by the landlord company
- Insurance costs
- Letting agent's fees
- Advertising for tenants
- Accountancy fees
- Legal and professional fees (see further below)
- The cost of cleaners, gardeners, etc, where relevant
- Ground rent, service charges, etc.
- Bad debts
- Pre-trading expenditure (see further below)
- Administrative expenditure (see further below)
- Salaries paid to staff or directors (covered more in Section 9.2)

All expenses must be incurred wholly and exclusively for the purposes of the company's business and, naturally, must actually be borne by the company itself (i.e. the company cannot claim any expenses if the tenant is paying them directly).

Interest and finance costs are not deducted from letting income received by a company, but are treated as general company overheads instead. We will look at how CT relief is obtained for these costs in Section 4.9.

Legal and Professional Fees

Most legal fees and other professional costs incurred for the purposes of the business may be claimed as a deduction against rental income. Typically, this will include items such as the costs of preparing tenants' leases and, perhaps, debt collection expenses.

Legal fees and other costs incurred on the purchase or sale of properties, however, may not be claimed against rental income. All is not lost though as these items may usually be claimed as allowable deductions for capital gains purposes (Chapter 6).

Wealth Warning

There remains the problem of abortive expenditure, such as the cost of building surveys on properties you do not, in fact, actually purchase. HMRC tends to regard these as capital items, which therefore cannot be claimed against rental income. But, since the property is never actually purchased, they cannot be claimed against any capital gain either.

In my view, such expenses are part of the general administrative cost of running a property investment company and should therefore still be claimed against rental income. This approach is generally supported throughout the tax profession, although some resistance may be encountered from HMRC.

Tax Tip

A more persuasive argument is that expenditure of this type only becomes capital if it is incurred after the decision to acquire the property has been taken. The best approach, therefore, is to ensure that, wherever possible, you record the fact that such expenditure is being incurred 'with a view to deciding whether the property should be purchased by the company': i.e. that no such decision has yet been made.

This can be done by way of directors' board minutes or within an email instructing the surveyor (or other professional, as the case may be) to carry out the work.

Another Tax Tip

Part of the professional fees arising on the purchase of a property will often relate to the raising of finance. It may therefore be worth arranging to have this element of the fees invoiced separately, so they can be claimed as a finance cost within general overheads, as detailed in Section 4.9. This will provide CT relief for these costs without having to wait until the property is sold.

Pre-trading Expenditure

You may incur some expenses for the purposes of your property business before you form your company or start to let out any properties.

In general, deductible expenses incurred within seven years before the commencement of a business may still be allowable if they would otherwise qualify under normal principles. In such cases, the expenses can be claimed as if they were incurred on the first day of the business.

Tax Tip

In the case of a new company, a number of 'pre-trading' expenses will often have been paid for by the investor personally before the company has been formed.

The best thing to do in these circumstances is:

i) Keep track of the relevant expenditure, retaining receipts, etc, as usual.
ii) Once the company has been formed, 'recharge' the expenses to the company. What this means in practice is that a 'director's loan account' is set up in the company recording the expenditure previously incurred by the director.
iii) The expenses recharged by the director may (subject to the normal principles of deductibility) be claimed in the company's first accounting period.
iv) The director may be repaid the 'loan account' as soon as the company has available funds.

Administrative Expenditure

This heading is perhaps the broadest, and can extend to the cost of running an office, motor, and travel costs. In the case of a company, it will also cover costs associated with running the company itself (as opposed to running its business). This would include filing fees payable to Companies House and audit fees, if applicable. Costs of the company formation (see Section 13.1) are not allowable as these are a capital item.

As usual, the general rule is any expenditure must be incurred wholly and exclusively for the purposes of the business. Unfortunately, business entertaining expenditure is specifically excluded. (Staff entertaining is allowed though: and will not even give rise to Income Tax charges for the staff in some cases, unless HMRC's prescribed limits are exceeded.)

4.4 CAPITAL EXPENDITURE YOU CAN CLAIM

The main type of disallowable expenditure in a property-letting or property-investment business is capital expenditure on property purchases, property improvements, and furniture, fixtures and fittings.

Relief is, however, available for certain types of capital expenditure in the form of capital allowances.

Sadly, capital allowances are extremely restricted when it comes to residential property or assets within it, but there are some important exceptions. Furthermore, companies renting out commercial property or furnished holiday lets can benefit enormously from capital allowances.

Apart from the fact that any changes usually apply from 1st April for companies (instead of 6th April), the rules on capital allowances for companies are pretty much the same as for individuals or partnerships.

There are three main types of capital expenditure for which property companies may be able to claim capital allowances:

- Plant and machinery: this includes equipment, machinery, furniture, fixtures, fittings and 'integral features'. The capital allowances regime for plant and machinery is explored in Section 4.5.
- Motor vehicles: strictly, these are regarded as a special type of 'plant and machinery', but there are a few quirks to be aware of which we will examine in Section 5.5.
- Structures and buildings: the 'structures and buildings allowance' provides valuable relief for those constructing or purchasing new non-residential property after 28th October 2018, or carrying out improvements to existing non-residential property after the same date. We will take a look at this new allowance in Section 4.6.

4.5 PLANT AND MACHINERY ALLOWANCES

The main type of capital allowances are 'plant and machinery allowances'. These allowances are available on qualifying plant, machinery, furniture, fixtures, fittings, computers and other equipment used in a business. Since 2008, plant and machinery allowances have also been available on 'integral features' within qualifying property. This term is explained further below.

More details on the type of expenditure qualifying for plant and machinery allowances are given in the Taxcafe.co.uk guide *'How to Save Property Tax'*.

Plant and Machinery Allowances on Rental Properties
Plant and machinery allowances are available on qualifying expenditure within rented commercial property (shops, offices, etc) and furnished holiday lets (see Section 4.8).

Wealth Warning

Landlords may lose the right to plant and machinery allowances on fixtures and fittings within a commercial property if they grant a lease of two years or more to a tenant and charge a lease premium. As such a premium is wholly or partly regarded as a capital sum for tax purposes, the landlord will be treated as having made a partial disposal of the property and may therefore lose the right to claim plant and machinery allowances on assets within it.

A landlord may also lose the right to claim plant and machinery allowances on items not qualifying as 'background' plant and machinery when a property is leased for more than five years. However, this should not generally apply to assets on which the landlord had been able to claim allowances previously, before the commencement of the lease.

Finally, landlords may also lose the right to plant and machinery allowances on fixtures or fittings they lease to the tenant separately under a different agreement to the lease of the property itself. However, this particular problem can often be avoided by making a joint election with the tenant. Furthermore, this can also be a useful method to enable the landlord to retain the right to plant and machinery allowances on assets within the property where a lease has been granted at a premium, as described above.

Residential Property

Sadly, expenditure on assets for use within a rented 'dwelling-house' is ineligible for plant and machinery allowances. Hence, plant and machinery allowances cannot generally be claimed on expenditure within a residential rental property. There are some important exceptions to be aware of however, including furnished holiday lets (Section 4.8), and expenditure within communal areas (e.g. lift machinery or a utility room in a block of flats).

A company that rents out residential property may also claim plant and machinery allowances on equipment purchased for its own business use outside its rental properties, such as computers and office furniture.

Like other landlords, companies may claim the cost of replacement furniture, furnishings and equipment within rented residential property. See Section 4.7 for further details.

The Amount of Allowances Available

The amount of plant and machinery allowances available depends on the date the qualifying expenditure is incurred. At present, the most important allowance for the majority of businesses is the annual investment allowance.

The Annual Investment Allowance

Qualifying companies are currently entitled to an annual investment allowance of up to £1m. This limit was due to fall to just £200,000 from 1st January 2021, but the reduction in the limit has been postponed for a year and is currently expected to take place on 1st January 2022 (although it is possible it may be postponed again).

(The allowance is also available to sole traders and most partnerships. Note, however, that where a company is a member of a partnership, the allowance will not be available to that partnership.)

The annual investment allowance provides 100% tax relief for qualifying expenditure on plant and machinery up to a specified limit in each accounting period. The specified limits for recent and current periods, and proposed limits for future periods, are as follows:

1st January 2016 to 31st December 2018:	£200,000
1st January 2019 to 31st December 2021:	£1,000,000
From 1st January 2022:	£200,000

Transitional rules apply where a company's accounting period spans a change in the specified limit.

For accounting periods straddling 1st January 2019, the maximum annual investment allowance is calculated on a pro rata basis. For example, a company with a twelve month accounting period ending 31st October 2019 will be entitled to a maximum annual investment allowance for the whole year of:

61/365 x £200,000	£33,424
304/365 x £1m	£832,877
Total:	£866,301

But, an additional rule applies to expenditure incurred before 1st January 2019. The maximum amount that can be claimed in respect of expenditure incurred in the part of the accounting period falling before that date is restricted to £200,000.

For accounting periods straddling 31st December 2021, the maximum annual investment allowance is again calculated on a pro rata basis. For example, a company with a twelve month accounting period ending 28th February 2022 is entitled to a maximum annual investment allowance for the whole year of:

306/365 x £1m	£838,356
59/365 x £200,000	£32,329
Total:	£870,685

But, an additional rule applies to expenditure incurred after 31st December 2021. The maximum amount that can be claimed in respect of expenditure incurred in the part of the accounting period falling after that date is restricted to the appropriate proportion of the £200,000 limit. Hence, in the case of the company described above, the maximum annual investment allowance that could be claimed on expenditure incurred between 1st January and 28th February 2022 is just £32,329.

The maximum annual investment allowance applying for some other popular accounting periods is as follows:

Year ended	31-Mar	30-Apr	30-Jun	30-Sep	31-Dec
2019					
For the year as a whole	£397,260	£463,014	£596,712	£798,356	£1m
Before 1/1/2019	£200,000	£200,000	£200,000	£200,000	n/a
2020 & 2021					
For the year as a whole	£1m	£1m	£1m	£1m	£1m
2022					
For the year as a whole	£802,740	£736,986	£603,288	£401,644	£200,000
After 31/12/2021	£49,315	£65,753	£99,178	£149,589	£200,000

Wealth Warning

As we can see, the annual investment allowance available on expenditure in the early part of 2022 will, in some cases, be quite restricted. Any excess will attract writing down allowances at just 18%, or possibly as little as 6% where it falls in the 'special rate pool' (see below). It is therefore important for companies with accounting periods spanning 31st December 2021 to plan the timing of their capital expenditure carefully.

In contrast to the immediate 100% relief provided by the annual investment allowance, expenditure attracting writing down allowances at 18% may take twelve years to achieve even 90% relief. For assets falling into the 'special rate pool' (see below), it may take almost forty years!

Restrictions on the Annual Investment Allowance

The annual investment allowance is restricted where a company has an accounting period of less than twelve months' duration. This will often apply to a new company's first accounting period.

For example, a company drawing up accounts for the six month period ending 31st December 2020 will be entitled to a maximum annual investment allowance of £502,732 (£1m x 184/366).

The annual investment allowance must also be shared between companies that are members of the same group, or which are otherwise closely related to each other.

The annual investment allowance is not available for expenditure on cars.

Enhanced Capital Allowances

Expenditure on qualifying energy-saving or environmentally beneficial equipment incurred before 1st April 2020 was eligible for 100% enhanced capital allowances.

Enhanced capital allowances continue to be available for:

- Qualifying expenditure in designated Enterprise Zones within assisted areas (this usually applies for a period of eight years after the zone is launched, but this has been extended to at least 31st March 2021 in all cases)
- Gas refuelling stations (to 31st March 2025)
- Zero emissions goods vehicles (to 5th April 2025)

Enhanced capital allowances are available in addition to the annual investment allowance and are not generally subject to any monetary limits.

Writing Down Allowances

Apart from expenditure qualifying for enhanced capital allowances, other qualifying expenditure in excess of the annual investment allowance is eligible for 'writing down allowances'. Writing down allowances also apply to expenditure on qualifying plant and machinery that is not eligible for either the annual investment allowance or enhanced capital allowances.

The rate of writing down allowances on most plant and machinery is currently 18%.

Qualifying expenditure not covered by either the annual investment allowance or enhanced capital allowances is pooled together with the unrelieved balance of qualifying expenditure brought forward from the previous accounting period. This pool of expenditure is known as the 'main pool'.

The writing down allowance is then calculated at the appropriate rate on the total balance in the main pool.

The remaining balance of expenditure is carried forward and the appropriate percentage of that balance may be claimed in the next accounting period. And so on.

However, where the balance in the main pool reduces to £1,000 or less, the full balance may then be claimed immediately.

The Special Rate Pool
Certain expenditure must be allocated to a 'special rate pool' instead of the main pool. This includes:

- Certain defined categories of 'integral features' (see below)
- Expenditure of £100,000 or more on plant and machinery with an anticipated working life of 25 years or more
- Thermal insulation of an existing building used in a qualifying trade

Expenditure in the special rate pool is eligible for a writing down allowance of just 6% instead of the usual 18%.

The rate of writing down allowances on the special rate pool was reduced from 8% to 6% with effect from 1st April 2019. For accounting periods spanning the date of change, a hybrid rate applies. For example, the rate applying for a twelve month accounting period ended 31st December 2019 is 6.493% (8% x 90/365 + 6% x 275/365).

Where the balance on the special rate pool reduces to £1,000 or less, the full balance may then be claimed immediately in the same way as for the main pool.

Tax Tip
The annual investment allowance may be allocated to expenditure falling into the special rate pool in preference to expenditure qualifying for the normal rate of writing down allowance. This will be extremely beneficial in most cases (see example below), with the exception of a few instances where a disposal of assets within the special rate pool is anticipated in the near future.

Integral Features
Expenditure on assets included in a defined list of 'integral features' within commercial property, qualifying furnished holiday accommodation, or communal areas within rented residential property, falls into the special rate pool.

However, as explained in the 'Tax Tip' above, these assets remain eligible for the annual investment allowance, so up to £1m per year of qualifying expenditure on assets in this category could currently attract immediate 100% relief.

The following items are classed as integral features:

- Electrical lighting and power systems
- Cold water systems
- Space or water heating systems, air conditioning, ventilation and air purification systems and floors or ceilings comprised in such systems
- Lifts, escalators and moving walkways
- External solar shading

The integral features regime applies to expenditure incurred by companies after 31st March 2008, including fixtures within second-hand buildings purchased after that date (but see further below regarding second-hand buildings).

It is worth noting that some of the items within the list of 'integral features' were not previously eligible for plant and machinery allowances, particularly cold water systems (i.e. basic plumbing) and most electrical lighting and power systems.

In other words, these items represent significant additions to the categories of expenditure on commercial property, qualifying furnished holiday accommodation, and communal areas within rented residential property, that attract plant and machinery allowances.

Combining this with the annual investment allowance, many property investment companies are able to benefit quite significantly.

Example
Hook Ltd is a property investment company drawing up accounts to 31st March each year. In August 2020, the company buys an old factory and converts it into office units to rent out, completing the work by December.

Hook Ltd's surveyors calculate the company has spent £1.2m on 'integral features' and £1m on other fixtures qualifying as plant and machinery. At first, the company draws up a draft CT computation for the year ending 31st March 2021 claiming a £1m annual investment allowance on the assets falling into the 'main pool' and writing down allowances at 6% on the integral features. This results in a total claim of £1,072,000 (£1m + £1.2m x 6%), saving the company £203,680 in CT (at 19%).

*However, before submitting the final computation, the company's accountant revises the capital allowances claim by allocating the annual investment allowance to the integral features instead of assets falling into the 'main pool'. The company may now claim an annual investment allowance of £1m **plus** writing down allowances at 6% on the remaining £200,000 of integral features expenditure **and** writing down allowances at 18% on the other qualifying fixtures. This produces a total claim of £1,192,000 (£1m + £200,000 x 6% + £1m x 18%), saving the company £226,480 in CT, or £22,800 more than the original computation.*

Furthermore, the company will continue to benefit from greater writing down allowances in future years, as illustrated below:

Year end 31st March	Allowances Claimed		Extra CT Saving
	Original Method	Revised Method	
2021	£1,072,000	£1,192,000	£22,800
2022	£67,680	£158,880	£17,328
2023	£63,620	£131,636	£12,923
2024	£59,802	£109,214	£9,388
2025	£56,214	£90,751	£6,562
2026	£52,842	£75,541	£4,313

The total CT saving achieved in the year of expenditure and the following five years amounts to over £73,000. Hence, as we can see, allocating the annual investment allowance to integral features and other assets falling into the special rate pool can prove hugely beneficial.

Thermal Insulation of Commercial Property

Expenditure on thermal insulation of an existing commercial building used in a qualifying business also falls into the special rate pool. The annual investment allowance is again available on this expenditure, currently providing immediate tax relief on up to £1m each year.

Planning with the Annual Investment Allowance

The annual investment allowance is available to each qualifying business entity. Any individual or company with a property rental business is a qualifying business entity.

Individuals or companies who own joint shares in rental properties, but who are not operating as a partnership, are each deemed to have their own separate property business.

A couple buying property jointly (but not as a partnership) during the 2020/21 tax year could therefore claim annual investment allowances of up to £1m each. Such a couple paying additional rate tax at 45% could therefore potentially benefit from a total tax saving of up to £900,000, simply by buying the right property!

A company can only claim one single annual investment allowance, regardless of how many shareholders it has. Even this is subject to the 'related company' rules.

Unincorporated businesses (i.e. not companies) under the control of the same person, or persons, are also subject to restrictions in the amount of annual investment allowance they can claim. However, for the purposes of the annual investment allowance, a company cannot be treated as being related to an unincorporated business.

Hence, an individual could buy property jointly with his or her own company (but not as a partnership) and the company might currently be eligible for an annual investment allowance of up to £1m while the individual still enjoys his or her own allowance of up to £1m.

Furthermore, a couple could even form a company together, buy property jointly with that company (but not as a partnership) and claim three separate annual investment allowances (one for each of the couple and one for the company), thus potentially providing immediate 100% tax relief on up to £3m of qualifying expenditure.

Taking this idea one step further, each member of the couple could form their own company and all four entities (two individuals and two companies) could buy property jointly (but not as a partnership), thus providing scope to claim immediate 100% tax relief on up to £4m of qualifying expenditure in total!

Late Claims

The annual investment allowance can only be claimed in the period the qualifying expenditure is incurred. However, it is worth noting that writing down allowances may be claimed at any time provided the relevant asset is still in qualifying use (which includes a property letting business). Hence, it is often possible to claim writing down allowances on assets purchased in earlier years where a claim was not originally made: provided the assets qualified in the first place. This is particularly relevant to purchases of second-hand property and there are companies that specialise in assisting property owners with this type of claim. There are, however, a few additional restrictions to be aware of.

Second-Hand Property

Generally speaking, a purchaser may only claim plant and machinery allowances on integral features and other qualifying fixtures within second-hand property where:

i) The seller has also claimed plant and machinery allowances on those fixtures, and
ii) The seller and purchaser agree a fixed value for the qualifying fixtures by making a joint election (a 'Section 198 Election')

The Section 198 Election must specify separate values for the items in the main pool and the special rate pool. The values specified may be anywhere between £1 and the original qualifying cost of the fixtures. Agreeing values for the election is a matter for negotiation and may also depend on the seller's tax position. Typically, however, most sellers will want to use low values (e.g. £1 for each pool) to avoid balancing charges (see below) or future restrictions in their writing down allowances.

Such low values effectively leave the purchaser unable to claim plant and machinery allowances on the fixtures in the property.

There are, however, a number of important exceptions to the rules on second-hand property. In these cases, the purchaser is free to allocate an appropriate element of the purchase price to any qualifying fixtures not covered by the rules. When making such an allocation, the best approach depends on the value of the property. For larger properties, it usually makes sense to ask a surveyor to establish the value of qualifying fixtures. For smaller properties, a reasonable estimate based on average proportions typically applying to the same type of property will usually suffice.

The rules on second-hand property set out above do not apply where:

- Neither the seller nor any other person owning the property since April 2012 was entitled to claim plant and machinery allowances on the fixtures. The most common incidence of this is likely to be where the seller had acquired the property before April 2008 and was therefore not entitled to claim allowances on cold water plumbing or electrical lighting and power systems.
- The property has not been in qualifying use at any time since April 2012. This often occurs where the purchaser acquires a residential property and adopts it as a furnished holiday let.
- The property was purchased between April 2012 and March 2014 and neither the seller nor any other previous owner since April 2012 has claimed plant and machinery allowances on the fixtures.
- The property was purchased before April 2012 and the purchaser did not enter into a Section 198 Election in respect of the fixtures (such elections were optional prior to April 2012, but binding on the purchaser if they were made).

Balancing Charges

When a property is sold, the proportion of sales proceeds relating to qualifying fixtures and fittings within the property must be deducted from the company's main and special rate pools. (The deductions applying to each pool are calculated separately.) In most cases, these sums will be the fixed values agreed by way of a Section 198 Election, as discussed above. Items of expenditure on which no allowances have been claimed do not need to be included.

If the sum to be deducted exceeds the balance on the relevant pool, the excess is added to the company's income for CT purposes. This is known as a 'balancing charge'.

Example

At 1st April 2020, Williams Ltd has balances of £10,000 brought forward on its main pool and £20,000 on its special rate pool. In September that year, the company sells Shane House, a commercial property, and enters into a Section 198 Election with the purchaser, Warburton Ltd. The agreed fixed values in the election are £17,000 for the items in the main pool and £15,000 for the items in the special rate pool.

After deducting the relevant amounts, Williams Ltd will be left with a balance of £5,000 on its special rate pool and can therefore still claim a writing down allowance of £300 (6%) on this pool.

When we turn to the company's main pool, however, the £17,000 deduction relating to Shane House exceeds the balance by £7,000. Williams Ltd will therefore be subject to a balancing charge of £7,000, will not be able to claim any writing down allowance on the main pool and will be left with a nil balance carried forward on this pool.

(I have assumed, for the sale of illustration, that Williams Ltd does not purchase any new qualifying assets during the same accounting period)

Note that a remaining balance on one pool (e.g. the special rate pool in the example above) cannot be used to reduce the balancing charge arising on the other pool. This makes it especially important to ensure the fixed values agreed in any Section 198 Election are considered very carefully.

Balancing charges have become more common for small property investment companies selling properties in recent years, due to the fact that most qualifying expenditure has previously been claimed in full by way of the annual investment allowance.

Other Equipment Used in the Business
See Section 5.5 for more details on the practical aspects of claiming plant and machinery allowances on the company's own plant and equipment, including motor cars.

4.6   THE STRUCTURES AND BUILDINGS ALLOWANCE

The structures and buildings allowance ('SBA') applies to expenditure on the construction, renovation, improvement or conversion of qualifying non-residential property after 28th October 2018. It is available to landlords renting out non-residential property, as well as businesses using commercial property in their own trade or profession.

The SBA is given as a straight-line allowance on qualifying cost at the following rates:

For the period 29th October 2018 to 31st March 2020:   2% per annum
For periods falling after 31st March 2020:   3% per annum

The above rates apply regardless of when the expenditure was incurred (subject to the rules set out below). Hence, for example, £1m of expenditure first qualifying for the allowance on 1st April 2019 will attract SBA of £200,000 in the year ended 31st March 2020 (2%) and £300,000 each year thereafter (3%) until the claim expires (see below).

The main provisos are:

- All contracts for construction works on the relevant project must have been entered into after 28th October 2018
- The structure or building is used in a business chargeable to UK CT or Income Tax; including a trade, profession, or 'ordinary' property business (i.e. not a furnished holiday let)
- The cost of land, including rights over land, does not qualify
- Property in residential use does not qualify (see further below)

Where any contract for the construction of a property was entered into before 29th October 2018 then the first point above means the SBA cannot be claimed on the property itself. However, this does not prevent later projects for renovation, conversion or improvement work on the property from qualifying.

SBA is limited to the 'net direct costs relating to physically constructing the asset'. Where relevant, this will include demolition costs, the costs of land alterations or preparations necessary for the construction and other direct costs of bringing the structure or building into existence. However, in addition to excluding the cost of land, SBA does not cover the cost of:

- SDLT and other purchase costs
- Obtaining planning permission
- Other land alterations beyond what is necessary for the construction (e.g. landscaping, although landscaping that results in the creation of a separate structure does qualify)
- Land reclamation
- Land remediation (a separate relief may be available for this cost)

The SBA cannot be claimed on expenditure that qualifies for plant and machinery allowances, including 'integral features' and other qualifying fixtures (Section 4.5).

The SBA claim generally commences on the later of the date the expenditure is incurred, and the date the building or structure is first brought into qualifying use. However, in the case of renovations or improvements to property already in qualifying use, the claim may commence on any of:

i) The last day works are carried out in relation to the project,
ii) The first day of the next accounting period commencing after (i), or
iii) The first day of the next accounting period after the day the expenditure is incurred

For example, in the case of a company with a 31st December accounting date carrying out improvements to a property over the period from October 2020 to 31st March 2021, the company may choose to claim the SBA:

- From 31st March 2021 using option (i),
- From 1st January 2022 using option (ii), or
- From 1st January 2021 for expenditure incurred up to 31st December 2020 and from 1st January 2022 for the remainder, using option (iii)

Expenditure incurred prior to the commencement of the owner's business is treated as if it were incurred on the date of commencement. Unlike the pre-trading rules for expenditure that is not capital in nature (see Section 4.3), there is no limit to how long prior to commencement the expenditure was incurred (subject to the rule that all contracts must have been entered into after 28th October 2018, as stated above).

The SBA is reduced on a time apportionment basis:

- In any accounting period of less than twelve months' duration,
- If the building or structure had not yet been brought into qualifying use at the beginning of the period, or
- Where the SBA claim commences part way through the period (as detailed above)

The current owner may continue to claim the SBA where a property falls into disuse, provided the property was in qualifying use immediately beforehand. However, a new owner must bring the property into qualifying use before they can claim the SBA.

For property investment companies (and other landlords), a property is in 'qualifying use' when it is being let out at full market rent.

The existing owner may continue to claim the SBA during a void that follows a period of 'qualifying use', but a new owner must let the property out (at full market rent) before they may claim the SBA. In all cases, the property must not be in residential use (see below).

The SBA ceases when a full claim for all periods since the relevant expenditure first qualified for the allowance would total 100%. For expenditure first qualifying for the SBA after 31st March 2020, this will take thirty-three and a third years, so the allowance remains a 'long player' (if you don't understand that reference, dear reader, ask one of your parents!) The SBA also ceases if a qualifying building or structure is demolished.

Following the increase in the rate of SBA from 1st April 2020, the earliest possible claims are now due to expire in August 2052, although I strongly suspect we will see more changes before then!

When a building or structure is sold, entitlement to the SBA transfers to the new owner. The SBA available for the year of sale is apportioned between the seller and purchaser, with the seller retaining entitlement for the day of transfer. There are no balancing allowances or charges at the point of sale.

Where a qualifying property is purchased from a developer, SBA may be claimed on the purchase price, but with appropriate exclusions for the cost of the land, integral features, and other fixtures qualifying for plant and machinery allowances (see Section 4.5). The expenditure is deemed to be incurred on the date of purchase in these cases.

Example 1

Townsend Ltd purchases a new office building from a developer for £13m. £2m of this cost relates to the land, and £1m represents 'integral features' and other fixtures qualifying as 'plant and machinery', so the amount qualifying for SBA is £10m. Townsend Ltd has a 31st December year end and starts to rent out the building on 1st February 2020.

On 30th June 2022, Townsend Ltd sells the building to Hogg Ltd for £20m. Hogg Ltd uses the property in its business until selling it to the Attuclac Relief Foundation for £17m on 31st March 2025. Hogg Ltd's accounting year end is 31st March.

The Attuclac Relief Foundation is a charity and does not pay CT or Income Tax, so cannot claim any allowance. It retains the property for several years before selling it to Darcy Ltd for £40m on 31st December 2050. Darcy Ltd uses the property in its business for many years. The company draws up accounts to 30th June 2051, then to 31st December each year from 2052 onwards.

The following SBA claims may be made:

Townsend Ltd

Year ending 31st December 2020		
1st February to 31st March	*£10m x 2% x 60/366*	*£32,787*
1st April to 31st December	*£10m x 3% x 275/366*	*£225,410*
Year ending 31st December 2021		*£300,000*
Year ending 31st December 2022	*£10m x 3% x 181/365*	*£148,767*

Hogg Ltd

Year ending 31st March 2023	*£10m x 3% x 274/365*	*£225,205*
Year ending 31st March 2024		*£300,000*
Year ending 31st March 2025		*£300,000*

Darcy Ltd

Year ending 30th June 2051	*£10m x 3% x 181/365*	*£148,767*
Period ending 31st December 2052	*£10m x 3% x 550/366*	*£450,820*
Year ending 31st December 2053		
1st January to 20th June*	*£10m x 3% x 171/365*	*£140,548*

The property's 'tax life' expires on 20th June 2053, the date on which 100% of the expenditure would have been claimed if it had been in qualifying use throughout the period since its purchase in 2020.

The SBA claims add up to £2,272,304. A further £7,727,696 could have been claimed between 2025 and 2050 if the property had been in qualifying use but since the Attuclac Relief Foundation was not in charge to UK CT or Income Tax, SBA could not be claimed during this period.

Whether, in practice, the information will be available to enable Darcy Ltd to make its claim is uncertain, but technically it will be eligible (assuming the SBA regime lasts that long).

The prices paid for the property by Hogg Ltd, the Attuclac Relief Foundation, and Darcy Ltd are irrelevant. SBA is based only on the original cost of the building (although separate claims may be made for subsequent improvement expenditure).

Where the original owner incurring the qualifying expenditure is not in charge to UK tax, or not using the property in a qualifying business, subsequent owners may still claim the SBA provided the first use of the property after the qualifying expenditure is not residential use. However, the first use of the property will still determine when the property's 'tax life' expires.

Residential Use
The SBA is not available when a property is in residential use. This includes:

- A dwelling house (i.e. normal residential property including houses, flats, apartments, etc.)
- Residential accommodation for school pupils
- Student accommodation (property that was either purpose built or converted for student use and is available for occupation by students at least 165 days per year)
- Residential accommodation for the armed forces
- Homes providing residential accommodation (but see the exception below)
- Prisons or similar institutions

There is an exception for care homes providing residential accommodation together with personal care for the elderly, disabled, people with mental disorders, or people suffering from alcohol or drugs dependency.

A 'dwelling house' is a building, or part of a building, that has all the facilities required for normal day to day living. Typically, therefore, hotel rooms do not usually constitute dwellings and a hotel would usually qualify for SBA. A guest house would, however, usually be a dwelling house and would not usually qualify.

Any structure on land in residential use, such as the garden or grounds of a house, is itself deemed to be in residential use. Additional facilities provided with serviced apartments (such as a gym or swimming pool) are also deemed to be in residential use and excluded from the SBA.

If the first use of a property following the qualifying expenditure is residential (as defined above), the SBA will never be available on that expenditure. Later expenditure on the same property may qualify, however.

Example 2
Farrell Ltd purchases a block of flats from a developer in December 2020 and starts to rent it out. No SBA is available on the cost of the flats as they are in residential use. In 2022, the company spends £250,000 converting the bottom two floors of the block into shops and offices. The SBA will be available on the conversion costs giving Farrell Ltd a tax deduction of £7,500 (£250,000 x 3%) per year.

Where a building or structure has both qualifying and non-qualifying use, the qualifying costs must be apportioned and the SBA may be claimed on an appropriate proportion. However, no relief is available on workplaces within a dwelling house; or where the proportion in qualifying use is 'insignificant' (generally taken to mean 10% or less).

Example 3
Beaumont Ltd purchases a property from the local authority for £800,000. The property was originally constructed in 2020 at a cost of £900,000, with the local authority taking possession in September that year. The property has six storeys, with shops on the ground floor and flats in the floors above. Beaumont Ltd may therefore claim an annual SBA of £4,500 (£900,000 x 1/6 x 3%).

Beaumont Ltd's SBA claim is based on the original cost of the property and is unaffected by the fact the original owner was not in charge to CT or Income Tax. The SBA claim will, however, cease thirty-three and a third years after the date the local authority first brought the property into use.

The Allowance Statement
SBA claims require an 'allowance statement'. This is a written statement identifying the relevant building or structure, together with:

    a) The date of the earliest contract relating to the relevant project
    b) The amount of qualifying expenditure
    c) The date the property was first brought into qualifying use

The owner who incurs the qualifying expenditure makes the allowance statement. Subsequent owners must obtain a copy.

Further Points

Where the owner grants a lease for thirty-five years or more at a premium then the right to claim the SBA on the property transfers to the tenant if the element of the premium treated as a capital disposal for tax purposes (see Section 4.12) is at least three times greater than the value of the owner's reversionary interest in the property. A tenant will also be able to claim SBA on any qualifying expenditure they incur themselves, regardless of the length of their lease.

The SBA is available on both UK and overseas property (provided the property is used in a business chargeable to UK CT or Income Tax).

The claimant must have a relevant legal interest in the land on which the building or structure is located (e.g. a freehold or leasehold interest).

Unclaimed relief is simply lost and cannot be carried forward.

The amount of qualifying expenditure for the purposes of SBA is subject to a market value 'cap'. In other words, expenditure in excess of market value does not qualify. This rule is only likely to be relevant where work is carried out by a connected party.

Interaction with Capital Gains

The amount of SBA claimed by a seller must be added to their sale proceeds for the purposes of calculating the chargeable gain arising on a disposal of the property. Hence, in Example 1, when Townsend Ltd sold the property, the total SBA of £706,964 claimed by the company would be added to its sale proceeds, increasing them from £20m to £20,706,964 and giving it a chargeable gain of £7,706,964 (£20,706,964 less £13m).

The relief provided by SBA is therefore effectively clawed back on the sale of a property.

Where a property is transferred by way of a 'no gain/no loss' transfer, the transferee will also have to add the SBA claimed by the transferor to any future sale proceeds on the ultimate disposal of the property. The most common incidence of a 'no gain/no loss' transfer is a transfer between spouses. The same principal applies where 'incorporation relief' is claimed on a transfer into a company (see Section 14.9).

A holdover relief claim on a transfer will have a similar, although slightly different effect, as the SBA claimed by the transferor will effectively be deducted from the cost of the property. We will take a closer look at this in Section 14.8.

4.7   REPLACING FURNITURE, FURNISHINGS & EQUIPMENT

'Replacement of domestic items relief' (formerly known as 'replacement furniture relief'), is available:

- To all companies with residential lettings
- On qualifying replacement expenditure within fully furnished lets, partly furnished lets and even unfurnished lets (but not furnished holiday lets)
- To cover replacements of all moveable items (i.e. all furnishings, as detailed below)

Any sale proceeds received on the disposal of the old item being replaced must be deducted from the replacement cost claimed.

The relief does not cover the cost of the original furnishings when the property is first let out, or the cost of additional items. Companies may, however, claim part of the cost of a replacement item that performs additional functions compared to the old item it replaces. For example, where a landlord company replaces an old fridge with a fridge-freezer costing £300, but could have purchased a new fridge for £200, it will still be able to claim the £200 direct replacement cost.

Furnished holiday lets are subject to a different regime, which I will examine in Section 4.8 (the key difference is that qualifying items within furnished holiday lets are eligible for plant and machinery allowances).

Items within 'communal areas' lying outside any individual dwelling (e.g. the common parts of a house divided into self-contained flats) are also subject to a different regime and may be eligible for plant and machinery allowances (see Section 4.5 for details).

What Are Furnishings?
The first thing to understand is that fixtures, fittings, and, generally speaking, anything else that is permanently fixed to the building, are not classed as 'furnishings' and replacing these items will often be claimable as a repair expense.

Items classed as 'furnishings' for tax purposes include:
- Furniture
- Electrical equipment
- Free-standing 'white goods', such as fridges, dishwashers, etc.
- Carpets and other floor coverings
- Curtains, blinds, etc.
- 'Soft furnishings', such as cushions, lampshades, etc.
- Cutlery, crockery and cooking utensils
- Bed linen

Carpets often cause a lot of confusion as many people see them as a 'fitting' rather than a 'furnishing'. For tax purposes, however, they are classed as furnishings.

Items classed as fixtures and fittings for tax purposes include:
- Baths, toilets, sinks, showers, etc.
- Fitted kitchens, including fitted (not free-standing) cookers, fridges and other items that are an integral part of a fitted kitchen
- Central heating equipment (boilers, radiators, etc.)
- Air conditioning
- Light fittings

Replacement or Repair?

It is important to stress nothing in this section affects the company's ability to claim repairs expenditure under normal principles. In particular, it is worth noting the following types of expenditure may usually be claimed as repairs:

- Replacement of fixtures and fittings (provided there is no element of improvement involved)
- Repairs to furniture, white goods, equipment, carpets, curtains and other furnishings

For further details on the principles applying to repairs expenditure, see the Taxcafe.co.uk guide *'How to Save Property Tax'*.

4.8   FURNISHED HOLIDAY LETS

Properties qualifying as 'furnished holiday lets' are subject to a special tax regime, with many of the tax advantages usually only accorded to a trade. Where I refer to furnished holiday lets or lettings throughout this guide, it is assumed the property, or properties, qualify for this special regime by meeting the criteria set out below.

The advantages of furnished holiday lets have been slightly curtailed as a result of changes to loss relief that we will look at in Section 4.10. Nonetheless, several other key advantages remain, including the ability to claim capital allowances on furniture and equipment and rollover relief for capital gains purposes.

The benefits for a shareholder owning a company mainly engaged in furnished holiday lets were considered in Section 3.2.

For the purposes of both loss relief and capital allowances, furnished holiday lets must be treated as a separate business to any other lettings the company has. Furthermore, furnished holiday lets in the UK must also be treated as a separate business to furnished holiday lets in the European Economic Area.

Qualifying Criteria

The qualification requirements for a 'furnished holiday let' are the property must be:

i)   Situated in the UK or the European Economic Area (see below)

ii)   Fully furnished (see below)

iii) Let out on a commercial basis with a view to the realisation of profits

iv)   Available for letting as holiday accommodation to the public generally for at least 210 days in a twelve-month period

v)   Actually let as holiday accommodation to members of the public for at least 105 such days (but see further below)

vi)   Not in 'longer term occupation' for more than 155 days during the same twelve-month period as that referred to in (iv) above

The European Economic Area comprises the 27 member states of the European Union, plus Iceland, Liechtenstein, and Norway.

'Longer term occupation' means any period of more than 31 consecutive days during which the property is in the same occupation, unless this arises due to exceptional circumstances (e.g. the tenant falls ill, or their flight home is delayed). Periods of longer term occupation cannot be counted towards the 105 days required under condition (v).

While the property need not be in a recognised holiday area, the lettings should strictly be to holidaymakers and tourists in order to qualify.

Companies with more than one UK furnished holiday let (or more than one furnished holiday let in the European Economic Area, as the case may be), may use a system of averaging to determine whether they meet condition (v).

Companies may elect for properties that qualified in the previous accounting period (including those qualifying by using averaging, as above) to stay within the furnished holiday letting regime for up to two further accounting periods, despite failing to meet condition (v). In effect, this means properties generally only need to meet this condition once every three years. The property must meet the other qualifying conditions and the company must have had a genuine intention to meet condition (v) each year. This extension to the qualifying conditions is likely to be particularly useful in 2020, due to the coronavirus crisis, but it remains important for companies with furnished holiday lets to meet the other conditions set out above and to make their best efforts to meet condition (v) wherever possible.

What Is a Fully Furnished Letting?

To be classed as a 'fully furnished letting', the landlord must provide sufficient furnishings so the property is capable of 'normal residential use' without the tenant having to provide their own. Typically, this will include beds, chairs, tables, sofas, carpets or other floor coverings, curtains or blinds, and kitchen equipment.

The key phrase here is whether the property is capable of 'normal residential use' and the level of furnishings and equipment required must be considered in this context. In essence, the landlord must provide the tenant with some privacy, somewhere to sit, somewhere to sleep, somewhere to eat, and the facilities required to feed themselves.

4.9   INTEREST AND FINANCE COSTS

As explained previously, interest and finance costs incurred by a company in connection with its property investment or property letting business are treated as general overheads rather than expenses of the letting business (except in the case of furnished holiday lets: see below). This provides a tremendous advantage for property investment businesses run through a company when compared with the same type of business run by an individual or partnership.

The interest and finance costs incurred by the company in connection with its property investment business may be set off against any income or capital gains received by the company during the same accounting period.

If we contrast this with the position for an individual or partnership where these same costs can only be set against rental income, and only attract basic rate tax relief (where the costs relate to residential lettings), we can readily see what an enormous advantage this provides.

Furthermore, as an alternative, the company may instead:

i)   Carry the costs back for set off against any interest, and certain other limited categories of income, received in the previous year,

ii)   Carry the costs forward for set off against *any* income *or* capital gains in future periods, or

iii)   Surrender the costs as 'group relief' (where the company is a member of a group of companies)

For costs arising before April 2017, any amounts carried forward under (ii) can only be set off against non-trading income or capital gains in future periods. However, since this includes rental profits, it will seldom cause much of an issue for property investment companies.

The carry forward rules under (ii) are subject to the proviso that the company must continue to carry on an investment business. An investment business for this purpose includes any form of property letting other than furnished holiday lets, as well as the other categories of investment business referred to in Section 4.10, although the investment business must not be 'small'. Here there is no definition of what 'small' means, although it seems safe to assume it means very small indeed.

If the company ceases to have an investment business, or it becomes 'small' then amounts carried forward under (ii) will again only be eligible for set off against non-trading income and capital gains.

Note that furnished holiday letting profits (see Section 4.8) are classed as trading income for the purposes of (ii) and are thus ineligible for the set off of brought forward interest and finance costs arising before April 2017 (or later costs when the company's investment business has ceased or become 'small').

Tax Tip
Option (ii) enables a property investment company to effectively 'roll up' its accumulated interest costs and set them off against the capital gains arising on the sale of its investment properties. This represents a massive advantage over individual investors who cannot set rental losses or interest costs against capital gains. We will look at the benefits of this in practice in Chapter 12.

What do we mean by 'Finance Costs'?
In addition to interest, other costs falling within this category include:
- Guarantee fees
- Loan arrangement fees
- Early redemption fees
- Reimbursement of lender's expenses
- Professional costs relating to the raising of finance

Loans and other Facilities Provided by the Company's Owner
In general terms, interest and finance costs (as described above) may continue to be claimed for CT purposes even when paid to one of the company's directors, shareholders, or another connected person. There are two important provisos, however:

i) The amount paid must not exceed a normal commercial rate
ii) Payment must actually be made within twelve months of the end of the company's accounting period

We will consider the issue of loans from the owner to the company in more detail in Chapter 12.

Non-Commercial Lettings

CT relief for interest and finance costs incurred in connection with any 'non-commercial' lettings (see Section 4.1) will be restricted so that, broadly speaking, relief is only given against income from those lettings.

Furnished Holiday Lets

Interest and finance costs relating to furnished holiday lets (see Section 4.8) are treated as a direct expense of that business and NOT as general company overheads in the manner described above.

This means these costs may only be set off against income from the company's furnished holiday lets. Further restrictions also apply where the company has both UK furnished holiday lets and furnished holiday lets in the European Economic Area (see Section 4.10).

It is also important to remember income from furnished holiday lets is classed as trading income for the purposes of relief for carried forward surplus interest and finance costs relating to other lettings.

> #### Practical Pointer
>
> Interest and finance costs incurred by individuals or partnerships in connection with furnished holiday lets remain fully allowable for Income Tax purposes and are not subject to the restrictions discussed in Section 12.12. This reduces the benefit of running this type of business through a company, since one key element of the difference between the corporate and personal property tax regimes is no longer present. Nonetheless, many other advantages do remain and, as we will see in Chapter 14, it is also much easier to transfer furnished holiday lets into a company.

Corporate Interest Relief Restrictions

Restrictions on interest relief apply to large multinationals or groups of companies. Companies or groups with no more than £2m of annual interest costs, or no overseas associated companies, are not affected.

4.10 TAX TREATMENT OF RENTAL LOSSES

Given the fact that interest and finance costs incurred in connection with a company's property rental business are not generally treated as an expense of that business (see Section 4.9), rental losses within a company should be a fairly rare occurrence. In this section, however, we will look at what happens when such losses do arise. For loss relief purposes, we must divide the company's property lettings into four categories:

i)   Ordinary UK property lettings
ii)   Ordinary overseas lettings
iii)   UK furnished holiday lets
iv)   Furnished holiday lets in the European Economic Area

For the purposes of (i) and (ii) above, 'ordinary' simply means not a furnished holiday let (as defined in Section 4.8).

Ordinary UK Property Lettings

Subject to the exception for non-commercial lettings set out below, for CT purposes, all of a company's 'ordinary' UK property lettings are treated as a single UK property business. Hence, the loss on any one such property is automatically set off against profits on other commercially let UK properties for the same period.

Any overall net losses arising from a company's 'ordinary' UK property-letting business will be set off against the company's other income and capital gains for the same period (if any).

This again represents a major advantage over individual property investors, or partnerships, who can only carry forward any net rental loss (other than losses derived from capital allowances).

Any remaining surplus rental loss incurred by the company is carried forward and set off against the company's **total** profits (including capital gains) for the next accounting period, then the next, and so on. Rental losses may be carried forward for as long as is necessary in this way, provided the company is still carrying on an 'ordinary' UK property-letting business in the accounting period for which the claim to offset the losses is made.

If the company's 'ordinary' UK property-letting business ceases, but the company still has an 'investment business', then any unused UK rental losses are converted to 'management expenses'. 'Management expenses' may also be carried forward and set off against the company's total profits, including capital gains, for as long as the company continues to have an 'investment business'.

An 'investment business' is any business that consists of making investments. For example, the company may have an 'investment business' if it owns subsidiary companies, has foreign investment property, or holds a portfolio of stock market investments. It is questionable, however, whether simply holding cash on deposit constitutes an 'investment business'.

Wealth Warning

It is unclear whether furnished holiday lets constitute an 'investment business' for these purposes; so it would perhaps be unwise to rely on them as a means to preserve rental losses from an 'ordinary' UK property-letting business.

Nevertheless, it is clear there are many ways for a company to preserve the value of its 'ordinary' UK rental losses and ensure CT relief is ultimately obtained. This contrasts with individual investors who effectively lose the value of any 'ordinary' UK rental losses if they cease to carry on an 'ordinary' UK rental business.

A company will only lose the value of its unused rental losses if it ceases to carry on both its 'ordinary' UK letting business and any other type of 'investment business'.

Tax Tip
As long as the company continues to have an 'ordinary' UK letting business or an 'investment business', it may continue to set brought forward rental losses off against other income and capital gains. Hence, a company with 'ordinary' UK rental losses may often be used as a vehicle to generate what will effectively be tax-free income or capital gains.

Either an 'ordinary' UK letting business or an 'investment business' must be continued, but this could be on a much smaller scale than previously, if desired.

Wealth Warning
Rental losses incurred in a company can only be set off against the company's income of the same or future periods. There is no scope for setting such losses off against rental profits the owner of the company may have as an individual.

Ordinary Overseas Lettings
All of a company's 'ordinary' overseas lettings are treated as a single business for CT purposes. This is treated as a separate business to the company's UK property letting business (if any).

Any loss on this business may be carried forward and set off against future profits from the same business: i.e. against future 'ordinary' overseas rental profits received by the company.

Furnished Holiday Lets
All of a company's UK furnished holiday lets are treated as a single business. All of its furnished holiday lets in the European Economic Area are also treated as a single business: but a different one. Losses arising on a furnished holiday letting business may only be carried forward and set off against future profits from the same business.

Non-Commercial Lettings
Losses arising on any non-commercial lettings (i.e. lettings not made on normal, commercial, 'arm's length' terms) may only be set against future profits from the same letting.

Corporate Loss Relief Restrictions
The total amount of relief a company, or group of companies, may claim for brought forward losses and unrelieved interest and finance costs is

restricted to a maximum of £5m plus 50% of any profits in excess of that amount. The £5m limit applies on an annual basis (e.g. the limit would be £2.5m for a six month period).

4.11 OTHER PROPERTY INVESTMENT INCOME

Any form of income, profit or gains derived from property that the company receives will generally be subject to CT.

We will look at property trading profits in Chapter 5 and capital gains in Chapter 6, but in this section, it is worth considering some other items that may arise.

In Section 4.2, we saw the company's rental income will include any tenant's deposits retained at the end of a lease. HMRC also takes the view that any dilapidation payments received should usually be treated as rental income unless the payment is put towards the cost of repairs, when they consider it should be netted off those costs.

This view is questionable. Some experts argue dilapidation payments are a capital receipt: i.e. effectively a part disposal of the property, meaning the sum received represents a capital gain and part of the property's original cost is properly deductible.

HMRC does agree with this view if the property is not rented out again after receipt of the payment and is subsequently sold or adopted for some other purpose (e.g. as the company's own office premises).

Some items are specifically excluded from treatment as property income, including:

- Any amounts taxable as trading income or capital gains
- Profits from farming and market gardening
- Income from mineral extraction rights

Wayleave payments received in respect of access rights (e.g. for the electric company to have access to an electricity pylon on the company's land) are, however, sometimes included as property income.

Another important source of property income is lease premiums, which we will examine in the next section.

4.12 LEASE PREMIUMS

Lease premiums have a particularly complex treatment for CT purposes.

Granting a Short Lease

Premiums received for the granting of short leases of no more than 50 years' duration are treated as being partly property income and partly capital disposal proceeds, potentially giving rise to a capital gain.

The proportion of the premium treated as capital disposal proceeds is equal to 2% of the total premium received for each full year of the lease's duration in excess of one year. The capital gain arising is calculated on the basis of a part disposal of the relevant property. The remainder of the premium is treated as rental income.

Example

Telstra Ltd owns the freehold to a property. The company grants a 12-year lease to Fiji Ltd for a premium of £50,000. The lease exceeds one year by 11 years and hence 22% of this sum (£11,000) falls within the capital gains regime. This will be treated as a part disposal of the property and may or may not give rise to a taxable capital gain for Telstra. What is certain is that Telstra will be subject to CT on deemed rental income of £39,000 (i.e. £50,000 less 22%).

A tenant paying a premium for the grant of a short lease of less than 50 years' duration may claim a deduction in respect of the proportion of the premium treated as rental income in the grantor's hands (i.e. £39,000 in the above example).

This claim must be spread over the length of the lease (e.g. £3,250 per annum for twelve years in Fiji Ltd's case) and is only available if the tenant has a taxable business of their own.

If the tenant subsequently assigns the lease, they must restrict their base cost for capital gains purposes (see Section 6.3) to the element of the original lease premium treated as capital disposal proceeds in the grantor's hands (e.g. £11,000 in our example above). This base cost will then be subject to further restriction as explained below.

Granting a Long Lease

The grant of a lease of more than 50 years' duration is treated purely as a capital disposal. The base cost (see Section 6.3) to be used has to be restricted under the 'part disposal' rules. In essence, this means the base cost is divided between the part disposed of (i.e. the lease) and the part retained (the 'reversionary interest') in proportion to their relative values at the time the lease is granted.

Example

JPR Ltd owns the freehold of a commercial property in Llanelli. The company grants a 60-year lease to Brian, a businessman from Belfast moving into the area. Brian pays a premium of £900,000 for the lease. The value of JPR Ltd's reversionary interest is established as £100,000. The base cost to be used in calculating JPR Ltd's capital gain on the grant of the lease is therefore 90% of its base cost for the property as a whole.

66

Assigning a Long Lease

Assigning a lease with no less than 50 years' duration remaining is a straightforward capital disposal. The capital gain arising is calculated in more or less the same way as for a freehold property sale (see Chapter 6). Any applicable capital gains reliefs may be claimed in the usual way.

Assigning a Short Lease

Again, this is treated entirely as a capital disposal. However, leases with less than 50 years remaining are treated as 'wasting assets'. The company is therefore required to reduce its base cost in accordance with a statutory schedule (see the Taxcafe.co.uk guide *'How to Save Property Tax'* or search on www.gov.uk).

For example, for a lease with 20 years remaining, and which had more than 50 years remaining when first acquired, the base cost must be reduced to 72.77% of the original premium paid for the lease (plus other applicable purchase costs).

Where the lease had less than 50 years remaining when originally acquired, the necessary reduction in base cost is achieved by multiplying the original cost by the factor applying at the time of sale and dividing by the factor applying at the time of purchase.

Example

Calcutta Cup Ltd pays a premium of £100,000 for the assignment of a lease with ten years remaining. Five years later, the company assigns the lease to Murrayfield Ltd at a premium of £60,000.

When calculating the capital gain, the amount Calcutta Cup Ltd may claim as its base cost is: £100,000 x 26.722/46.695 = £57,227

Where the base cost is reduced on assignment of a lease with less than 50 years remaining, any SBA claim that must be added to sale proceeds (see Section 4.6) is also reduced in the same proportion.

Chapter 5

Property Trading Income and Expenses

5.1 HOW PROPERTY TRADING PROFITS ARE TAXED

Some property companies are not taxed under the rules for rental profits set out in Chapter 4, but are, instead, taxed on the basis the income from their property business represents trading profit.

The most important differences in being a 'trading company' are probably the implications for the owner, which we looked at in Chapter 3. As far as the computation of profits is concerned, the differences are not huge and there is therefore little point in repeating all the rules from scratch.

What I will do in this chapter, however, is consider the differences for a company between the taxation of trading profits and the taxation of rental profits.

Trading losses are also subject to a different set of rules to rental losses and we will look at these in Section 5.6.

5.2 TRADING PROFITS VERSUS RENTAL PROFITS

The major differences between the taxation of rental profits and trading profits in a company may be summarised as follows:

- In the case of property development or property trading, the disposal proceeds received on the sale of a property represent trading income. Likewise, the cost of properties acquired represents 'cost of sales' and may be deducted from sale proceeds at the time of the property's sale.
- Legal and professional fees and other costs incurred on the purchase or sale of properties may also be included within 'cost of sales'.
- Any abortive costs relating to property purchases or sales may be claimed as company overheads.
- The costs related to any unsold properties are included in the company's accounts as 'trading stock'. We will look at the implications of this in more detail in the next section.
- Interest and finance costs relating to a company's trading activities are treated as a trading expense. They are deducted from trading profits and will also form part of any trading loss, to be dealt with as explained in Section 5.6 below. (Costs in excess of £2m per year continue to be subject to the restriction explained in Section 4.9.)

- Capital allowances may only be claimed in respect of assets acquired as long-term fixed assets of the business. We will look at this further in Section 5.5.
- The cost of any furnishings purchased and sold with a property may be deducted as 'cost of sales' against the disposal proceeds from that property.
- All of the company's business will usually be treated as a single business, regardless of where its properties are located. This will all be treated as UK trading income if the business is all run from the UK. (Non-UK resident companies are subject to CT on trading profits derived from UK land and property.)

Notwithstanding any of the above, any costs related to a property acquired as a long-term fixed asset of the business (such as its own offices, for example) remain capital in nature and do not form part of the company's trading stock or 'cost of sales'. A disposal of the company's own trading premises would continue to be dealt with under the rules for capital gains.

5.3   PROPERTIES AS TRADING STOCK

Properties held for development or sale in a property development or property dealing company are not regarded as long-term capital assets. They are, instead, regarded as the company's *trading stock*.

For tax purposes, all the company's expenditure in acquiring, improving, repairing or converting the properties becomes part of the cost of that trading stock. Many of the issues we need to deal with in a property investment company regarding the question of whether expenditure is revenue or capital in nature therefore become completely irrelevant. Most professional fees and repairs or improvement expenditure are treated as part of the cost of the company's trading stock.

(The term 'revenue expenditure' means expenditure deductible from income, whereas capital expenditure is subject to different rules.)

When properties are sold, the related costs become 'cost of sales' and may be deducted from the company's sale proceeds. Sometimes, however, it may be some considerable time before this occurs. In the meantime, the property will have to be dealt with as 'trading stock'. In this section, we will take a detailed look at what this means in practice.

The way trading stock works for tax purposes can best be illustrated by way of an example.

Example

In November 2020, Grand Slam Ltd buys a property in Manchester for £275,000. The company pays SDLT of £8,250 and legal fees of £1,500. Previously, in October, it had also paid a survey fee of £750. Grand Slam Ltd is a property development company and draws up accounts to 31st December each year. In the accounts to 31st December 2020, the Manchester property will be included as trading stock with a value of £285,500, made up as follows:

Property purchase	£275,000
SDLT	£8,250
Legal fees	£1,500
Survey fee	£750
Total	£285,500

Points to Note

While all Grand Slam Ltd's expenditure is regarded as revenue (because it's a property development company), the company cannot yet claim any deduction for it because it still holds the property.

Example Continued

Early in 2021, Grand Slam Ltd incurs further professional fees of £7,000 obtaining planning permission to divide the property into two separate residences. Permission is granted in July and by the end of the year, Grand Slam Ltd has spent a further £40,000 on conversion work. In the accounts to 31st December 2021 the property will still be shown in trading stock, as follows:

Costs brought forward	£285,500
Additional professional fees	£7,000
Building work	£40,000
Total	£332,500

Grand Slam Ltd still doesn't get any tax relief for any of this expenditure.

By March 2022, Grand Slam Ltd has spent another £5,000 on the property and is ready to sell the new houses. One of them sells quickly for £190,000. Grand Slam Ltd incurs a further £3,500 in estate agent and legal fees in the process. The taxable profit on this sale is calculated as follows:

Total cost brought forward:	£332,500
Additional building costs:	£5,000
Trading stock prior to sale of first property	£337,500
Allocated to property sold (50%):	£168,750
Add additional costs:	£3,500
Total cost of sales	£172,250
Profit on sale (£190,000 – £172,250)	£17,750

This will form part of Grand Slam Ltd's trading profit for the year ending 31st December 2022.

Points to Note
The additional building spend of £5,000 was allocated to trading stock as this still related to the whole property.

The legal and estate agent's fees incurred on the sale, however, were specific to the part that was sold and may thus be deducted in full against those sale proceeds.

In the example, I have split the cost of trading stock equally between the two new houses. If the houses are identical then this will be correct. Otherwise, the costs should be split between the two properties on a reasonable basis: e.g. total floor area, or in proportion to the market value of the finished properties.

The latter approach would be the required statutory basis if these were capital disposals. Although it is not mandatory here, it might still be a useful yardstick.

The most important point, however, is that even if Grand Slam Ltd fails to sell the second house before 31st December 2022, its profit on the first house will still be taxable in full. There is one exception to this, as we shall now examine.

Net Realisable Value
Trading stock is generally shown in the accounts at its cumulative cost to date. On this basis, Grand Slam Ltd's second house, if still unsold at 31st December 2022, would have a carrying value of £168,750 in its accounts.

If, however, the market value of the property is less than its cumulative cost then its carrying value in the accounts may be reduced appropriately.

Furthermore, since the act of selling the property will itself give rise to further expenses, these may also be deducted from the property's reduced value in this situation. This gives us a value known in accounting terminology as 'net realisable value'.

> **Practical Pointer**
> Trading stock should be shown in the accounts at the lower of cost or net realisable value.

To see the effect of this in practice, let's return once more to our example.

Example
The second house doesn't sell so quickly. Grand Slam Ltd therefore decides to take it off the market and build an extension to make it more attractive to potential buyers. Unfortunately, there are some problems with the foundations for the extension and the costs turn out to be more than double what Grand Slam Ltd had expected.

By 31st December 2022, the company has spent £34,250 on the extension work and it still isn't finished. The total costs to date on the second house are now £203,000. Furthermore, the further expenditure required to complete the extension is estimated at £12,000.

The estate agent reckons the completed property will sell for around £210,000. The agent's own fees will amount to £3,150 and there will also be legal costs of around £850.

The net realisable value of the property at 31st December 2022 is thus:

Market value of completed property	£210,000
Less: Costs to complete	£12,000
Professional costs to sell	£4,000
Net Realisable Value at 31/12/2022	£194,000

Since this is less than the company's costs to date, this is the value that should be shown as trading stock in the 2022 accounts.

The result of this is Grand Slam Ltd will show a loss of £9,000 (£203,000 less £194,000) on the second house in its 2022 accounts. This loss will automatically be set off against the £17,750 profit on the first house.

By June 2023, the second house is ready for sale. Fortunately, there is an upturn in the market and Grand Slam Ltd manages to sell the property for £225,000 in October 2023.

The actual additional expenditure on the extension work amounted to £11,800 and the professional fees incurred on the sale were actually £4,350.

Grand Slam Ltd's taxable profit on this property in 2023 is thus calculated as follows:

Value of trading stock brought forward, as per accounts:	£194,000
Additional building cost	£11,800
Professional fees on sale	£4,350
Total cost of sales	£210,150
Taxable profit (£225,000 – £210,150)	£14,850

Points to Note
When preparing the accounts, we use the most accurate estimates available at that time to calculate net realisable value. In the case of sale price, however, we use the completed property's market value at the accounting date (i.e. 31st December 2022 in this example).

When calculating Grand Slam Ltd's profit for 2023, we use actual figures for everything that took place after 31st December 2022, the company's last accounting date (i.e. the sale price, the final part of the building work, and the professional fees on the sale). The property's net realisable value in the accounts at 31st December 2022 is, however, substituted for the costs incurred up to that date.

In this example, as often happens in practice, the selling price and actual costs incurred after the last accounting date turned out to be different to the estimates previously available. As a result, the apparent loss the company was able to claim in 2022 effectively reversed and became part of its profits in 2023.

In the end, overall, the true net profit Grand Slam Ltd actually made on the development has been taxed. The effect of the net realisable value calculation, however, was to provide some early CT relief for a loss that was reasonably anticipated at that time. For this reason, it will always be worth considering whether properties held as trading stock have a net realisable value less than cost at each accounting date.

5.4   WORK-IN-PROGRESS & SALES CONTRACTS

Generally, for speculative property developers, their company's trading stock, as we have seen, is valued at the lower of cumulative cost to date or net realisable value. However, if a contract for the sale of the property exists, the development company has to follow a different set of rules.

This is a complex area of accounting, but, broadly speaking, the company is required to value properties under development, for which a sale contract already exists, at an appropriate percentage of their contractual sale value. This is done by treating the completed proportion of the property as having already been sold.

The same proportion of the expected final costs of the development can be deducted from the sale. Any remaining balance of development costs is included in the accounts as 'Work-in-Progress', which is simply a term for trading stock that is only partly completed.

Example
Aayan Ltd is building a new house on a plot of land and has already contracted to sell it for £500,000. The company draws up accounts to 31st March each year. At 31st March 2021, the house is 75% complete. Aayan Ltd's total costs to date are £320,000, but further costs of £80,000 are anticipated before the house is completed.

Aayan Ltd will need to show a sale of £375,000 (75% of £500,000) in its accounts to 31st March 2021. The company will, however, be able to deduct costs of £300,000, which equates to 75% of its anticipated final total costs of £400,000 (£320,000 + £80,000).

In other words, Aayan Ltd will show a profit of £75,000 in its accounts to 31st March 2021, which is equal to 75% of the expected final profit on the development of £100,000.

The remaining £20,000 of Aayan Ltd's costs to date will be shown in its accounts at 31st March 2021 as Work-in-Progress.

The following year, Aayan Ltd completes the property at a cost of £77,000.

The company's accounts for the year ending 31st March 2022 will show a sale of £125,000, i.e. the remaining 25% of the total sale proceeds of £500,000.

From this, Aayan Ltd can deduct total costs of £97,000, which is made up of £20,000 of Work-in-Progress brought forward and actual costs in the year of £77,000. This gives Aayan Ltd a development profit of £28,000 for the year ending 31st March 2022.

As we can see from the example, the effect of this accounting treatment is to accelerate part of the profit on the development. As there is no specific rule to the contrary, the tax position will follow the accounting treatment, so the development company is taxed on part of its property sale in advance.

It follows that the whole profit on a property for which a sales contract exists will need to be included in the company's accounts once the property is fully completed. Where this accounting treatment applies, the company may nevertheless claim deductions to reflect:

- Any doubt over the purchaser's ability, or willingness, to pay
- Rectification work still to be carried out
- Administration and other costs relating to completion of the sale

5.5   CAPITAL ALLOWANCES FOR TRADING COMPANIES

As explained in Section 5.2, a property trading company can generally only claim capital allowances on its *own* long-term fixed assets. Properties held for development or sale, together with any furniture, furnishings or equipment within them, will form part of its trading stock.

In general terms, property development companies are likely to have greater scope for claiming capital allowances than companies with residential property investment businesses but possibly less scope than those with commercial property investments. Property dealing companies and property management companies are unlikely to be able to claim very many allowances.

The principles outlined below also apply equally to assets a property investment company purchases for use in its own business.

Plant and Equipment

Subject to the general comments above, plant and equipment purchased for use in the trade will be eligible for the plant and machinery allowances described in Section 4.5.

'Plant and equipment' may include the following items used in the company's trade:

- Building equipment and tools
- Computers
- Office furniture, fixtures and fittings
- Vans and motorcycles

Example

During the year ending 31st March 2021, Triple Crown Ltd spends £1.03m on plant and equipment for use in its trade. The company is entitled to an annual investment allowance of £1m (see Section 4.5) and may claim writing down allowances on the remaining £30,000 of its expenditure.

The company's writing down allowances amount to £5,400 (£30,000 x 18%) giving it total plant and machinery allowances for the year of £1,005,400 (£1m + £5,400). (For the sake of illustration, I am assuming the company has no balance brought forward on its main pool.)

The remaining £24,600 of expenditure is carried forward to the year ending 31st March 2022, when it is eligible for writing down allowances of 18%, or £4,428. This leaves £20,172 to be carried forward to the year ending 31st March 2023, when it will attract writing down allowances of 18%, or £3,631.

Thereafter, the unrelieved balance of expenditure will continue to be carried forward and attract writing down allowances of 18% each year until the remaining unrelieved balance on the company's main pool reduces to £1,000 or less (see Section 4.5).

It is worth noting it will take twelve years before Triple Crown Ltd has obtained tax relief for 90% of the expenditure not covered by the annual investment allowance. If that expenditure had been incurred in the company's previous, or next, accounting period, 100% tax relief may have been obtained immediately!

(Although the company's expenditure in the year ending 31st March 2022 will be subject to the transitional rules examined in Section 4.5)

Motor Cars

The capital allowances regime for cars purchased by companies may be summarised as follows:

- Cars are not eligible for the annual investment allowance
- Cars with CO_2 emissions over the 'higher threshold' fall into the special rate pool and attract writing down allowances at just 6%
- Cars with CO_2 emissions over the 'lower threshold' but not over the 'higher threshold', fall into the main pool and attract writing down allowances at 18%
- Cars with CO_2 emissions of no more than the 'lower threshold' attract enhanced capital allowances at 100%

See Section 4.5 for further details on the main and special rate pools.

The 'higher threshold' for cars purchased between 1st April 2018 and 31st March 2021 is 110 g/km; thereafter it will fall to just 50g/km.

The 'lower threshold' for cars purchased between 1st April 2018 and 31st March 2021 is 50g/km. Thereafter, it will fall to zero, meaning only fully electric cars will qualify for the 100% first year allowance.

Private Use
For cars owned by a company, there is no restriction in the amount of capital allowances available to reflect any private use of the vehicle.

Instead, however, the person enjoying that private use is subject to Income Tax on a 'Benefit-in-Kind' charge. For 2020/21 this charge will generally be somewhere between 13% and 37% of the original purchase cost of the car when new (between 0% and 14% for hybrid cars with CO_2 emissions not exceeding 50g/km; 0% for fully electric cars).

In addition to the Income Tax charge on the individual, the company will have to pay Class 1A NI at 13.8% on the same 'Benefit-in-Kind'.

In total, the annual Income Tax and NI costs of running a company car could add up to over 27% of the cost of that car when it was brand new.

Company cars are a complex subject in their own right. Suffice to say, you should carefully review your situation before deciding to buy a car through your company.

The Structures and Buildings Allowance
Companies with property trades may claim the SBA on their own trading premises and other properties and structures held as long-term assets, following the principles outlined in Section 4.6. The SBA cannot be claimed on property held as trading stock, however.

Capital Allowance Disclaimers
Generally speaking, capital allowances are not mandatory, and any proportion of the available allowance may be claimed, from zero to 100%. Allowances not claimed are generally referred to as 'capital allowance disclaimers'.

As the SBA (see Section 4.6) cannot be carried forward, there would rarely be any benefit in not claiming the full allowance available (unless the allowance is unlikely to provide any relief for the company but would increase a taxable capital gain).

Where plant and machinery allowances are disclaimed, however, a greater balance of expenditure is carried forward to the next period, thus increasing later plant and machinery allowance claims. Nonetheless, plant and machinery allowance disclaimers are generally only worth considering where claiming the allowances would result in losses that are likely to go to waste and the increased allowances available in future periods are likely to be of some benefit.

5.6   TRADING LOSSES

Trading losses may be set off against the company's other income *and capital gains* of the same accounting period.

Loss Carry Back
If the claim for set-off of trading losses within the same accounting period has been made, the company may additionally claim to carry back any surplus loss against its total profits and capital gains in the twelve months preceding the accounting period that gave rise to the loss.

If, however, the loss-making trade was not being carried on by the company throughout the previous twelve months, the relevant period for loss set-off is the period beginning with the commencement of that trade.

An added benefit of setting a trading loss off against other income in the current and previous years is that the resultant tax saving is more or less immediate.

Loss Carry Forward

Any further trading losses still remaining unrelieved after any claim for set-off in the current year or carry back to the previous year, will be carried forward for set-off in future periods as follows:

- Losses arising after March 2017 may be set off against the company's total income and capital gains, provided the trade that gave rise to the loss has not ceased or become 'small'. Where the trade has become 'small', the carried forward losses may only be set off against future profits from that trade. There is no definition of what 'small' means, although it seems safe to assume it means the trade has become far smaller than it was when it gave rise to the losses.
- Losses arising before April 2017 may only be set off against future profits from the same trade.

Companies must now claim these set-offs and are subject to the limits on amounts in excess of £5m discussed in Section 4.10.

Companies that are members of a group of companies may also surrender some or all of their trading losses as group relief.

Loss relief claims must be made within two years of the end of the loss-making accounting period in the case of losses set off against profits and capital gains within the same period or the previous twelve months; or within two years of the end of the period for which relief is claimed in the case of losses carried forward.

Finally, it is worth noting that, while companies are subject to the limit on losses in excess of £5m carried forward (discussed in Section 4.10), they are not subject to the rather more restrictive limitations on individuals discussed in Section 12.11.

Chapter 6

Corporation Tax on Capital Gains

6.1   WHEN DOES A CAPITAL GAIN ARISE?

In Chapter 3, we examined the various different types of property companies and we saw that some property disposals give rise to trading profits.

We also saw, however, that property disposals made by property investment companies (see Section 3.2) give rise to capital gains instead.

Furthermore, other property companies disposing of their long-term fixed assets, such as their own office premises, for example, will also be subject to capital gains treatment.

In each case, the calculation of the amount of capital gain chargeable to CT is:

Capital Gain Equals Proceeds Less Base Cost

The date of sale for capital gains purposes is when an unconditional contract for sale comes into being.

6.2   HOW TO CALCULATE THE 'PROCEEDS'

In most cases, the amount of 'Proceeds' to be used in the calculation of a capital gain will be the actual sum received on the disposal of the asset. However, from this, the company may deduct incidental costs in order to arrive at 'net proceeds', which is the relevant sum for the purposes of calculating the capital gain.

Example
Yachvilli Ltd sells a house for £375,000. In order to make this sale, the company spends £1,500 advertising the property, pays £3,750 in estate agent's fees and pays £800 in legal fees. Yachvilli Ltd's net proceeds are therefore £368,950 (£375,000 less £1,500, £3,750 and £800).

There are, however, a number of cases where the proceeds we must use in the calculation of a capital gain are not simply the actual cash sum received. Four of the most common such exceptions are set out below.

Exception 1 – Connected Persons

Where the person disposing of the asset is 'connected' with the person acquiring it, the open market value of the asset at the time of transfer must be used in place of the actual price paid (if any).

A company is deemed to be 'connected' with any person who controls that company, either alone, or acting together with other persons. We will take a look at the concept of a 'connected company' in Section 14.2.

Example

Beckham Ltd is a property investment company and is wholly owned by Victoria. The company sells a property to Victoria for £500,000. The market value of the property at the time of sale is £800,000. The company pays legal fees of £475 on the sale. Beckham Ltd will be deemed to have received net sale proceeds of £800,000 (the market value). The legal fees the company has borne are irrelevant, as this was not an 'arm's-length' transaction.

The concept of 'connected persons' is important for a number of reasons, as we will see throughout this guide. A list of the persons deemed to be 'connected' with each other is given in Appendix B.

Exception 2 – Transactions not at 'arm's-length'

Where a transaction takes place between 'connected persons', as above, there is an automatic assumption that the transaction is not at 'arm's-length' and hence market value must always be substituted for the actual proceeds. There are, however, other instances where the transaction may not be at 'arm's-length', such as:

- A sale of an asset to an employee
- A transaction that is part of a larger transaction
- A transaction that is part of a series of transactions

The effect of these is much the same as before: the asset's market value must be used in place of the actual proceeds, if any.

The key difference from Exception 1 above is that the onus of proof that this is not an 'arm's-length' transaction is on HMRC, rather than there being an automatic assumption that this is the case.

Example

Brooklyn Ltd owns an investment property with a market value of £200,000. If the company sold the property at this price, it would have a capital gain of £80,000. Not wishing to incur a CT liability, Brooklyn Ltd sells the house to Romeo Ltd for £120,000. However, Brooklyn Ltd only does this on condition that Romeo Ltd gives it an interest-free loan of £80,000 for an indefinite period. The condition imposed by Brooklyn Ltd means this transaction is not at 'arm's-length'. The correct position is therefore that Brooklyn Ltd should be deemed to have sold the property for £200,000 and still have a capital gain of £80,000.

Exception 3 – Non-cash proceeds

Sometimes all or part of the sale consideration will take a form other than cash. The sale proceeds to be taken into account in these cases will be the market value of the assets or rights received in exchange for the asset sold.

Example

Little Property Company Ltd owns an office block in central London. Big Properties plc (a quoted company) wants to buy the property from Little Property Company Ltd but, as it is experiencing some short-term cashflow difficulties, it offers Little Property Company Ltd 500,000 shares for the property rather than cash. Little Property Company Ltd accepts this offer and takes the shares, worth £12.50 per share at the date of sale. The company's sale proceeds for CT purposes will therefore be £6.25m (500,000 x £12.50).

Wealth Warning

Note that if, as in the above example, you take non-cash consideration for a sale, you will be taxed on the value of that consideration at that date. If the value of the non-cash asset you receive should subsequently fall you will still be taxed on the original value! This problem can sometimes be alleviated by disposing of the asset that has fallen in value and thus generating a capital loss, but this is not always desirable. A capital loss cannot be carried back to an earlier accounting period.

Exception 4 – Structures and Buildings Allowance Claims

As explained in Section 4.6, a seller who has claimed SBA on a property must add the amount claimed to their sale proceeds.

6.3 HOW TO CALCULATE THE 'BASE COST'

The 'Base Cost' is the amount that may be deducted in the capital gains calculation in respect of an asset's cost. The higher the base cost, the lower the chargeable gain and the less CT payable!

The basic starting point in most cases will be the amount paid to purchase the asset. Added to the actual amount paid are:

i) Incidental costs of acquisition (e.g. legal fees, SDLT, etc)
ii) Enhancement expenditure (e.g. the cost of building an extension)
iii) Expenditure incurred in establishing, preserving or defending title to, or rights over, the asset (e.g. legal fees incurred as a result of a boundary dispute)

Base Cost – Special Situations

There are again a number of special situations where base cost is determined by reference to something other than the actual amount paid for the asset.

The major exceptions fall into three main categories:

- The asset was not acquired by way of a 'bargain at arm's length'
- The asset was acquired for non-cash consideration
- The asset was acquired before April 1982

Where one of these exceptions applies, the actual amount paid for the asset is replaced by the amount derived under the rules set out below.

Assets Not Acquired by Way of a 'Bargain at Arm's Length'
In the case of an acquisition that is not a 'bargain at arm's length', the acquiring company's base cost will generally be the asset's market value at the time of purchase, as this will be the deemed 'proceeds' on which the person selling the asset is taxed.

Example
Martin owns a property investment company, Johnson Investments Ltd. The company buys a warehouse from Martin for £100,000. The warehouse, which Martin held as an investment, has a market value of £200,000. Johnson Investments' base cost for the warehouse will be £200,000. (Martin's personal CGT liability will be based on a sale for deemed 'proceeds' of £200,000.)

Gifts of Business Assets
In the case of a property that qualifies as a 'business asset' for CGT purposes, the usual rule for an acquisition that is not a 'bargain at arm's length' may be over-ridden by a 'hold-over' relief claim (see Section 14.8). This would alter the position and the acquiring company would usually be treated as acquiring the property for a sum equal to the property's open market value less the amount of 'held over' gain.

This treatment can generally only apply to furnished holiday lets or property used as a long-term fixed asset in the transferor's own trading business. We will return to this subject in more detail in Chapter 14.

Where an asset is not acquired by way of a 'bargain at arm's length' (whether 'hold-over' relief is claimed or not), subsequent expenditure incurred by the purchaser under headings (ii) and (iii) above continues to be added to the base cost in the normal way.

Assets acquired for non-cash consideration
Where an asset was acquired for non-cash consideration, its base cost will be determined by reference to the market value of the consideration given. Expenditure incurred by the purchaser under headings (i) to (iii) above is still added to the base cost in the normal way.

Assets acquired before April 1982
Generally speaking, the base cost will usually be the asset's open market value at 31st March 1982. Expenditure incurred by the purchaser under

headings (ii) and (iii) above is added to the base cost: but only when incurred after March 1982. Earlier expenditure is ignored as it is effectively replaced by the asset's market value at 31st March 1982.

6.4   HOW AND WHEN TO CALCULATE INDEXATION RELIEF

Property acquired after November 2017 is not eligible for indexation relief. If you were not already operating a property company by November 2017, you can safely ignore this section.

Indexation relief was introduced in 1982 to eliminate the purely inflationary element of capital gains. It was abolished for individuals in 2008 but companies in existence before December 2017 may still benefit to a limited extent.

Indexation relief has been frozen for company disposals taking place after December 2017 and the relief is now based on the increase in the retail prices index from the date of purchase until the earlier of the date of sale or December 2017.

So if a property purchased in January 2005 is sold in December 2020, indexation relief will be available from January 2005 to December 2017, but no indexation relief will be available for the period from January 2018 to December 2020.

Companies that have held properties for many years and expect to sell them in the near future will still enjoy a sizeable amount of indexation relief. By contrast, companies that sell properties many years from now will be more exposed to paying tax on purely inflationary gains.

The following example illustrates how indexation relief is calculated. Note that, where the base cost of the asset is made up of the original cost and later enhancement expenditure (incurred before December 2017), each element of the base cost will attract indexation relief at its own appropriate rate.

Example
Wilkinson Ltd bought a property for £100,000 in June 2000. In August 2005 the company spent £50,000 building an extension. The property is sold for £300,000 in December 2025.

The retail prices index was 171.1 in June 2000, 192.6 in August 2005 and 278.1 in December 2017 (from which date indexation relief is frozen).

The retail prices index increased by 62.5% between June 2000 and December 2017, so the indexation relief due on the company's original purchase cost is £62,500 (£100,000 x 62.5%). No indexation relief is available for the period January 2018 to December 2025.

The retail prices index increased by 44.4% between August 2005 and December 2017, so the indexation relief due on the company's enhancement expenditure (the cost of the extension) is £22,200 (£50,000 x 44.4%).

Wilkinson Ltd's chargeable gain is therefore calculated as follows:

	£	£
Sale proceeds		300,000
Less:		
Original cost	100,000	
Enhancement expenditure	50,000	

		150,000
Indexation relief		
On original cost	62,500	
On enhancement expenditure	22,200	

Total:		84,700

Chargeable gain:		£65,300

Wilkinson Ltd does not enjoy any indexation relief from January 2018 to December 2025. But what if it did? If the retail prices index were to increase by roughly 20% over this period then we would expect it to stand at around 334 in December 2025.

If indexation relief were available for those extra eight years then we would have expected the company to enjoy relief of around £95,000 on the original cost of the property and £36,700 on the enhancement expenditure: a total of £131,700; or £47,000 more than it will actually receive. Hence, the freezing of indexation relief has potentially added an extra £47,000 to the company's chargeable gain.

Clearly, the freezing of indexation relief will have an ever greater impact on property companies' tax bills the further we progress into the future.

Indexation relief may not be used to create or increase a capital loss. Hence, in some cases, the amount of relief has to be restricted. Where a capital loss already arises, no relief is given at all. Where there is a capital gain before indexation, the relief cannot exceed the amount of gain before indexation.

If a property was acquired before April 1982, the relief is based on the increase in the retail prices index from March 1982 only.

The Retail Prices Index
A table of retail prices index factors for use in calculating indexation relief on capital disposals by companies is reproduced in Appendix C.

The rate of indexation relief to be claimed is calculated as follows:

Indexation Relief Rate = (RD – RA)/RA

RA is the retail prices index for the month of acquisition, or other allowable expenditure. If the property's open market value at 31st March 1982 is being used for its base cost (see Section 6.3), use 79.44 for RA. RD is the retail prices index for the month of disposal. If the month of disposal is December 2017 or later, use 278.1 for RD.

Example
To calculate the indexation relief rate applying to the cost of a property purchased by a company in May 2000 and sold by that company in October 2020, we find from Appendix C that RA is 170.7 and RD is 278.1. The indexation relief rate is therefore (278.1 – 170.7)/170.7 or 107.4/170.7, which equates to 62.9%.

6.5   MAKING THE MOST OF CAPITAL LOSSES

We have already seen how companies can set their rental losses or trading losses off against their capital gains (see Sections 4.10 and 5.6). Unfortunately, the opposite does not hold true: companies cannot set their capital losses off against their rental income or trading profits.

Any capital losses that arise may be set off against capital gains (after indexation relief) arising in the same accounting period.

Surplus capital losses are then carried forward for set off against capital gains arising in later accounting periods. Any carried forward capital losses set off against gains arising after 31st March 2020 must be counted towards the £5m annual limit on brought forward losses of all types (Section 4.10). Once the £5m limit is exhausted, the set off of further carried forward capital losses is limited to 50% of remaining capital gains.

Capital losses cannot be carried back to earlier accounting periods and nor can they be set against capital gains made by the company owner, even on shares in the company making the capital losses.

Tax Tip
It may be worth considering disposing of loss-making properties before the end of an accounting period in which the company has made capital gains.

Another Tax Tip
Unless there are strong commercial reasons for doing so, a company which has unused capital losses carried forward should not be wound up as there will always be a possibility of realising tax-free capital gains through it in the future.

Chapter 7

Capital Gains Tax on Company Shares

7.1　INTRODUCTION

Company owners are not generally subject to CGT on capital gains their company makes on the disposal of properties. As we have seen in previous chapters, the company pays CT on those gains instead. (But see Section 15.5 regarding exceptions sometimes applying to UK resident individuals operating through non-UK resident companies.)

Company owners are, however, subject to CGT on the disposal of shares in their property company. A 'disposal' for this purpose includes:

- A sale of the company,
- A winding up of the company (but see the points in Section 7.7), or
- A transfer of shares to another person

In the case of a transfer to a connected person (see Appendix B), or any other transfer that is 'not a bargain at arm's length' (see Section 6.2), the market value of the shares is substituted in place of the actual sale proceeds for CGT purposes.

Holdover relief may sometimes be available in these circumstances (see Section 7.6). Transfers to the owner's spouse are also generally exempt from CGT.

As we saw in Chapter 3, some property company shares will also be eligible for business asset disposal relief, which we shall be looking at in detail in Section 7.3.

Throughout this chapter, and indeed the majority of this guide, we will be basing all our calculations, forecasts, etc, on the current CGT regime. However, it is important to be aware that CGT is one of the prime candidates for some significant changes in the future. We will look at those potential changes, and their impact on property investors using, or deciding whether to use, a company, in Chapter 17.

7.2　CAPITAL GAINS TAX RATES

For disposals made by individuals, CGT is currently charged at five rates:

- 10% where business asset disposal relief is available (Section 7.3)
- 18% on residential property gains made by basic rate taxpayers
- 28% on residential property gains made by higher rate taxpayers
- 10% on most other gains made by basic rate taxpayers
- 20% on most other gains made by higher rate taxpayers

The 18% and 28% rates apply to:

- Any interest in land or property that has ever included a residential dwelling at any time during the taxpayer's ownership
- Contracts for off-plan purchases of residential property
- A few other, very limited, cases

The lower rates for basic rate taxpayers apply to the extent that the individual has any remaining basic rate tax band available after accounting for their total taxable income for the tax year.

The good news is that, although the rates applying to residential property are 18% and 28%, the 10% and 20% rates apply to disposals of shares in property investment companies: even if the company is investing in residential property.

Each individual is also entitled to an annual CGT exemption each tax year. The annual exemptions for 2019/20 and 2020/21 are £12,000 and £12,300 respectively.

Example
In March 2021, Andy sells some shares in his property investment company and makes a capital gain of £50,000. The shares do not qualify for business asset disposal relief.

Andy's total taxable income for 2020/21 is £30,000. After deducting his personal allowance of £12,500, his income uses up £17,500 of his basic rate band, leaving £20,000 available for CGT purposes (see Appendix A for details of Income Tax allowances, bands, etc).

After deducting his annual exemption of £12,300, Andy is left with a taxable capital gain of £37,700. His CGT bill is therefore as follows:

£20,000 x 10%   £2,000
£17,700 x 20%   £3,540
Total   £5,540

7.3 BUSINESS ASSET DISPOSAL RELIEF (FORMERLY KNOWN AS ENTREPRENEURS' RELIEF)

Business asset disposal relief (formerly known as entrepreneurs' relief) operates by substituting a CGT rate of 10% in place of the usual rates.

Each individual may claim business asset disposal relief on a maximum cumulative lifetime total of £1m of qualifying capital gains (£10m for gains on disposals made before 11th March 2020). Thereafter, the CGT rate on all further capital gains reverts to the normal rates.

The Qualifying Period

Where I refer to the 'qualifying period' for the tests detailed in this section, this is generally two years, but it is one year where the disposal took place before 6th April 2019, or the business ceased before 29th October 2018.

Personal Companies

While companies themselves do not qualify for business asset disposal relief, property company owners may benefit from this relief when they dispose of shares in a qualifying 'personal company'.

The definition of a 'personal company' for the purposes of business asset disposal relief is broadly as follows:

i)   The individual holds at least 5% of the ordinary share capital

ii)   The holding under (i) provides at least 5% of the voting rights

iii)   The company is a trading company (see below)

iv)   The individual is an officer or employee of the company (an 'officer' includes a director or company secretary)

v)   For disposals after 28th October 2018, the individual must either:
        a) Have at least a 5% interest in both the distributable profits and net assets of the company by virtue of their holding under (i), or
        b) Be entitled to at least 5% of the sale proceeds arising on a disposal of the company's entire ordinary share capital (but this option was not available for disposals before 21st December 2018)

Each of these rules must be satisfied for at least the 'qualifying period' prior to the disposal in question or, where the company has ceased trading, for at least the 'qualifying period' prior to the cessation. In the latter case, the disposal must take place within three years after cessation.

Where a qualifying business has been transferred to a company and the gains arising have been held over under 'incorporation relief' (see Section 14.9), or could have been held over if the relief had not been disclaimed, then the individual's period of ownership of the business prior to the transfer can be counted towards the 'qualifying period' for their shares in the company where those shares are disposed of after 5th April 2019.

Where the company ceases to qualify as an individual's 'personal company' as a result of a fresh issue of shares after 5th April 2019, made wholly for cash and for genuine commercial reasons, the individual may elect for the gain arising on their shares up to that point to 'crystallise' and become chargeable. However, they may further elect to hold over this gain until the ultimate disposal of their shares. The effect of this (assuming both elections are made) is that they will only be subject to CGT on the ultimate disposal of their shares, but will then be eligible for business asset disposal relief on the proportion of the gain arising up to the date of the fresh share issue.

The Short Version

The 'personal company' rules have grown pretty complex but, for a small private company with only a single class of ordinary shares, tests (i), (ii) and (v) are usually satisfied simply by holding at least 5% of the ordinary shares. Hence, assuming you are also a director of the company, the only test you will generally need to worry about is (iii) – do you have a 'trading company' for the purposes of business asset disposal relief.

The Importance of Trading Status

As we saw in Chapter 3, property development companies, property management companies and, in theory, property dealing companies, all qualify as trading companies. Furnished holiday lets are also deemed to be a trade for the purposes of business asset disposal relief.

Example

Redpath Ltd and Delaglio Ltd are property development companies. Both were set up with an initial investment of just £1,000 each and started trading immediately afterwards. Both companies also have some rental income, meaning, in HMRC's view, they have some non-trading activity. Redpath Ltd manages to keep its non-trading activity below the level HMRC regards as 'substantial' (see Section 3.6), meaning it is accepted as a trading company. The shares in Redpath Ltd therefore qualify for business asset disposal relief.

Brian, who owns all the shares in Redpath Ltd, decides to sell the company in 2021 and receives net proceeds of £1.001m, giving him a capital gain of exactly £1m. Assuming he has already used his annual exemption on other gains, his CGT liability on the sale will be £100,000 (£1m x 10%).

Lawrence, the sole shareholder of Delaglio Ltd, also sells his company in 2021 and makes a capital gain of £1m. However, Delaglio Ltd's non-trading activities are deemed to be 'substantial', meaning the company is not regarded as a trading company for business asset disposal relief purposes.

Hence, assuming Lawrence is a higher rate taxpayer and has used his annual exemption on other gains, his CGT liability on the sale of Delaglio Ltd will be £200,000 (£1m x 20%).

*That's **double** Brian's CGT liability on a sale of a very similar company!*

Some Final Points

The cumulative lifetime limit (currently £1m; formerly £10m) applies to all business asset disposal relief (or entrepreneurs' relief) claims on capital gains arising after 5th April 2008.

Where a basic rate taxpayer claims business asset disposal relief the relevant gain uses up their remaining basic rate band in priority to other gains. In effect, this pushes more (or perhaps all) of their other gains into the 20% or 28% CGT bracket, thus reducing, or possibly even eliminating, any potential saving.

Business asset disposal relief is not mandatory. Taxpayers may choose whether to claim it. It therefore makes sense to refrain from making claims where there is no saving.

Furthermore, with the lifetime limit now much reduced, it may also make sense to avoid making claims that only produce a small saving relative to the amount of capital gain involved. On the other hand, there is a risk the relief may be abolished altogether in future, so it may make sense to make any potential claims while you still can, provided there is at least *some* saving: 'a bird in the hand may be worth two in the bush!'

7.4 BUSINESS ASSET DISPOSAL RELIEF FOR PROPERTY INVESTMENT COMPANIES

Subject to the cumulative lifetime limit, business asset disposal relief is available on the whole capital gain arising on the disposal of shares in a company that meets the 'personal company' conditions set out in Section 7.3 for the relevant 'qualifying period', even if the company did not previously meet those conditions.

Hence, business asset disposal relief will be available in full as long as the company qualifies as a 'trading company' for the two year period prior to the disposal of the shares, or cessation of its business, as the case may be (provided the other qualifying conditions are met).

> **Tax Tip**
>
> Business asset disposal relief would be available on shares in a former property investment, or other 'non-trading', company that changes its business and becomes a qualifying 'trading company' for the two year period prior to the disposal of the shares or cessation of the company's business.
>
> As usual, furnished holiday lets (see Section 4.8) count as 'trading' for this purpose and may therefore provide an easier way for a residential property investment company to undergo the necessary conversion.

7.5   BUSINESS ASSET DISPOSAL RELIEF AND COUPLES

With the cumulative lifetime limit for business asset disposal relief now reduced to just £1m, it is more important than ever to remember this limit applies on a 'per person' basis.

If both members of a couple own at least 5% of the ordinary shares in a qualifying 'trading company', they may potentially be able to claim business asset disposal relief on total capital gains of up to £2m, thus providing total CGT savings of up to £200,000.

Alternatively, if 5% or more of the ordinary shares in a qualifying 'trading company' are transferred to the owner's spouse at least two years prior to cessation or sale the spouse may again be entitled to business asset disposal relief, once more giving potential relief on gains of up to £2m.

> **Wealth Warning**
> For a disposal of shares to qualify for business asset disposal relief, the company must generally have qualified as the 'personal company' of the individual making the disposal for at least two years prior to cessation or sale.
>
> A pre-sale transfer of shares to a spouse might therefore result in the loss of business asset disposal relief if the spouse did not meet all the necessary qualifying conditions (see Section 7.3) for at least two years prior to cessation or sale.
>
> It is also important to remember that pre-sale transfers to a spouse are only effective if the transferee genuinely obtains beneficial ownership. In other words, the transferee must be free to do as they wish with the transferred shares and must be beneficially entitled to their share of the sale proceeds.

7.6   HOLDOVER RELIEF

Holdover relief is available on the transfer of shares in an unquoted trading company (except a transfer to or from another company).

Where the transfer is an outright gift, the transferor and transferee may jointly elect to 'hold over' the entire capital gain arising. No CGT is then payable by the transferor and the transferee is treated as having acquired the shares for the same base cost (see Section 6.3) as the transferor.

For sales made for a consideration less than market value, a partial hold over is available. Broadly speaking, the amount of gain held over is equal to the difference between the market value and the sales price. The effect of this is that the transferor pays CGT based on the actual sales price and the transferee's base cost is equal to that price.

The definition of a 'trading company' for holdover relief purposes is the same as for business asset disposal relief purposes (see Chapter 3 and Section 7.3 for further details). It follows that most unquoted shares which qualify for business asset disposal relief will qualify for holdover relief (but not necessarily vice versa). However, it is important to note that holdover relief will be restricted if the company has not qualified as a 'trading company' throughout the transferor's entire period of ownership.

Holdover Relief and Business Asset Disposal Relief
A holdover relief claim could be used to make a transfer of shares in a qualifying 'trading company' to another individual other than the owner's spouse free from CGT (e.g. to transfer shares to an unmarried partner or an adult child).

If the transferee then held the transferred shares for at least two years, and met all the other qualifying conditions set out in Section 7.3, they would be entitled to business asset disposal relief on those shares.

7.7   WINDING UP THE COMPANY

When a company is wound up, any remaining assets or funds within the company are distributed to its shareholders. This is known as a 'capital distribution on winding up'. The basic rule is that such distributions are subject to CGT.

Hence, for example, if a property company owner had originally subscribed for their shares for £100 and they receive a distribution of £100,100 when that company is wound up, they will have a capital gain of £100,000. Like any other gain, this will be taxed at the rates set out in Section 7.2. Business asset disposal relief may even be available if the criteria discussed in Section 7.3 are met.

Winding up a company can be a very expensive process in terms of fees, especially if the company still has assets and liabilities, or has recently been in active business.

In simple cases, where the company has been inactive for some time and perhaps only holds cash, you can, alternatively, apply to have it struck off. This is a simpler, cheaper and quicker process. However, striking off (or 'dissolving') a company has some important legal implications. Furthermore, any sums in excess of £25,000 (in total) distributed to shareholders must be taxed as income (as if they were a dividend: see Section 9.3 for details of the tax rates applying to dividends).

For these reasons, it is usually sensible to go for a winding up (a 'members' voluntary liquidation', to give it its formal name) in all but the very simplest cases, so we will assume that is the case for the remainder of this guide (unless specifically stated to the contrary). Either way though, it is wise to seek professional advice before you act!

Even in the case of a winding up, 'anti-phoenixing' legislation applies to treat certain distributions as income distributions subject to Income Tax, as if they were dividends; instead of capital distributions subject to CGT.

The provisions apply where:

i) The recipient held at least 5% of the share capital and voting rights in the company immediately before the winding up,

ii) The company was a 'close company' (see Section 15.2) at any time within the two year period prior to the winding up,

iii) The recipient of the distribution participates in a new business operating in a similar trade or business to the company being wound up at any time within the period of two years following the winding up, and

iv) It is reasonable to assume the main purpose, or one of the main purposes, of the winding up is to reduce Income Tax, OR
The winding up forms part of arrangements, one of the main purposes of which is to achieve a reduction in Income Tax

Given that higher rate taxpayers will always pay a lower rate of tax on a capital distribution (10% or 20%, depending on whether business asset disposal relief is available), than on an income distribution (32.5% or more), many commentators fear that HMRC will nearly always regard condition (iv) as having been satisfied.

As we shall see in Section 15.2, most small private companies are close companies, so condition (ii) will usually be satisfied as well.

Hence, if condition (i) applies, it will generally be essential to ensure you do not fall foul of condition (iii). In other words, if you own at least 5% of the company, it will be important to avoid 'participating' in any similar trade or business for at least two years after the winding up.

Where the company being wound up was a property investment company, this means you can't invest in property for the next two years! For these purposes 'participating' in a trade or business includes:

- Acting as a sole trader/investor
- Investing jointly with one or more other people
- Being a partner in a partnership
- Being a member of an LLP
- Owning at least 5% of the shares in a company

Worst of all, you may also be caught by condition (iii) if a 'connected person' (see Appendix B) participates in a similar trade or business within the critical two year period.

Chapter 8

Stamp Duty for Property Companies

8.1 INTRODUCTION

Stamp Duty is the oldest tax on the statute books. It was several centuries old already when Pitt the Younger introduced Income Tax in 1799. Even today, we are still governed (to a limited extent) by the Stamp Act 1891.

Since 2003, however, for transfers of real property (i.e. land and buildings or any legal interest in them), Stamp Duty has been replaced by SDLT (see Section 8.3).

8.2 STAMP DUTY ON SHARES

Despite talk of its abolition a few years ago, this ancient tax continues to apply to transfers of shares. The rate of Stamp Duty on purchases of shares and securities is still unchanged at a single uniform rate of only 0.5%. This has led to many tax-avoidance strategies, designed to avoid the excessive rates applied to property transactions by making use of this more palatable rate. Anti-avoidance legislation has effectively blocked most of the more popular methods, however.

Nevertheless, for those investing in property through a company, there remains the possibility of selling shares in that company at a much lower rate of Duty than would apply to the sale of individual properties within the company.

Sales of private company shares for no more than £1,000 are exempt from Stamp Duty.

8.3 STAMP DUTY LAND TAX AND COMPANIES

Stamp Duty Land Tax ('SDLT') is charged on purchases and transfers of land and buildings (or any form of legal interest in them) in England or Northern Ireland. The tax applies regardless of where the vendor or purchaser are resident, and regardless of where the transfer documentation is drawn up. (See Sections 8.10 and 8.11 regarding property in Scotland and Wales respectively)

The type of company you have generally has no impact on the rate of SDLT and the rates applying are mostly the same for companies as they are for individuals except that:

- The higher charges on residential property introduced in 2016 *always* apply to purchases by companies (subject to the exemptions set out in Section 8.12)
- A special rate of 15% may apply to certain purchases of residential property for over £500,000 (see Section 8.6)
- The proposed non-resident surcharge could apply to some UK companies: see Section 8.5 for details

Generally speaking, SDLT charges are based on the actual consideration paid for the purchase: whether in cash or by any other means.

However, in the case of a transfer of property to a 'connected company' (see Section 14.2), the deemed consideration for SDLT purposes will generally be the greater of the actual amount of consideration paid and the property's market value. We will explore the implications of this in Chapter 14 including, in Section 14.6, the major exception that will often apply if the transferor is a partnership.

The rates of SDLT to be applied must be determined after taking account of any 'linked transactions'. However, this is not always as disastrous as it once was, following the introduction of 'multiple dwellings relief'. We will examine this issue further in Section 8.8.

8.4   STAMP DUTY LAND TAX ON RESIDENTIAL PROPERTY

Like any other purchaser, companies are currently able to benefit from the temporary reduction in SDLT rates applying to residential property for the period from 8th July 2020 to 31st March 2021 (sometimes referred to as the SDLT 'holiday').

Subject to the points in Section 8.3, the rates of SDLT for residential property purchases by companies during both the 'holiday' (reduced) and before and after that period (normal) are as follows:

Purchase Consideration	Reduced	Normal
Up to £125,000	3%	3%
£125,000 to £250,000	3%	5%
£250,000 to £500,000	3%	8%
£500,000 to £925,000	8%	8%
£925,000 to £1.5m	13%	13%
Over £1.5m	15%	15%

The current SDLT 'holiday' means savings of up to £15,000 are available on purchases of residential property in England or Northern Ireland (the maximum saving arises on purchases for £500,000 or more).

Tax Tip
The same level of saving is also available on transfers of residential property into a company, and might potentially lead to savings of up to £15,000 *per property!* We will look at the tax-saving potential of this incredible 'window of opportunity' in more detail in Section 14.22.

The rates set out above include the additional 3% that always applies where property is purchased by a company. These rates also generally apply to individual property investors, but for details of the limited circumstances under which the additional 3% charge may be avoided, see the Taxcafe.co.uk guide *'How to Save Property Tax'*.

Example
The SDLT arising on a residential property purchased by a company in March 2021 for £1.6m, for use in its business (see Section 8.6), would be:

First £500,000 @ 3%:	*£15,000*
Next £425,000 @ 8%:	*£34,000*
Next £575,000 @ 13%:	*£74,750*
Next £100,000 @ 15%:	*£15,000*
Total:	*£138,750*

What Is Residential Property?

For SDLT purposes, a property is classed as residential if it is used or suitable for use as a dwelling; or is in the process of being constructed or adapted for use as a dwelling.

The gardens or grounds of any such property are also subject to the residential rates, including any structures in those gardens or grounds.

An interest in or right over land that benefits a dwelling is also classed as residential property (e.g. a right of way needed to access a dwelling).

Residential accommodation for school pupils, students, or members of the armed forces are classed as dwellings for this purpose, as well as any institution that is the sole or main residence of at least 90% of its residents. However, these properties are subject to the following exceptions, which are instead classed as non-residential property and subject to the rates set out in Section 8.7:

i)   Children's homes
ii)   Halls of residence for students in further or higher education
iii)   Care homes for the elderly, disabled, or people suffering from alcohol or drugs dependency, or mental disorder
iv)   Hospitals and hospices
v)   Prisons and similar institutions
vi)   Hotels, inns, and similar properties

Tax Tip
In addition to the exceptions set out above, property with 'mixed use' (i.e. both residential and non-residential elements) is subject to SDLT at the non-residential rates. This can lead to substantial savings. We will look at this point further in Section 8.7.

8.5   THE NON-RESIDENT SURCHARGE

The Government is proposing to introduce a further, additional SDLT surcharge of 2% on purchases of residential property by non-UK residents. The charge will apply to purchases completed after 31st March 2021, although transitional rules may apply to cancel the surcharge where contracts were exchanged before 11th March 2020.

This further surcharge is in addition to the higher charges discussed in Section 8.4, which already apply to purchases by companies. Hence, affected companies purchasing residential property in England or Northern Ireland will face a total surcharge of 5%, and a maximum overall rate of 17% on purchase consideration in excess of £1.5m.

The exact scope of who will be caught by the new surcharge is still under development, but some UK companies could be included. The current proposals are broadly as follows:

- Individuals will be treated as non-UK resident for the purposes of the surcharge if they spend less than 183 days in the UK in both the calendar year ending on the date of purchase and in the calendar year commencing immediately after the date of purchase
- Non-UK resident companies will be subject to the surcharge
- 'Close companies' (see Section 15.2) will also be subject to the surcharge if they are under 'non-UK control', even if the company itself is deemed UK resident (see Section 15.5)

The current proposed definition of 'non-UK control' is extremely complex, but it is generally safe to say that, if none of the company's shareholders are non-UK resident (as defined above), the company will not be caught. In other cases, it will be wise to seek professional advice.

Exemptions

Under current proposals, the non-resident surcharge will not apply to purchases:

- Of leasehold interests with a fixed term of no more than 21 years left to run
- Of the superior interest in a property that is subject to a lease with a fixed term of more than 21 years left to run
- For less than £40,000

8.6 RESIDENTIAL PROPERTY PURCHASES BY 'NON-NATURAL' PERSONS

A special SDLT rate of 15% applies to the entire purchase price on purchases of residential properties in excess of £500,000 by companies and other 'non-natural' persons, such as collective investment schemes, unit trusts, and partnerships where any 'non-natural' person is a partner.

The rate only applies where a single dwelling is purchased for a price in excess of £500,000, or where one or more separate dwellings included in the purchase of a larger portfolio are worth more than £500,000 each.

Properties are exempt from this special rate when acquired for use in a business. This exemption covers both trading businesses and property investment businesses, so property investment companies should not generally have to pay this punitive rate. There are detailed rules governing this exemption, including the fact the property must not be occupied by a close relative of the company owner within three years of acquisition (close relatives are the individuals listed in Appendix B).

Where this special rate applies, neither multiple dwellings relief, nor the alternative treatment outlined in Section 8.8, is available.

Under current Government proposals, purchasers caught by both this special rate and the non-resident surcharge (see Section 8.5) will pay a total overall rate of 17% after 31st March 2021.

8.7 STAMP DUTY LAND TAX ON NON-RESIDENTIAL PROPERTY

There is no SDLT 'holiday' for non-residential property. The rates applying, which are again charged on a 'progressive' basis, are as follows:

Purchase Consideration

Up to £150,000	0%
£150,000 to £250,000	2%
Over £250,000	5%

As well as commercial property, such as shops, offices, warehouses, etc, the non-residential rates also apply to:

- 'Mixed use' property, such as a shop with a flat above it, where both parts are purchased as part of the same transaction
- Properties falling into one of the exceptions (i) to (vi) in Section 8.4
- Property not suitable to be lived in
- Agricultural land (see further below)
- Any other land or property not part of a dwelling's garden or grounds

There is also an option to use non-residential rates on a simultaneous purchase of six or more residential dwellings (see Section 8.8).

A farmhouse sold together with a working farm would be regarded as 'mixed use' and hence the whole transaction will be taxed at non-residential rates. However, residential rates will apply where land is simply sold as part of the garden or grounds of a dwelling: e.g. a cottage with fields. In borderline cases, seek professional advice.

8.8   LINKED TRANSACTIONS

The rates of SDLT to be applied must be determined after taking account of any 'linked transactions'.

'Linked transactions' can arise in a number of ways, including a simultaneous purchase of several properties from the same vendor.

The effect of the 'linked transactions' depends on whether 'multiple dwellings relief' is claimed. This relief is only available for multiple purchases of residential property. We will look at multiple dwellings relief later in this section, but first let's look at the basic rule applying to linked transactions where the relief is not claimed (or not available).

Basic Rule without Multiple Dwellings Relief
The basic rule where multiple dwellings relief is not claimed is the 'linked transactions' are treated as if they were a single purchase for SDLT purposes. In practice, this will mainly apply to multiple purchases of non-residential property, although it will also apply to any other 'linked transactions' where multiple dwellings relief is not available.

For example, if a property investment company were to buy three commercial properties from the same developer at the same time for £250,000 each, this would be treated for SDLT purposes as if it were one single purchase for £750,000. The SDLT charge would therefore be:

£100,000 @ 2%:	£2,000
£500,000 @ 5%:	£25,000
Total:	£27,000

Multiple Dwellings Relief
Multiple dwellings relief is available where multiple **residential** properties are purchased from the same vendor, or connected vendors, at the same time.

Where multiple dwellings relief is claimed, the rate of SDLT is based on the **average** consideration paid for each 'dwelling'. The relief is not automatic and must be claimed by the purchaser.

For companies, the higher charges detailed in Section 8.4 will always continue to apply to the average price.

Example 1

In January 2021, Carter Ltd buys five houses from a developer for a total consideration of £1.2m. Without multiple dwellings relief, SDLT would be charged as follows:

First £500,000 @ 3%:	£15,000
Next £425,000 @ 8%:	£34,000
Next £275,000 @ 13%:	£35,750
Total:	£84,750

However, as the average price for each property is just £240,000, Carter Ltd claims multiple dwellings relief. The SDLT calculation is then as follows:

Total per property: £240,000 @ 3%:	£7,200
x 5 =	£36,000

(Outside the current 'holiday' period, the company's SDLT liability, even with multiple dwellings relief, would be £47,500)

In a case like this, the charge with multiple dwellings relief is clearly much fairer (or perhaps one should say 'less unfair'). The relief goes even further, however, and could be used to reduce the SDLT charge on a single large property.

Example 2

Lamont Properties Ltd is planning to buy a new house in York at a cost of £1.25m. The company's SDLT bill will currently amount to:

First £500,000 @ 3%:	£15,000
Next £425,000 @ 8%:	£34,000
Next £325,000 @ 13%:	£42,250
Total:	£91,250

In order to reduce the SDLT cost, however, the company arranges to buy two small flats from the same developer at the same time. The flats cost £65,000 each, bringing the total consideration to £1.38m, but the average consideration is now just £460,000. Lamont Properties Ltd can therefore claim multiple dwellings relief to give a reduction in the SDLT charge to:

Total per property: £460,000 @ 3%:	£13,800
x 3 =	£41,400

Hence, by buying the flats at the same time as the house, the company has saved £49,850. That's equivalent to a discount of almost 40% on the flats!

(Outside the current 'holiday' period, the company's SDLT liability with multiple dwellings relief after buying the flats would be £80,400, compared with £106,250 if it had bought the house alone. The company would still have saved £25,850, almost 20% of the cost of the flats: but we can readily see how much more of a saving can be generated during the current SDLT 'holiday'!)

A Major Benefit for Property Investors

Self-contained flats within a single property each constitute a separate 'dwelling' for the purposes of multiple dwellings relief. This provides a major benefit for property investors buying larger properties.

For example, if a property investment company buys a property that has been divided into four flats, this would constitute four dwellings, so that multiple dwellings relief can be claimed and thus significantly reduce the SDLT due.

Granny Flats, Etc.

Multiple dwellings relief also extends to other cases where a single property is divided into more than one 'dwelling', such as when the property has a self-contained 'granny flat' or annex. The second 'dwelling' must be quite separate from the main property, such that it could be used by an unconnected third party as their residence. In a recent case, a property failed to qualify as two dwellings as there was no door on the corridor linking the annex to the main building. While that may not have been the only factor in that case, it does go to show it might sometimes be worth getting the seller to make a few minor alterations before the purchase proceeds!

Example 3

Wainwright Ltd is buying a house for £1m. The SDLT arising (during the current 'holiday' period) will be:

First £500,000 @ 3%:	*£15,000*
Next £425,000 @ 8%:	*£34,000*
Next £75,000 @ 13%:	*£9,750*
Total:	*£58,750*

However, the house has a self-contained 'granny flat', so the company is able to claim multiple dwellings relief on the basis the property comprises two 'dwellings' with an average value of £500,000 each. This reduces the SDLT charge to £30,000 (£500,000 x 3% x 2), giving the company a saving of £28,750.

Mixed Purchases

Multiple dwellings relief does not apply to non-residential, or partly non-residential, property: even when it forms part of a larger, 'mixed' purchase.

Alternative Treatment

A simultaneous purchase of six or more residential dwellings (from the same vendor, or connected vendors) can alternatively be treated as a non-residential property purchase. This may sometimes produce a better outcome than claiming multiple dwellings relief. For example, a purchase of six dwellings for a total of £1.8m after the current 'holiday' period has ended would attract SDLT of £84,000 at residential rates: even with multiple dwellings relief. The charge at non-residential rates would be reduced to £79,500.

8.9   STAMP DUTY LAND TAX ON LEASES

Lease **premiums** attract SDLT at the same rates as outright purchases.

Further SDLT may also be payable on the granting of a lease, based on the 'net present value' of the rent payable under the lease over its entire term. However, where the net present value does not exceed £500,000 (for residential property), or £150,000 (for non-residential property), no further SDLT will currently be payable. Outside the current 'holiday' period (see Section 8.4), the normal threshold for charges on residential leases is £125,000. See also below regarding the proposed non-resident surcharge.

For new leases with a net present value exceeding these limits, SDLT is payable at a rate of 1% on the excess. The rate increases to 2% on any amounts in excess of £5m.

VAT is excluded from the rent payable under the lease for the purposes of SDLT calculations <u>unless</u> the landlord has already exercised the option to tax (this applies to commercial property only: see Section 15.1).

Example

In April 2021, Woodward Ltd takes on a ten-year lease over a house in Kent at an annual rent of £18,000.

The SDLT legislation provides that the net present value of a sum of money due in twelve months' time is equal to the sum due divided by a 'discount factor'. The applicable discount factor is currently 103.5%.

For SDLT purposes, all of the first year's rent is treated as if it were one single lump sum due in twelve months' time. The 'net present value' of the first year's rent is therefore £17,391 (i.e. £18,000 divided by 103.5%).

Similarly, the second year's rent, which is due a further twelve months later, must be 'discounted' again by the same amount, i.e. £17,391/103.5% = £16,803.

This process is continued for the entire ten-year life of the lease and the net present values of all the rental payments are added together to give the total net present value for the whole lease. In this case, this works out at £149,699.

The SDLT payable by Woodward Ltd is therefore £246 (1% of £149,699 LESS £125,000, rounded down to the nearest whole £1).

(If Woodward Ltd had taken out the lease any time between 8th July 2020 and 31st March 2021, no SDLT would have been due)

The current 'discount factor' (103.5%) may be changed in the future, depending on a number of factors, including the prevailing rates of inflation and interest.

Non-Resident Surcharge on Leases
Under current Government proposals, the non-resident surcharge (see Section 8.5) will also apply to SDLT on the net present value of rent payable under a residential lease. However, leases with a fixed term of no more than 21 years will be exempt.

For leases with a term of more than 21 years, the surcharge will apply to the entire net present value of the rent due under the lease, not just the amount in excess of £125,000.

8.10   PROPERTY IN SCOTLAND

In Scotland, SDLT has been replaced by Land and Buildings Transaction Tax ('LBTT'), which operates in a broadly similar way to SDLT, subject to a few variations, as noted below.

Subject to the exemptions set out in Section 8.12, companies purchasing residential property in Scotland will always be subject to the Additional Dwelling Supplement ('ADS'), which adds an additional charge in a similar way to the higher rates of SDLT examined in Section 8.4. However, since January 2019, ADS has applied at 4% instead of the 3% added to SDLT.

ADS also applies to purchases of residential property made by individuals for business purposes: for further details see the Taxcafe.co.uk guide *'How to Save Property Tax'*.

Residential Property
The rates of LBTT on residential property have been temporarily reduced for the period from 15th July 2020 to 31st March 2021. The reduced rates are set out below, together with the 'normal' rates applying both before and after this period. Both sets of rates include the additional 4% ADS.

Purchase Consideration	Reduced	Normal
Up to £145,000	4%	4%
£145,000 to £250,000	4%	6%
£250,000 to £325,000	9%	9%
£325,000 to £750,000	14%	14%
Over £750,000	16%	16%

The maximum saving on a property purchase, or transfer, under these reduced rates is £2,100 (for purchase consideration, actual or deemed, of £250,000 or more).

Non-Residential Property
The rates of LBTT on non-residential property are as follows:

Purchase Consideration	Rate Applying
Up to £150,000	Nil
£150,000 to £250,000	1%
Over £250,000	5%

Example
Laidlaw Ltd buys a shop in Aberdeen for £275,000. The company pays LBTT totalling £2,250, made up of 1% on £100,000 (£250,000 – £150,000) and 5% on £25,000 (£275,000 – £250,000).

Key Differences
Apart from the rates applying, LBTT operates in broadly the same way as SDLT. Many of the principles examined in Sections 8.3 to 8.8 continue to apply. Nonetheless, there are a few important differences to be aware of.

LBTT does not apply to rent payable under residential leases. The rates on non-residential leases are the same as those for SDLT (see Section 8.9), except the 2% rate applies to net present value in excess of £2m.

Multiple dwellings relief operates differently under LBTT. Instead of taking an average price, the LBTT is calculated separately on each dwelling comprised in the purchase. The total LBTT due cannot be less than 25% of the amount due on the total consideration for the whole transaction. Purchases of six or more dwellings may again alternatively be taxed at non-residential rates based on the total consideration for the whole transaction.

The special rate of SDLT examined in Section 8.6 does not apply to LBTT and nor, as far as we are currently aware, will the non-resident surcharge when it comes into force.

This is by no means an exhaustive list of all the differences between LBTT and SDLT, so it remains essential to take legal advice when purchasing property in Scotland (just as it is when purchasing property anywhere else!)

8.11 PROPERTY IN WALES

In Wales, SDLT has been replaced by Land Transaction Tax ('LTT'), the first devolved tax for Wales.

Residential Property

The main rates of LTT on residential property have been temporarily reduced for the period from 25th July 2020 to 31st March 2021. However, all purchases of residential property in Wales by companies are subject to an additional 3% charge and, where this charge applies, the temporary reduced rates are not available.

Hence, the rates of LTT applying to residential property purchases by companies, including the additional 3% charge, remain as follows:

Purchase Consideration	Rate Applying
£0 to £180,000	3%
£180,000 to £250,000	6.5%
£250,000 to £400,000	8%
£400,000 to £750,000	10.5%
£750,000 to £1.5 million	13%
Over £1.5 million	15%

Non-Residential Property

The rates of LTT on non-residential property are as follows:

Purchase Consideration	Rate Applying
£0 to £150,000	0%
£150,000 to £250,000	1%
£250,000 to £1 million	5%
Over £1 million	6%

As with LBTT, there are a few other differences in the way LTT operates, so it is again essential to take legal advice when purchasing property in Wales.

8.12 EXEMPTIONS

The following purchases are exempt from both SDLT and LBTT (including ADS):

- Interests in property worth less than £40,000
- Caravans, mobile homes and houseboats

Chapter 9

Saving Tax When You Extract Profits

9.1   PROFIT EXTRACTION PRINCIPLES

As I explained at the beginning of the guide, the need to extract profits from your property company (or, indeed, any company) poses a major drawback. This is why property companies generally work better if the owners do not continually draw out all or most of the profits.

Clearly, if you are able to retain all the profits within the company, profit extraction is not a problem. However, sooner or later, almost everyone will want to take something out of the company, or else there wouldn't be much point in having a property business in the first place!

To extract profits from your company tax efficiently, you need to take account of:

a)   Your own personal tax costs,
b)   Any tax costs falling on the company, and
c)   Any CT relief available to the company

Factors (a) and (b) depend on your personal tax position for the tax year in which the payments are made to you; but factor (c) generally depends on the company's CT position, and the rate of CT, for the accounting period in which it makes those payments.

There are two main methods for extracting profits from your company: paying yourself a salary or bonus (i.e. employment income), or paying yourself dividends.

Where the owner has loaned funds to the company, there is also the option of charging interest on those funds, or taking capital repayments. In many cases, interest charges provide the most tax efficient method for extracting funds from the company where this option is available. Capital repayments are, of course, tax free (the company is simply repaying the sums you have loaned to it), but have longer term implications. We will look at the subject of interest charges and capital repayments in more detail in both Section 9.7 and Chapter 12.

In most other cases, dividends usually represent the most tax efficient method for extracting funds from your company; although it is generally worth paying yourself a small salary first.

9.2   SALARIES, ETC

Employment income is subject to three taxes:

i)   Income Tax
ii)   Employee's Class 1 NI
iii)   Employer's secondary Class 1 NI

The rates for each are set out in Appendix A. The combined cost of all three taxes can be quite prohibitive: 45.8% for a typical basic rate taxpayer; 55.8% for a typical higher rate taxpayer; more in some cases. There may also be student loan repayments and compulsory pension contributions to consider; although the latter are probably not relevant in the case of your own company.

Despite this, small salary payments can be very tax efficient, especially as, under the right circumstances, these will provide CT relief for the company.

Payments of wages, salaries or bonuses are deductible against the company's taxable profits for CT purposes, as long as they are incurred for the benefit of the company's business. Some care needs to be taken, therefore, if you do decide to pay yourself, your spouse, your partner, or any other members of your family, any wages or salaries, as no deduction will be available if there is no business justification for the payment.

In other words, yes, the recipient does have to actually work in the business!

Tax Tip
Subject to my comments above, payments of small salaries to yourself, your spouse, your partner, or another family member, can be a useful tax-planning measure, where justified.

Tax Efficient Salaries
The best level of salary to pay yourself or a family member depends on a number of factors. The issue has been rendered more complex from 2020/21 onwards since, in a spectacular display of their utter inability to ever genuinely simplify the tax system, the Government has chosen to allow the primary and secondary NI thresholds to drift apart again, after having been aligned at the same level from 2017/18 to 2019/20.

The secondary threshold is now lower, standing at £8,788 for 2020/21. Salaries up to this level can usually be paid free from both employer's and employee's NI. Hence, with a CT saving of 19% available, such salaries will generally be tax efficient, where justified.

Salaries in excess of £8,788 may be subject to employer's NI at 13.8% on the excess, although there are a number of exceptions (as detailed below).

However, payments up to the primary threshold (£9,500 for 2020/21) will usually be free from employee's NI.

Hence, assuming it is covered by the recipient's personal allowance, the payment of a further £712, to bring the salary up to a total of £9,500, will generally remain tax efficient.

Where employer's NI is due on this additional £712, it will cost £98 (£712 x 13.8%). However, the additional payment will produce a CT saving of £154 (£712 + £98 = £810 x 19% = £154); thus yielding an overall net saving of £56.

(Whether you feel this small net saving justifies the additional admin involved is a matter of personal choice; and possibly also dependent on who does your payroll and how they calculate their charges!)

In many cases, it will not be tax efficient to make salary payments in excess of the primary threshold (currently £9,500) since, unless one of the relevant exceptions applies, the excess will suffer a total NI cost of 25.8% (12% paid by the employee and 13.8% paid by the employer). This outweighs the CT saving produced by the payment.

There are, however, a number of exceptions, where it may be tax efficient to increase the salary payment to a level that fully utilises the recipient's personal allowance (£12,500 for 2020/21). These include cases where:

- The recipient is over state pension age (no employee's NI will be due)
- The recipient is aged under 16 (no NI will be due at all: but see further below)
- The recipient is aged under 21 (no employer's NI will be due on payments up to the higher rate tax threshold)
- The recipient is an apprentice aged under 25 (no employer's NI will be due on payments up to the higher rate tax threshold)
- The employment allowance is available (see below)

Any other taxable income received by the recipient needs to be taken into account when determining a salary level that fully utilises their personal allowance. For those over state pension age, this will usually include their state pension.

Children aged 14 or more (sometimes 13 where local by-laws permit) may be employed in your company and salary payments made to them.

As always, the amount paid must be justified by the work the recipient does in the business and there are legal restrictions on the type and amount of work children under school leaving age may carry out. Hence, in spite of the NI exemption for payments to children under 16, it will be very rare for a salary in excess of a few thousand pounds to be justified in any case.

For further details on the benefits and restrictions relating to employing children, see the Taxcafe.co.uk guide *'Small Business Tax Saving Tactics'*.

Salary payments to any family member (or indeed yourself) must always be justified by the amount of work they do for the company. Payments in excess of the recipient's personal allowance will seldom be tax efficient but may be necessary where the family member's employment duties are extensive.

Salaries paid to non-directors aged 16 or more must at least equal the national minimum wage; or the living wage in the case of those aged 25 or more.

Salaries and other payments to employees (including directors) are subject to strict reporting requirements under the PAYE regulations. Furthermore, with the exception of directors, NI liabilities are based on 'pay periods' rather than being an annual charge. This means, for non-directors, salary payments may need to be made in regular instalments rather than a single lump sum, in order to avoid giving rise to NI costs.

For further details on PAYE obligations, and NI thresholds for 'pay periods', see the Taxcafe.co.uk guide *'Small Business Tax Saving Tactics'*.

The Employment Allowance
Most employers are entitled to exemption from a total of up to £4,000 of employer's Class 1 NI each tax year from 2020/21 onwards (£3,000 in earlier years). This is subject to two exclusions:

i) Large businesses with employer's NI costs of £100,000 or more, and
ii) Companies where a single shareholder/director is the only employee

The second exclusion could affect many small property companies with a single shareholder/director. Furthermore, HMRC incorrectly interprets this rule as meaning at least one other person must be paid in excess of the secondary NI threshold whereas, in fact, what the legislation actually says is there simply needs to be at least one other employee (on any level of pay).

Nonetheless, to be on the safe side, in order to ensure the employment allowance is available where you are a single shareholder/director, it would be wise to make sure another person receives at least £1 more in salary than the secondary NI threshold (this means paying them at least £8,789 in 2020/21).

Tax Tip
Where the employment allowance is available, and has not already been used up on payments to other employees, it will often be worth increasing any salary payments to yourself, your spouse, or other family members, to a level that uses up their Income Tax personal allowance.

Although the recipient will usually suffer employee's NI at 12% on any payment in excess of the primary NI threshold (see Appendix A), the company will be exempt from employer's NI and will (subject to my comments above) be entitled to CT relief on the full amount paid: thus providing a net saving of 7%.

Where a couple, or any two family members, own a company together, they can each be paid salaries up to the personal allowance without any employer's NI arising, as long as the company either has no other employees, or has at least £1,025 of its employment allowance still available.

The same result can be achieved where one person is the sole owner of the company, but simply employs another family member in the business.

How Far Does the Employment Allowance Go?
Salary payments in excess of the personal allowance are not usually tax efficient, but there are some exceptions to this where the employment allowance is available, including cases where the property company owner is already earning a salary of at least £50,000 from another job, or is over state pension age.

We will be looking at these situations in more detail in Sections 9.6 and 10.15. In these cases, it may be worth paying the maximum salary that can be covered by the employment allowance; or at least it may be more tax efficient to pay salaries up to this level in preference to dividends in excess of the dividend allowance (see Section 9.3).

The maximum director's salaries that can be covered by the employment allowance will vary from company to company, but two of the most common scenarios, at 2020/21 rates, are:

- Single director with one other employee earning £1 over the secondary NI threshold: £37,772
- Two directors with no other employees: £23,280 each

These maximum salaries would be the same where the company has other employees, but those employees' salaries are exempt from employer's NI (e.g. employees aged under 21 and earning less than £50,000).

9.3   DIVIDENDS

Subject to the dividend allowance described below, dividends are subject to Income Tax at the following rates:

Basic rate taxpayers: 7.5%
Higher rate taxpayers: 32.5%
Additional rate taxpayers: 38.1%

The non-refundable tax credit which attached to dividends prior to April 2016 no longer applies: one of the few genuine pieces of simplification the Government has ever actually achieved! As a consequence, the amount of taxable dividend income is now the same as the dividend actually received and there is no longer any need to 'gross up' dividend income to take account of the tax credit. (If none of that means anything to you, don't worry: it's irrelevant now)

The Dividend Allowance

Each individual has an annual 'dividend allowance' (currently £2,000) that reduces the rate of Income Tax on the first part of their dividend income (up to the amount of the allowance) to nil. Dividends falling within the allowance are still included as taxable income for other purposes, however. This means dividends covered by the allowance will still:

- Use up the basic rate band
- Count in determining the level of your personal savings allowance (Section 9.4)
- Trigger or increase the High Income Child Benefit Charge, where appropriate
- Cause the loss of the individual's personal allowance if they push their total taxable income over (or further over) £100,000
- Count as income for the purposes of the £150,000 additional rate tax threshold
- Count as income for the purposes of restrictions on pension relief for individuals with total deemed income over £240,000

Example

In March 2021, Gabby takes dividends of £8,000 out of her property investment company. She has £49,000 of income from other sources for 2020/21.

The dividend allowance reduces the rate of Income Tax on the first £2,000 of Gabby's dividends to nil. However, adding her 'tax free' dividends to her other income produces a total of £51,000: which exceeds the higher rate tax threshold for 2020/21. Hence, the remaining £6,000 of Gabby's dividends are subject to higher rate tax at 32.5%.

An individual's personal allowance is used first before the dividend allowance is considered. Or, put another way, dividends covered by an individual's personal allowance do not use up their dividend allowance.

Example

In December 2020, Greg takes a dividend of £10,000 out of his property company. His other income for 2020/21 totals £9,000. The first £3,500 of Greg's dividend is covered by the remaining part of his personal allowance (£12,500 – £9,000); the next £2,000 is covered by his dividend allowance; and the last £4,500 is taxed at 7.5%.

It follows that an individual with no other income could take tax-free dividends of up to £14,500 out of their company during 2020/21. This is the total of their personal allowance (£12,500) and their dividend allowance (£2,000). As we shall see in Section 9.6, however, this will seldom be the optimal approach.

See Appendix A for details of the higher rate tax threshold and personal allowance, as used in the above examples.

Other Considerations

Dividends represent a distribution of a company's after-tax profits and no deduction is therefore allowed for CT purposes.

No business justification is required for dividends, although company law does require distributable profits to be available. Hence, having your spouse, partner, or another adult family member as a shareholder in your company may be a useful tax-planning measure. (Dividends paid to minor children from their parent's company will be treated as the parent's income for tax purposes.)

Jointly Held Shares

Where shares are held jointly by a married couple, it is no longer possible for the dividend income arising to be automatically split 50/50 for Income Tax purposes. The income must be split according to the couple's actual beneficial entitlement.

9.4   THE PERSONAL SAVINGS ALLOWANCE

The personal savings allowance is often relevant in determining a shareholder/director's optimum profit extraction strategy. Not only does it provide the opportunity to take tax-free interest income from your own company (as we shall see in Section 12.10), it can also impact the question of how much salary it is most tax efficient for you to take.

Interest and other savings income covered by your personal savings allowance is free from Income Tax. Note that, for tax purposes, pensions income is not classed as savings income.

Income falling within your personal allowance or starting rate band (see Section 12.10) does not use up your personal savings allowance: the allowance only applies to income that would otherwise give rise to an Income Tax charge. As with the dividend allowance (Section 9.3), income covered by the personal savings allowance remains taxable income and has the same effect on your overall tax position.

The amount of your personal savings allowance depends on how much total taxable income of all types you ultimately end up with for the tax year: both from your company and from other sources. To summarise, if you finish the tax year with total taxable income:

- Not exceeding the higher rate tax threshold (currently £50,000), your personal savings allowance is £1,000
- That exceeds the higher rate tax threshold but does not exceed £150,000, your personal savings allowance is £500
- Exceeding £150,000, your personal savings allowance is nil.

These thresholds mean, if you have £1,000 or more of interest and savings income, any income that takes your total taxable income over the higher rate tax threshold will cost an extra £100 (on top of the tax on that income itself). Similarly, if you have £500 or more of interest and savings income, any income that takes your total taxable income over £150,000 will cost either an extra £100 or £200.

9.5   MAXIMUM TAX-FREE SALARIES

Before we move on, I need to expand a little further on the question of what an individual's maximum tax-free salary is. This concept will be important when we start to look at optimum profit extraction strategies later in this chapter. In this section, I will only be considering Income Tax although, as we already know, salaries are also subject to both employer's and employee's NI.

An individual's maximum tax-free salary depends on how much taxable income they are receiving from outside the company. In this context, it is important to remember an individual's taxable income includes the profit **before** interest from any residential lettings, although we will look at this issue, and its potential relevance to the individual's maximum tax-free salary, in more detail in Section 12.12.

Where an individual's taxable income from outside the company, excluding dividends, interest, and other savings income, is more than, or equal to, the personal allowance (currently £12,500), their maximum tax-free salary is usually nil. In other words, generally speaking, any salary they take from their company will give rise to an Income Tax liability. (But see Section 12.12 for some potential exceptions.)

For an individual with no taxable income from outside the company, their maximum tax-free salary is equal to the personal allowance.

Where their only other taxable income is dividends of £2,000 or less and/or interest and other savings income of no more than £5,000 plus their personal savings allowance (Section 9.4), their maximum tax-free salary remains the same.

In other cases, where an individual has no more than £2,000 of dividend income from outside the company, their maximum tax-free salary is the lower of:

a) The amount that brings their total taxable income, excluding dividends, interest, and other savings income, up to the amount of the personal allowance
b) The amount that brings their total taxable income, excluding dividends, but including interest, and other savings income, up to an amount equal to £17,500 plus their personal savings allowance (see Section 9.4)

Example
Shaunagh has a small pension of £6,000 per year, dividends of £1,500 from outside her property company and interest income of £2,500.

For Shaunagh, the amount under (a) is £6,500, and the amount under (b) is £9,000 plus her personal savings allowance. The amount under (a) is therefore lower, so her maximum tax-free salary is £6,500.

Where an individual has more than £2,000 of dividend income from outside the company, their maximum tax-free salary is the amount that brings their total taxable income of all types up to £14,500.

Such individuals may also be able to take further salary at a maximum effective Income Tax rate of just 7.5%, and this will often be worthwhile, especially where the total salary remains below the primary NI threshold, or the employment allowance is available.

The additional salary taxed at this low effective rate will be the amount that brings the total salary up to the lowest of (a) and (b) above, and (c), the amount that brings the individual's total taxable income for the year up to the higher rate tax threshold. For the rest of this chapter, I will refer to this additional salary as a 'low tax salary'.

Example
Amy earns £5,000 from a part-time job. She also receives dividends of £3,800 from outside her property company and interest income of £1,500. Her maximum tax-free salary is £4,200.

For Amy, the amount under (a) is £7,500, the amount under (b) is £11,000 plus her personal savings allowance, and the amount under (c) is £39,700. The amount under (a) is the lowest, so she can increase her salary to £7,500 and the additional £3,300 over and above her maximum tax-free salary will be a 'low tax salary'.

9.6   OPTIMUM PROFIT EXTRACTION

There are a number of methods for extracting profits from your company but, in most cases, we are usually concerned with either salary or dividends, or a combination of both.

Assuming these are the only options available, a good rule of thumb to start with is to follow this order of priorities:

- A salary that doesn't suffer any of the three taxes described at the start of Section 9.2 is the best thing to pay first
- Salaries that suffer no Income Tax and only one type of NI are next best
- Dividends covered by the dividend allowance are next
- Salaries that suffer Income Tax but no NI are next
- Pay anything else you need as dividends

This 'rule of thumb' isn't entirely accurate, but you probably won't go far wrong by following it in most cases.

The rest of this section is for those who, like me, want a more precise analysis of the optimum method of profit extraction: although even this detailed analysis isn't perfect and is subject to a few rare exceptions (so much for 'tax simplification'!)

In this section, I have worked on the basis that the company owner needs a certain net sum, after tax, in their hands, and looked at the most tax efficient way to achieve this, taking all the relevant factors into account: Income Tax, employee's NI, employer's NI, and CT relief.

To avoid repeating the same phrase many times, the use of an asterisk (*) in this section means I am referring to income excluding dividends, interest, and other savings income.

The optimum method of profit extraction depends on many factors, including whether the employment allowance is available on any salary paid to the company owner (see Section 9.2). Let's start with the position where the employment allowance is **not** available.

Employment Allowance NOT Available

No Other Taxable Income
- Firstly pay a salary up to the amount of the primary NI threshold
- Pay any further amounts required by way of dividend

Other Taxable Income* Less Than the Personal Allowance
- Firstly pay a salary equal to the lower of:
  - The primary NI threshold, and
  - The individual's maximum tax-free salary plus any 'low tax salary' (Section 9.5)
- Secondly pay any dividend covered by the dividend allowance
- Thirdly pay any further salary required to bring the total salary up to the level of the **secondary** NI threshold
- Pay any further amounts required by way of dividend

Other Taxable Income* At Least Equal to Personal Allowance
- First pay any dividend covered by the dividend allowance
- Second pay a salary up to the amount of the **secondary** NI threshold
- Pay any further amounts required by way of dividend

Simple Summary
Some of that may seem a little complex but, in most cases, it can be vastly simplified. The simple version below applies where your taxable income from outside the company does **not** include more than £2,000 of dividends, or any interest and savings income not covered by your personal savings allowance (see Section 9.4).

The optimum profit extraction strategy for 2020/21 in most cases where the employment allowance is **not** available is as follows:

Other Income (1)			First Pay	Then	Then	Then
£0	To	£3,000	£9,500 Salary	Dividends		
£3,000	To	£3,712	Salary (2)	Dividends		
£3,712	To	£12,500	Salary (2)	Div Allce (3) £8,788	Salary (4)	Dividends
£12,500	Or	more	Div Allce (3)	Salary	Dividends	

Notes
1. Total taxable income from all sources outside the company, excluding dividends, interest, and savings income
2. Sufficient salary to bring taxable income* up to a total of £12,500
3. Dividends covered by the dividend allowance: i.e. £2,000 less any dividends received from other sources outside the company
4. Bring salary up to a total of £8,788 (when combined with amount at 2 above)

Employment Allowance IS Available

No Other Taxable Income
- Firstly pay a salary up to the amount of the personal allowance
- Pay any further amounts required by way of dividend

Other Taxable Income* Less Than the Personal Allowance
- Firstly pay the individual's maximum tax-free salary (Section 9.5)
- Secondly pay any further salary equal to the lower of:
  - o The amount required to bring the total salary up to the primary NI threshold
  - o Any 'low tax salary' (Section 9.5)
- Thirdly pay any dividend covered by the dividend allowance
- Fourthly pay the greater of:
  - o Any further salary required to bring the total salary up to the primary NI threshold
  - o Any remaining 'low tax salary'
- Pay any further amounts required by way of dividend

Other Taxable Income* At Least Equal to the Personal Allowance
- Firstly pay any dividend covered by the dividend allowance
- Secondly pay a salary up to the amount of the primary NI threshold
- Pay any further amounts required by way of dividend

Other Salary of £50,000 or more
There are some potential exceptions to the optimum strategy set out above where the company owner has a salary of £50,000 or more from another job outside the company.

In this situation, the company owner may be able to apply to reduce the rate of Class 1 NI on any salary from their property company. This means where, and to the extent that, the employment allowance is available, salary in excess of the primary NI threshold may be more tax efficient than dividends in excess of the dividend allowance.

However, the reduced Class 1 rate of 2% does not apply until the company owner has paid at least £5,019 in NI at the main rate of 12% (using 2020/21 rates).

Nonetheless, where the company owner is willing to go to the effort of applying for the reduced NI rate on the salary from their company, the optimum profit extraction strategy for those with a salary of at least £50,000 from outside the company will often be to increase the salary from their company to the level that exhausts the company's employment allowance.

However, this is only worth doing if the further net sum required after tax following payment of any dividend covered by the dividend allowance and a salary equal to the primary NI threshold, is sufficient to make it worthwhile. Naturally, there also needs to be enough of the company's employment allowance left to cover such a net salary (and remember £98 of the employment allowance will have already been used paying a salary equal to the primary NI threshold). The 'break-even' thresholds for this revised strategy are as follows.

Higher rate taxpayer with another salary of £50,000 or more: further net sum required at least £2,173; must have at least £549 of employment allowance still available.

Additional rate taxpayer with another salary of £50,000 or more: further net sum required at least £2,316; must have at least £638 of employment allowance still available.

Simple Summary
Once again, the above guidelines can be simplified in most cases. The simple version below again applies where your taxable income from outside the company does **not** include more than £2,000 of dividends, or any interest and savings income not covered by your personal savings allowance (see Section 9.4).

The optimum profit extraction strategy for 2020/21 in most cases where the employment allowance **is** available is as follows:

Other Income (1)			First Pay	Then	Then	Then
			£12,500			
£0			Salary	Dividends		
					Salary	
£1	to	£12,500	Salary (2)	Div Allce (3)	(4)	Dividends
				£9,500		
£12,500	or	more	Div Allce (3)	Salary	Dividends	
Unless:						
				£9,500	Salary	
Salary £50,000+			Div Allce (3)	Salary	(5)	Dividends

Notes
1. Total taxable income from all sources outside the company, excluding dividends, interest, and savings income
2. Sufficient salary to bring taxable income* up to a total of £12,500
3. Dividends covered by the dividend allowance: i.e. £2,000 less any dividends received from other sources outside the company
4. Bring salary up to £9,500 (when combined with amount at 2 above)
5. See above re cases where it will be more tax efficient to pay salary up to the level that exhausts the company's employment allowance. See Section 9.2 for some pointers on how much salary may be covered by the employment allowance.

Other Variations

Variations to the optimum profit extraction strategies set out above may occur where the company owner:

- Has a loan account balance with the company and is able to charge interest thereon (see Section 12.10)
- Is over state pension age (see Section 10.15)
- Is a Scottish taxpayer (see Section 15.8)
- Has more than £32,000 of dividend income from outside the company

See the Taxcafe.co.uk guide *'Salary versus Dividends'* for a full analysis of optimum profit extraction strategies. See Appendix A for the current NI thresholds, personal allowance, dividend allowance, and higher rate tax threshold.

9.7   BENEFICIAL PROFIT EXTRACTION

In the previous section, my approach was to show you the most tax efficient way to extract the funds you need, or desire, from your company.

There are some cases, however, where it is actually beneficial to extract profits, even when you don't need the cash yet. In these cases, the funds can be extracted and then loaned back to the company, providing you with the opportunity to take tax-free capital repayments in the future, or perhaps to explore the benefits of charging interest as an alternative, and more tax efficient, form of profit extraction. (We will explore the benefits of charging interest to your company further in Chapter 12.)

Often, in these cases, it is not necessary to actually withdraw the funds and loan them back: the same result can be achieved simply by preparing the relevant paperwork (including making the relevant PAYE reports etc), and making the appropriate entries in the company's accounting records and the owner's personal tax return. HMRC may, however, look to see if the company could have made the relevant payments (i.e. whether it had the cash available).

Negative Cost Options

Profit extraction that has an overall negative cost (after taking account of CT relief) is always worth doing, even if you don't need the cash. This includes the following options:

- Taking a salary up to the primary NI threshold that is covered by your personal allowance
- Taking any level of salary that is covered by both your personal allowance and the company's employment allowance (Section 9.2)
- Charging your company interest that is covered by your personal allowance, starting rate band, or personal savings allowance (see Section 9.4)
- Charging your company rent that is covered by your personal allowance (see Section 16.2)

Zero Cost Options

Anything that can be done at zero cost means you can take money out and lend it back to the company at no cost, providing opportunities for tax-free capital repayments in the future when you need to extract cash. This includes the following options:

- Dividends covered by your personal allowance
- Dividends covered by the dividend allowance (see Section 9.3)

Low Cost Options

Negative and zero cost profit extraction options are always worth pursuing. Less clear is whether it makes sense to pursue low cost options that, while they do have a cost, are less expensive than other methods you may be forced to pursue in the future.

Think about future years. Will you need to extract more than can be covered by the negative and zero cost options outlined above? Naturally, if you have loaned funds to the company, you can take tax-free loan repayments, but how long will they last? Would it make sense to supplement them by pursuing low cost profit extraction options now?

The following options have an overall net tax cost (after CT relief at 19%) of just 1%:

- Salaries up to the secondary NI threshold that are subject to basic rate Income Tax at 20% in the recipient's hands
- Salaries up to the primary NI threshold that are covered by the company's employment allowance and subject to basic rate Income Tax at 20% in the recipient's hands
- Charging your company interest that is subject to basic rate Income Tax at 20% in your hands (see Section 12.4)
- Charging your company rent that is subject to basic rate Income Tax at 20% in your hands (see Section 16.2)

Example
Stuart and Colin each have a property company, to which they have loaned £126,000. They also each have other sources of income that bring in taxable income of £30,000 each year, making them basic rate taxpayers. Each of them

plans to grow their property company for five years and will then need to start taking a net sum of £50,000 per year out of the company. Both companies have another employee, and enough employment allowance available to mean a director's salary of £9,500 would not suffer any NI.

Stuart pursues his negative and zero cost options. Each year he takes interest of £1,000 out of his company, which is covered by his personal savings allowance, and dividends of £2,000, which are covered by his dividend allowance. He loans these sums back to the company each year. The company saves £190 (CT relief on the interest) and Stuart has no Income Tax to pay on his company income.

After five years, Stuart's loan account balance stands at £141,000 and the company has saved a total of £950 due to the interest it has paid. He now needs a net sum of £50,000 each year. To get this, he starts taking a loan repayment of £47,000 each year in addition to his interest and dividends. However, after three years, his loan balance has been reduced to nil. His optimum profit extraction strategy (as per Section 9.6) is now to take:

i)   Salary of £9,500, giving rise to Income Tax, at 20%, of £1,900
ii)   Dividends of £58,704, which are taxed as follows:

£2,000 @ 0%	£0
£8,500 @ 7.5%	£638
£48,204 @ 32.5%	£15,666
Total	£16,304

His total income before tax (from the company) is £68,204 (£9,500 + £58,704) and his total Income Tax bill is £18,204 (£1,900 + £16,304), leaving him with the net sum of £50,000 he requires.

The only saving for the company is on Stuart's salary, which provides CT relief of £1,805 (£9,500 x 19%).

Colin, on the other hand, decides to also pursue his low cost options in addition to his negative and zero cost options. He therefore starts, right from the outset, by paying himself:

i)   Salary of £9,500, giving rise to Income Tax, at 20%, of £1,900
ii)   Dividends of £2,000, which are covered by his dividend allowance
iii)   Interest of £10,500

The interest he charges amounts to 8.33% of his loan account balance, which can be justified as a reasonable rate (see Section 12.10). The first £500 is covered by his personal savings allowance, which has been reduced to £500 because his total taxable income is now £52,000, i.e. more than the higher rate tax threshold. However, he doesn't actually pay any higher rate tax because his top £2,000 of income is covered by the dividend allowance.

The remaining £10,000 of Colin's interest income is taxed at 20%, giving rise to further Income Tax of £2,000. Colin's total Income Tax bill is thus £3,900.

He lends his net, after tax, income of £18,100 (£9,500 + £2,000 + £10,500 – £3,900) back to the company.

The company makes an annual CT saving of £3,800 by claiming relief for Colin's salary and interest charges. The overall net cost of the payments to Colin is thus £100 (£3,900 – £3,800).

Colin's company is worse off than Stuart's by £290 each year (the difference between Stuart's annual saving and Colin's overall net cost). This is effectively the cost of Colin's 'low cost options'. [His salary and interest charges in excess of £1,000 have a net cost of 1%. There is also an additional cost of £100 (£500 x 20%) due to the fact that, by increasing his taxable income above the higher rate tax threshold, he has lost £500 of his personal savings allowance. As we shall see later, this additional cost is worthwhile in the end.]

After five years, Colin's loan account stands at £216,500 (£126,000 + 5 x £18,100), and the company has benefitted from a total of £19,000 in CT relief on the salary and interest payments made to him. However, in cash terms, Colin's company is £1,450 worse off than Stuart's at this stage.

From year six onwards, Colin continues to pay himself the same salary, dividends, and interest, but also takes a loan repayment of £31,900 to give him the total net, after tax, sum of £50,000 he requires. Colin's Income Tax bill and the company's CT relief therefore remain the same. The £290 net cash deficit compared with Stuart's company also remains the same for the next three years.

But, when Stuart's loan balance has been exhausted at the end of year eight, Colin still has a loan balance of £120,800 (£216,500 – 3 x £31,900). Colin can therefore still carry on in much the same way, with perhaps a small reduction in his interest payments as his loan balance drops.

If we assume Colin's interest payments are capped at the lower of £10,500 or 10% of his outstanding loan balance (see Section 12.10), he can pay himself as follows over the next few years:

Year	Salary	Interest	Dividends	Loan Repay't	Income Tax
9	£9,500	£10,500	£2,000	£31,900	£3,900
10	£9,500	£8,890	£2,000	£33,188	£3,578
11	£9,500	£5,571	£2,000	£35,743	£2,814
12	£9,500	£1,997	£27,345	£19,969	£8,811

The last column indicates the Income Tax paid by Colin. The company will continue to enjoy CT relief at 19% on the interest and salary payments.

As we can see, in year twelve, Colin needs to start paying himself more than £2,000 in dividends in order to get the net sum of £50,000 he requires. Nonetheless, by this point he will have accumulated considerable tax savings:

and those savings translate into additional cash within his company available for investment in new properties.

*The **cumulative** position for both investors is summarised below:*

End of Year	Loan Balance	Stuart Income Tax	CT Relief	Net Tax Paid
5	£141,000	£0	£950	-£950
6	£94,000	£0	£1,140	-£1,140
7	£47,000	£0	£1,330	-£1,330
8	£0	£0	£1,520	-£1,520
9	£0	£18,204	£3,325	£14,879
10	£0	£36,408	£5,130	£31,278
11	£0	£54,612	£6,935	£47,677
12	£0	£72,816	£8,740	£64,076

End of Year	Loan Balance	Colin Income Tax	CT Relief	Net Tax Paid	Versus Stuart
5	£216,500	£19,500	£19,000	£500	-£1,450
6	£184,600	£23,400	£22,800	£600	-£1,740
7	£152,700	£27,300	£26,600	£700	-£2,030
8	£120,800	£31,200	£30,400	£800	-£2,320
9	£88,900	£35,100	£34,200	£900	£13,979
10	£55,712	£38,678	£37,694	£984	£30,294
11	£19,969	£41,492	£40,558	£935	£46,742
12	£0	£50,303	£42,742	£7,561	£56,515

As we can see from the last column, Colin eventually ends up more than £56,500 better off than Stuart, simply due to the fact he built those 'low cost options' into his profit extraction strategy. This enabled his loan balance to last almost four years longer than Stuart's.

From year thirteen onwards, both investors will be in the same position, meaning Colin's saving of over £56,500 is a permanent addition to the value of his company.

If, in the same scenario, Colin had restricted his interest payments to a maximum of £8,500 per year: the level that would have enabled him to retain his full personal savings allowance of £1,000; he would have ended up £50,166 better off than Stuart at the end of year twelve. In other words, increasing his interest payments by a further £2,000 per year as detailed above has ultimately saved an additional £6,349 (£56,515 – £50,166) despite meaning the loss of £500 of tax free allowance each year, and costing an extra £120 per year in net cash terms.

That net cost is the product of an extra £500 in Income Tax (tax at 20% on the £2,000 itself and on the £500 of lost allowance) less £380 in CT relief (£2,000 x 19%).

But, at an effective rate of 6%, (£120/£2,000) this is considerably less than Income Tax at 32.5% on a dividend paid to a higher rate taxpayer. Hence, the extra interest payment is worthwhile when it only pushes dividend income covered by the dividend allowance over the higher rate tax threshold and, as in Colin's case, no actual higher rate tax is due.

This is what one might call a 'medium cost option' and, in a case like Colin's, where the company owner will eventually need to resort to paying themselves dividends taxed at 32.5% (see Section 9.3), it is worth pursuing. In fact, in this situation, anything that can be added to a loan account balance (or used to preserve more of a loan account balance) at a lower cost will ultimately save tax overall.

Look at it this way: it cost a net sum of £120 to preserve an extra £1,500 of Colin's loan account balance (£2,000 of additional interest charged less the £500 additional Income Tax cost arising). That's an effective 'grossed up' rate of 8% (£120/£1,500).

For a higher rate taxpayer to get a net sum of £1,500 by way of dividend (once their dividend allowance is exhausted) means paying a dividend of £2,222. After paying £722 in Income Tax at 32.5%, they are left with the desired net sum of £1,500. That's an effective 'grossed up' rate of over 48%!

Hence, if you know you will ultimately end up having to pay yourself dividends taxed at 32.5% (or more), any 'medium cost options' with an effective 'grossed up' rate below 48% could be worth pursuing. The lower the 'grossed up' rate, the bigger and more obvious, the ultimate saving.

The simplest and one of the best 'medium cost options' is to pay yourself dividends that fall within your basic rate tax band and are thus taxed at 7.5%. That's equivalent to an effective 'grossed up' rate of just 8.1%. Hence, while dividends above the dividend allowance are no longer tax free for basic rate taxpayers, they are often still worth paying if it means reducing the amount of dividends subject to higher rate tax in the future.

By way of example, as we saw above, Colin's taxable income in year eleven was made up as follows:

Income from sources outside the company	£30,000
Salary	£9,500
Interest	£5,571
Dividends	£2,000
Total	£47,071

This means Colin could have taken further dividends of £2,929 (£50,000 – £47,071) that would have been taxed at just 7.5%, costing £220. He would then have had £2,709 (£2,929 – £220) more left in his loan account at the end of year eleven.

In year twelve, his higher opening loan account balance would have meant he could pay a further £271 in interest (at 10%) taxed at 20% (a cost of just £54), but providing CT relief at 19%: a net cost of a mere 1% (less than £3).

Most importantly, he would also have £2,709 more capital loan repayment to take. Hence, in all, a further £2,926 (£2,709 + £271 – £54) of his cash requirements would come from his loan account. This, in turn, means he would need £2,926 less dividends after tax.

However, his higher interest payments mean £271 more of his dividends go into the higher rate tax bracket. This increases the Income Tax on this element of his dividends by £68 (£271 x 25%: the difference between 7.5% and 32.5%).

Nonetheless, his requirement for after tax income from dividends taxed at the higher rate of 32.5% still reduces by £2,858 (£2,926 – £68), saving him £1,376 in Income Tax. (To get a net sum of £2,858 after tax, a higher rate taxpayer needs to pay a dividend of £4,234, on which the Income Tax, at 32.5% is £1,376.)

Colin's overall net saving in year twelve is thus £1,305 (£1,376 saved by paying less dividends, minus £68 extra paid on existing dividends, minus the £3 net cost of his additional interest payment).

So, investing £220 in year eleven yields a return of £1,305 in year twelve: a net saving of £1,085, or a return of almost 500%!

That's got to be worth doing, and it now puts Colin a total of £57,600 ahead of Stuart: just by preserving his loan account.

Guidance on Interest Charges
See Section 12.10 for further guidance on charging your company interest, the formalities to be observed, and suitable rates to charge.

Chapter 10

Personal versus Company Ownership

10.1 INTRODUCTION

In the previous chapters, we have worked through the principles of how a property company and its owners are taxed. In the next two chapters, we will be looking in detail at the decision itself: "Should I run my property business through a company?"

Before we do that, we are going to take a look in this chapter at the comparative levels of tax on a personal property investor and a company investing in property. There are a great many different criteria we could choose for our comparison; almost an infinite number, in fact. However, in order to keep things down to a manageable size, we are just going to look at a few different scenarios that, I believe, should be sufficient to amply demonstrate the principles involved.

In this chapter, we will mostly be looking at income, starting with rental profits and then moving on to income classed as trading profit. Once we get into capital gains, the situation becomes even more complicated and can only really be assessed through the use of detailed examples. This will form a major part of the next chapter.

In each of Sections 10.3 to 10.17, I will look at a different scenario and produce a set of conclusions for that scenario. I will then summarise those conclusions in Section 10.18 at the end of the chapter.

It is important to remember however, as you consider the tables in this chapter, that these only represent one-off annual 'snapshots' of the position. While they do provide useful illustrations of the potential tax savings involved, I must urge you to also consider the more detailed and longer-term issues we will be looking at in the next two chapters.

As explained in the foreword, I have based all my calculations on current tax rates, bands, and allowances. This, I believe, is now the best approach because, while the tax regime is likely to undergo significant changes in the medium to long-term future:

- Apart from minor inflationary adjustments, current rates may persist for some time before any significant changes take place
- We do not know what changes will occur, or when

- The question of whether a property company is beneficial is dependent on the **_differences_** between the corporate and personal tax regimes, not on those regimes themselves

There is good reason to believe that, while significant changes to both regimes are likely, the overall differential between the two regimes will probably remain fairly consistent.

While I am using current tax rates for my calculations, we are still using them to produce forecasts of the long-term future position. This is important to remember because it is the long-term position you need to consider when deciding whether a property company will be beneficial.

We will look at likely future tax changes and their potential impact on using a property company in Chapter 17.

10.2   PERSONAL TAX RECAP

As explained in the previous section, I am basing all my calculations in this chapter on current (2020/21) tax rates, bands, and allowances. As we know, this means using the current CT rate of 19%, but it is also worth recapping the personal tax rates we will be using for our comparisons. These are also summarised in Appendix A.

Income Tax Rates (Except on Dividends)
Up to £12,500:	0%	
£12,500 to £50,000:	20%	
£50,000 to £100,000:	40%	
£100,000 to £125,000:	60%	(see Note 1)
£125,000 to £150,000:	40%	
Over £150,000:	45%	

Dividend Tax Rates
Dividend allowance:	£2,000
Basic rate taxpayers:	7.5%
Higher rate taxpayers:	32.5%
Additional rate taxpayers:	38.1%

NI Rates for Self-Employed Traders
Up to £6,475:	Nil	
£6,475 to £9,500:	£159	(see Note 2)
£9,500 to £50,000:	9%	
Over £50,000:	2%	

Employee's Primary Class 1 NI
Up to £9,500:	Nil
£9,500 to £50,000:	12%
Over £50,000:	2%

Employer's Secondary Class 1 NI
Up to £8,788:   Nil
Over £8,788:   13.8%

Note 1
An individual loses £1 of their personal allowance for every £2 by which their total taxable income exceeds £100,000. This creates the effective rate of 60% referred to above. The additional cost of losing your entire personal allowance is £5,000 and you will see this amount appear in a number of examples throughout this guide. In other cases, you will see the additional cost of a partial loss of personal allowance where the individual's total taxable income is between £100,000 and £125,000.

Note 2
Self-employed taxpayers with trading businesses currently pay both Class 2 and Class 4 NI. Class 4 is paid at the 9% and 2% rates set out above.

Class 2 NI is currently payable at the rate of £3.05 per week (£158.60 for a year), where trading profits exceed the 'small profits threshold' of £6,475. This tax was due to be abolished but, after two stays of execution, the last thing we heard was that it would continue for the rest of the current Parliament. Now, like everything else, its long-term future is uncertain but, in keeping with our general philosophy of sticking to current tax rates, I will include it in my comparisons, where appropriate.

Keeping it Simple
For the sake of illustration, unless expressly stated to the contrary, some additional complexities in the UK tax system will be ignored for the purpose of all forecasts, comparisons, examples, etc, throughout the remainder of this guide. These include:

- The High Income Child Benefit Charge (see Section 10.16)
- The £4,000 NI employment allowance (see Section 9.2)
- Different Income Tax rates applying to Scottish taxpayers (see Section 15.8 for a detailed exploration of their impact on the issues discussed in this guide)
- The marriage allowance (which allows spouses to transfer 10% of their personal allowance where neither the transferor nor transferee is a higher rate taxpayer)
- Student loan repayments
- 'Auto-enrolment' pension contributions

The last two are not really tax, but are closely related. 'Auto-enrolment' pension contributions only apply automatically to salaries in excess of £10,000. Furthermore, when taking a salary out of your own company it is, of course, possible to opt out in any case. Nonetheless, there may be some extra admin to deal with if you pay yourself a salary over £10,000 (which, as we saw in Chapter 9, can sometimes be the best strategy): see the Taxcafe.co.uk guide *'Small Business Tax Saving Tactics'* for further details.

We will also ignore grants under the Self-Employed Income Support Scheme ('SEISS') and other grants available during the coronavirus crisis as, one fervently hopes, these are not relevant to our long-term forecasts.

It is, however, perhaps worth noting that many self-employed individuals or business partners with property trades (e.g. property development or property management) will have been eligible for SEISS grants, whereas shareholder/directors are not. A director might have been eligible for payments under the Coronavirus Job Retention Scheme, but these will have been pretty puny for most directors following an optimum profit extraction strategy (see Section 9.6). One has to wonder if the Government has been relishing this opportunity to get their revenge on those who have carefully planned their tax affairs in the past!

For landlords, of course, there is very little help available whether you are using a company or not!

10.3   RENTAL PROFITS KEPT IN THE COMPANY

In this section, we will start out with the simplest situation (albeit a little hypothetical). Here, we look at the tax burden on an individual receiving rental income and compare it with the tax that would have been paid by a company set up to run their property portfolio.

For the time being, in this section, we are also assuming:

i)   All profits are retained within the company
ii)   The individual has no other taxable income
iii)   No interest or finance costs are incurred

Annual Rental Profits	Tax Paid Personally	Tax Paid By Company	Tax Saving/(Cost)
£20,000	£1,500	£3,800	(£2,300)
£30,000	£3,500	£5,700	(£2,200)
£40,000	£5,500	£7,600	(£2,100)
£50,000	£7,500	£9,500	(£2,000)
£60,000	£11,500	£11,400	£100
£75,000	£17,500	£14,250	£3,250
£100,000	£27,500	£19,000	£8,500
£125,000	£42,500	£23,750	£18,750
£150,000	£52,500	£28,500	£24,000
£200,000	£75,000	£38,000	£37,000

Conclusions

As we can see, using a company is of no benefit to a basic rate taxpayer landlord with no interest or finance costs.

A benefit does begin to accrue once the landlord's income exceeds the higher rate tax threshold.

These conclusions are, however, based on the fact that no part of the company's profits are being extracted; neither as salary, dividend, nor by any other means.

For a taxpayer with no other income, this is probably unrealistic. Furthermore, as we saw in Section 9.7, it would actually be beneficial for such an individual to extract some profit from the company. In the next section, we will therefore factor in some limited profit extraction that has a beneficial, or neutral, effect overall.

10.4   RENTAL PROFITS EXTRACTED WHERE BENEFICIAL

In this section, we will assume as follows:

i)   The individual takes a salary of £9,500 (the primary NI threshold) and dividends of £2,000 (the dividend allowance) out of the company
ii)   The remaining profits are retained within the company
iii)   The individual has no other taxable income
iv)   No interest or finance costs are incurred

Annual Rental Profits	Tax Paid Personally	Tax Paid By Company	Tax Saving/(Cost)
£20,000	£1,500	£2,075	(£575)
£30,000	£3,500	£3,975	(£475)
£40,000	£5,500	£5,875	(£375)
£50,000	£7,500	£7,775	(£275)
£60,000	£11,500	£9,675	£1,825
£75,000	£17,500	£12,525	£4,975
£100,000	£27,500	£17,275	£10,225
£125,000	£42,500	£22,025	£20,475
£150,000	£52,500	£26,775	£25,725
£200,000	£75,000	£36,275	£38,725

'Annual Rental Profits' are before paying the individual's salary. 'Tax Paid By Company' includes employer's NI of £98, but is reduced by CT relief for both the salary and the NI.

The outcome would be the same if the individual took no dividends, or any amount up to £2,000. However, as we saw in Section 9.7, taking dividends covered by the dividend allowance is generally beneficial in the long run.

Conclusions

Taking a small salary equal to the primary NI threshold produces a saving of £1,725 compared with the results in Section 10.3.

However, as we can see, using a company is still of no benefit to a basic rate taxpayer landlord with no interest or finance costs.

The benefit to higher rate taxpayers remains and, indeed, has been slightly improved. Furthermore, the company owner now has up to £11,500 of tax-free income. This might be sufficient in some cases, such as where the owner's spouse or partner has substantial income.

But, in many cases, it would be impractical to live off a maximum of £11,500 per year. In the next section, we will therefore consider the position for a taxpayer who already has sufficient other income to make them a higher rate taxpayer.

10.5   HIGHER RATE TAXPAYERS WITH RENTAL PROFITS

This time, we will assume:

i)   All profits are retained within the company
ii)   The individual has other taxable income totalling £50,000 (the higher rate tax threshold)
iii)   No interest or finance costs are incurred

Annual Rental Profits	Tax Paid Personally	Tax Paid By Company	Tax Saving
£10,000	£4,000	£1,900	£2,100
£20,000	£8,000	£3,800	£4,200
£30,000	£12,000	£5,700	£6,300
£40,000	£16,000	£7,600	£8,400
£50,000	£20,000	£9,500	£10,500
£60,000	£26,000	£11,400	£14,600
£75,000	£35,000	£14,250	£20,750
£100,000	£45,000	£19,000	£26,000
£125,000	£56,250	£23,750	£32,500
£150,000	£67,500	£28,500	£39,000
£200,000	£90,000	£38,000	£52,000

'Tax Paid Personally' represents the additional tax arising due to the individual's rental profits. It does not include the tax on their other income.

The above figures are also based on the assumption the individual's other income does not include dividends, interest or other savings income. Modest amounts of these income sources would only make a slight difference to the forecast savings shown above however.

A dividend wholly covered by the dividend allowance (see Section 9.3) could be paid without affecting the savings outlined above.

Conclusions
A company produces considerable tax savings for a higher rate taxpayer landlord prepared to retain their profits within the company.

For an investor whose existing taxable income is already at least £50,000 (which they could potentially augment with a tax-free dividend of up to £2,000), this is not entirely unreasonable, although the day must surely come when they will wish to extract some profits. This is something we will be exploring further in the next chapter. In the next section, however, we will look at the position for those who cannot wait so long.

10.6   RENTAL PROFITS EXTRACTED FROM THE COMPANY

In Section 10.5, we looked at the position where rental profits are retained within the company. In this section we will take the opposite approach and assume the company owner extracts all the company's after tax profits.

We already know using a company is of no benefit to a basic rate taxpayer landlord with no interest or finance costs, so we will also assume the landlord has sufficient other income to make them a higher rate taxpayer.

The table below is therefore based on the following assumptions:

i)   All the company's after tax profits are paid out to the owner in the optimum manner, as described in Section 9.6 (and assuming the employment allowance is not available)

ii)   The individual has other taxable income totalling £50,000 (the higher rate tax threshold)

iii)   That other income does not include any interest or dividends (although, as noted before, modest amounts of these income sources will only make a slight difference to the outcome)

iv)   No interest or finance costs are incurred

Annual Rental Profits	Tax Paid Personally	Tax Paid Via Company	Tax Saving/(Cost)
£10,000	£4,000	£3,481	£519
£20,000	£8,000	£7,947	£53
£30,000	£12,000	£12,480	(£480)
£40,000	£16,000	£17,012	(£1,012)
£50,000	£20,000	£21,545	(£1,545)
£60,000	£26,000	£26,273	(£273)
£75,000	£35,000	£35,502	(£502)
£100,000	£45,000	£49,207	(£4,207)
£125,000	£56,250	£60,742	(£4,492)
£150,000	£67,500	£73,207	(£5,707)
£200,000	£90,000	£98,137	(£8,137)

'Tax Paid via Company' summarises the total tax burden using the company route, including CT payable by the company, employer's NI, and the individual's Income Tax on the salary and dividends received.

Conclusions

As we can see, using a property investment company is of little or no value where the investor extracts all the profits from the company each year and there are no interest or finance costs.

Wealth Warning

If dividends are paid without there being supporting accounts available to show the company had sufficient distributable profits (**after tax**) at that time, they are illegal under company law. 'Illegal' dividends may then be treated as salary, resulting in Income Tax and NI at a combined total rate of at least 42% for a higher rate taxpayer, plus a further 13.8% in NI for the company.

In reality, therefore, it is usually best not to extract all the company's after-tax profits as dividends every year.

It is also important to ensure the company quite clearly has sufficient distributable profits before any dividend is paid and has the necessary supporting accounts to demonstrate this fact. Supporting accounts would generally consist of either the previous year's statutory accounts or up to date management accounts (e.g. to the end of the previous calendar month). Documentation minuting the payment of a dividend is also advisable.

10.7   HALFWAY HOUSE

In Section 10.5 we saw the potential benefits available to higher rate taxpayers using a property investment company where all the profits are retained within the company. In Section 10.6, however, we saw there is little or no benefit in using a property investment company if all the profits are extracted each year.

Between these two extremes, there are many other potential scenarios. The table below illustrates just one of those scenarios: where precisely half the company's profits after tax are extracted each year. All other assumptions remain the same as in Section 10.6 and we assume that profits are extracted in the optimum manner (see Section 9.6).

Annual Rental Profits	Tax Paid Personally	Tax Paid Via Company	Tax Saving
£10,000	£4,000	£2,376	£1,624
£20,000	£8,000	£5,215	£2,785
£30,000	£12,000	£8,259	£3,741
£40,000	£16,000	£11,476	£4,524
£50,000	£20,000	£14,692	£5,308
£60,000	£26,000	£17,908	£8,092
£75,000	£35,000	£22,733	£12,267
£100,000	£45,000	£30,773	£14,227
£125,000	£56,250	£39,106	£17,144
£150,000	£67,500	£49,171	£18,329
£200,000	£90,000	£67,936	£22,064

Conclusions

As we can see, retaining half the after tax profits in the company has returned our investor to a position where using the property investment company is quite beneficial, although the savings here are considerably reduced compared with those in Section 10.5.

In fact, small savings persist at all profit levels with up to 86.5% of after tax profits extracted from the company. However, it remains important to understand, the more profits are extracted, the smaller the savings become. Here, for example, is the position where 75% of after tax profits are extracted:

Annual Rental Profits	Tax Paid Personally	Tax Paid Via Company	Tax Saving
£10,000	£4,000	£2,898	£1,102
£20,000	£8,000	£6,495	£1,505
£30,000	£12,000	£10,369	£1,631
£40,000	£16,000	£14,244	£1,756
£50,000	£20,000	£18,118	£1,882
£60,000	£26,000	£21,993	£4,007
£75,000	£35,000	£27,804	£7,196
£100,000	£45,000	£39,891	£5,109
£125,000	£56,250	£52,176	£4,074
£150,000	£67,500	£61,862	£5,638
£200,000	£90,000	£82,508	£7,492

Arguably, in this scenario, the costs and additional admin involved in running a company outweigh the small savings at annual profit levels under £60,000.

10.8 THE IMPACT OF INTEREST AND FINANCE COSTS

Individual property investors now only get basic rate tax relief for interest and finance costs relating to residential lettings.

These horrendous restrictions are examined in a little more detail in Section 12.12. For a more thorough examination of their impact, see the Taxcafe.co.uk guides 'How to Save Property Tax' and 'The Big Landlord Tax Increase'.

The restrictions do not apply to borrowings relating to non-residential property or furnished holiday lets, so the conclusions we have already drawn in Sections 10.3 to 10.7 will remain the same for any investor renting out those types of property.

But, for residential lettings, the different treatment of interest and finance costs will make an enormous difference and that is what we will now examine.

To do this, we are going to have to make an assumption about the level of interest being paid by the investor.

We will start with a highly geared investor whose interest and finance costs amount to 75% of their profit before interest. Hence, each £10,000 of rental profit in the table below is made up as follows:

Profit before interest	£40,000		
Less: Interest and finance costs	£30,000		
Profit after interest	£10,000		

The personal investor will pay tax on their profit before interest of £40,000 and only receive basic rate tax relief on their interest costs of £30,000. For a higher rate taxpayer, this produces an Income Tax liability of £10,000 on a profit of the same amount!

The table below is also based on the following further assumptions:

i)   All the company's after tax profits are paid out to the owner in the most tax efficient manner (see Section 9.6)
ii)   The employment allowance is not available
iii) The individual has no other taxable income

Annual Rental Profits	Tax Paid Personally	Tax Paid Via Company	Tax Saving/(Cost)
£10,000	£0	£175	(£175)
£20,000	£7,500	£2,331	£5,169
£30,000	£21,500	£4,839	£16,661
£40,000	£33,000	£7,346	£25,654
£50,000	£45,000	£9,854	£35,146
£60,000	£57,000	£12,443	£44,557
£75,000	£75,000	£19,242	£55,758
£100,000	£105,000	£30,573	£74,427
£125,000	£135,000	£42,388	£92,612
£150,000	£165,000	£58,086	£106,914
£200,000	£225,000	£81,916	£143,084

It is worth noting that in this scenario, once the individual investor's profits after interest exceed £75,000, their Income Tax liability is *over 100%!*

The savings in the table above are pretty spectacular but we must remember this is based on a highly geared investor. Keeping all our other assumptions the same, let's now look at the position where the level of interest is lower. Firstly, where interest costs amount to 50% of profits before interest:

Annual Rental Profits	Tax Paid Personally	Tax Paid Via Company	Tax Saving/(Cost)
£10,000	£0	£175	(£175)
£20,000	£1,500	£2,331	(£831)
£30,000	£5,500	£4,839	£661
£40,000	£11,500	£7,346	£4,154
£50,000	£17,500	£9,854	£7,646
£60,000	£27,500	£12,443	£15,057
£75,000	£37,500	£19,242	£18,258
£100,000	£55,000	£30,573	£24,427
£125,000	£72,500	£42,388	£30,112
£150,000	£90,000	£58,086	£31,914
£200,000	£125,000	£81,916	£43,084

Next, where interest costs amount to just 25% of profits before interest:

Annual Rental Profits	Tax Paid Personally	Tax Paid Via Company	Tax Saving/(Cost)
£10,000	£0	£175	(£175)
£20,000	£1,500	£2,331	(£831)
£30,000	£3,500	£4,839	(£1,339)
£40,000	£6,167	£7,346	(£1,180)
£50,000	£10,833	£9,854	£979
£60,000	£15,500	£12,443	£3,057
£75,000	£22,500	£19,242	£3,258
£100,000	£39,167	£30,573	£8,594
£125,000	£51,667	£42,388	£9,279
£150,000	£65,000	£58,086	£6,914
£200,000	£91,667	£81,916	£9,750

Conclusions

The tables in this section clearly demonstrate the fact that major savings are available to higher rate taxpayers by using a property investment company to hold residential rental property where there are borrowings against the properties.

Furthermore, as we know from earlier sections, these savings will be greatly enhanced if some or all of the after tax profits are retained within the company.

The tables also show, once again, that a property investment company is of no use to basic rate taxpayers: **BUT** we must remember anyone with *profits before interest* in excess of the higher rate tax threshold is now a higher rate taxpayer!

For example, in our first table in this section, where interest costs amounted to 75% of profit before interest, even a landlord with just £20,000 of profit after interest achieved significant savings by using a company.

This is because the restrictions on interest relief for individual landlords result in them having £80,000 of taxable profit: well in excess of the higher rate tax threshold; and they will only receive basic rate tax relief for their interest.

10.9   HIGHER INTEREST RATES IN COMPANIES

The previous section demonstrated the clear advantage of using a property investment company for residential rental property with borrowings against it.

Unfortunately, however, the cost of borrowing within a company is usually higher. Although lenders that offer mortgages to companies tend to use the same rates, there are fewer lenders willing to lend to a company in the first place. As a result, the rates available across the market as a whole are higher.

Depending on market conditions, loan-to-value ('LTV'), and rental yields, the interest rates for a company are typically greater than those available to individual buy-to-let investors by a factor of anything up to a half.

For the sake of illustration, we will therefore assume the company's interest and finance costs are greater than the individual's costs by a factor of one quarter.

In the table below, we have also assumed the individual's interest costs amount to 50% of their profit before interest.

This table has to be presented slightly differently to the tables in previous sections as the company's profit before tax is now different to the individual's. Hence, the best thing to compare is the ultimate net income after both tax and interest.

As before, we will also continue to assume:

i)   All the company's after tax profits are paid out to the owner in the most tax efficient manner, as described in Section 9.6
ii)   The employment allowance is not available
iii)   The individual has no other taxable income

Annual Rental Profits	Net Income Personally	Net Income Via Company	Tax & Interest Saving/(Cost)
£10,000	£10,000	£7,500	(£2,500)
£20,000	£18,500	£13,875	(£4,625)
£30,000	£24,500	£19,542	(£4,958)
£40,000	£28,500	£25,161	(£3,339)
£50,000	£32,500	£30,780	(£1,720)
£60,000	£32,500	£36,400	£3,900
£75,000	£37,500	£44,829	£7,329
£100,000	£45,000	£55,758	£10,758
£125,000	£52,500	£66,010	£13,510
£150,000	£60,000	£76,262	£16,262
£200,000	£75,000	£91,914	£16,914

You may notice, in this scenario, the individual's net income is the same with an annual rental profit of £50,000 or £60,000. This is not an error: I am sorry to say this is correct! (It is due to the fact the individual's taxable income before deducting interest is pushed over £100,000, causing the loss of their personal allowance, as discussed in Section 10.2.)

Conclusions
The higher interest cost in the company has significantly reduced the overall savings available. However, substantial savings are still evident at higher levels of profit. It must also be remembered that the savings are greatly enhanced when some or all of the profits are retained in the company. The savings will, of course, also be improved if the company's interest and finance costs are not as high as we have predicted.

10.10 THE 'OPTIMUM SCENARIO'

This scenario is what one might call the 'best of both worlds', where we use the lessons from the previous sections in this chapter to produce an optimum position. That optimum position is basically as follows:

Firstly, the investor builds a 'private' portfolio, held in their own name, as an individual, which is large enough to use up their basic rate band. At current rates, this means the following amounts will total £50,000:

a)   Profits from residential lettings *before* interest
b)   Profits from non-residential and furnished holiday lettings *after* interest
c)   Income from other sources

If (c) alone exceeds £50,000 then the individual is already a higher rate taxpayer and we will assume there is no 'private' portfolio.

The benefit of any residential lettings within the 'private' portfolio will, of course, be maximised if these properties are debt free and this is an ideal position for the investor to aim for.

The tables below compare the position arising on any further property investments beyond the 'private' portfolio included under (a) and (b) above. For ease of reference, we will refer to these further investments as the 'second portfolio'. The tables are based on the following assumptions:

i)   The investor has £50,000 of taxable income from other sources (including income from their 'private' portfolio, as described under (a) and (b) above)

ii)   That other income does not include any interest or dividends (although, as noted before, modest amounts of these income sources will only make a slight difference to the outcome)

iii)   The properties in the 'second portfolio' are all residential lettings

iv)   The rental profits arising on the 'second portfolio' when held as an individual are shown after interest costs equal to 50% of the profits before interest

v)   The interest costs incurred by the company are greater than those incurred by an individual by a factor of one quarter

vi)   When profits are extracted from the company, this is done optimally, as described in Section 9.6, and on the basis that no employment allowance is available

The first table shows the position where all after tax profits are extracted:

Annual Rental Profits	Net Income Personally	Net Income Via Company	Tax & Interest Saving
£10,000	£4,000	£5,019	£1,019
£20,000	£8,000	£9,319	£1,319
£30,000	£10,000	£13,420	£3,420
£40,000	£11,000	£17,520	£6,520
£50,000	£15,000	£21,621	£6,621
£60,000	£18,000	£25,722	£7,722
£75,000	£22,500	£31,873	£9,373
£100,000	£30,000	£39,640	£9,640
£125,000	£37,500	£47,376	£9,876
£150,000	£45,000	£57,627	£12,627
£200,000	£60,000	£76,833	£16,833

Next, we look at the position where half the after tax profit is extracted from the company:

140

Annual Rental Profits	Net Income Personally	Net Income Via Company	Tax & Interest Saving
£10,000	£4,000	£5,834	£1,834
£20,000	£8,000	£11,204	£3,204
£30,000	£10,000	£16,575	£6,575
£40,000	£11,000	£21,741	£10,741
£50,000	£15,000	£26,828	£11,828
£60,000	£18,000	£31,916	£13,916
£75,000	£22,500	£39,548	£17,048
£100,000	£30,000	£52,267	£22,267
£125,000	£37,500	£64,987	£27,487
£150,000	£45,000	£77,706	£32,706
£200,000	£60,000	£100,829	£40,829

'Net Income Via Company' now includes after tax profits retained within the company. Finally, let's look at the position where all the after tax profits are retained within the company:

Annual Rental Profits	Net Income Personally	Net Income Via Company	Tax & Interest Saving
£10,000	£4,000	£6,075	£2,075
£20,000	£8,000	£12,150	£4,150
£30,000	£10,000	£18,225	£8,225
£40,000	£11,000	£24,300	£13,300
£50,000	£15,000	£30,375	£15,375
£60,000	£18,000	£36,450	£18,450
£75,000	£22,500	£45,563	£23,063
£100,000	£30,000	£60,750	£30,750
£125,000	£37,500	£75,938	£38,438
£150,000	£45,000	£91,125	£46,125
£200,000	£60,000	£121,500	£61,500

If the individual's other income is made up of rental income or pensions and they have no interest or finance costs on any residential lettings within their 'private' portfolio, they will have net income after tax of £42,500, so the idea of leaving all the profits in the company is not unreasonable.

Small dividends covered by the dividend allowance will make no difference to the outcome in the last table, so there is the opportunity to bring net income up to £44,500 and still retain these savings.

If that's not enough for you, a salary of £8,788 would only reduce the savings shown above by £1,845 and would bring your total net after tax income up to £49,773.

Conclusions
Even after factoring in the probability that higher interest rates will apply to borrowings within a company, we see that a property investment company can provide major savings for a higher rate taxpayer.

Remember, when we refer to higher rate taxpayers, this now includes any residential landlords whose profit *before interest* pushes them over the higher rate tax threshold.

The tables also show that the available savings are greatly enhanced when some or all of the after tax profits are retained within the company.

10.11   TRADING PROFITS

Having covered rental profits, we will now look at the same comparison where the income is treated as trading income. This makes no difference to the rates of CT applying. The individual's tax position is significantly altered, however, due to the fact that Class 2 and 4 NI is payable where this income is received personally (unless the individual is over state pension age: see Section 10.15).

For our first trading scenario, we will consider the position where the individual has no other income and all the company's after tax profits are paid out in the most tax efficient manner, as described in Section 9.6 (but see the 'Wealth Warning' in Section 10.6). As usual, we will also assume the company's employment allowance is not available.

Annual Trading Profits	Tax Paid Personally	Tax Paid Via Company	Tax Saving/(Cost)
£10,000	£204	£175	£29
£20,000	£2,604	£2,331	£272
£30,000	£5,504	£4,839	£665
£40,000	£8,404	£7,346	£1,057
£50,000	£11,304	£9,854	£1,450
£60,000	£15,504	£12,443	£3,061
£75,000	£21,804	£19,242	£2,562
£100,000	£32,304	£30,573	£1,731
£125,000	£47,804	£42,388	£5,416
£150,000	£58,304	£58,086	£218
£200,000	£81,804	£81,916	(£113)

Conclusions

Many people will be surprised by the results shown in the above table, but it is clear, with a few exceptions, there is generally little or no tax benefit in putting a trading business into a company if all the profits are to be extracted each year (bearing in mind there are extra costs involved in running a company that have not been factored into the figures).

This is mostly due to the overall marginal rate of tax applying to profits that are first taxed in the company and then taxed again when paid out to a higher rate taxpayer as dividends.

That marginal rate is currently 45.3%, as shown below:

Corporation Tax	19.0%
Income Tax on after tax profit paid as dividend (81% x 32.5%)	26.3%
Overall marginal rate	45.3%

This compares with the overall marginal tax rate (Income Tax and NI) of 42% applying to a self-employed higher rate taxpayer. In other words, the company is ***costing extra tax!***

As we can see from the table above, there are some quirks in the tax system, which mean reasonable savings can arise at certain profit levels but, generally speaking, the overall picture suggests it is not worth using a company for a property trade where all the profits are being extracted each year.

10.12   RETAINING TRADING PROFITS IN THE COMPANY

In the previous section, we saw that a property trading company was of little or no benefit where all the profits were being extracted each year.

A taxpayer with no other income will almost certainly need to extract some profits but, in this section, we will assume the amount extracted is not enough to make the company owner a higher rate taxpayer. The table below is therefore based on the following assumptions:

i)   The taxpayer has no other income
ii)   Company profits are extracted by first taking a salary of £9,500, then taking any remaining profits as a dividend up to a maximum of £40,500 (thus bringing the taxpayer's income up to the higher rate tax threshold of £50,000)
iii)   The employment allowance is not available

For trading profits of £50,000 or less, the outcome is the same as in the previous section. Hence, here, we will just look at higher profit levels.

Annual Trading Profits	Tax Paid Personally	Tax Paid Via Company	Tax Saving
£60,000	£15,504	£12,337	£3,167
£75,000	£21,804	£15,187	£6,617
£100,000	£32,304	£19,937	£12,367
£125,000	£47,804	£24,687	£23,117
£150,000	£58,304	£29,437	£28,867
£200,000	£81,804	£38,937	£42,867

Conclusions

A property trading company can produce considerable tax savings where the profits extracted are limited to an amount that prevents the company owner's income from exceeding the higher rate tax threshold.

This leaves the owner with net income after tax of £47,338 (once the company's trading profits reach at least £59,958).

10.13 HIGHER RATE TRADERS

Where a property investor already has sufficient income from other sources to make them a higher rate taxpayer, they could make considerable savings by using a property trading company: provided they do not extract all the profits each year.

Some savings are possible where only part of the profits are extracted, but the best savings arise where all the after tax profits are retained in the company: which is what we will look at in this section. Hence, the tables below are based on the following assumptions:

i)   The trader has £50,000 of taxable income from other sources (as detailed further for each table below)
ii)   All the company's after tax profits are retained

The nature of the trader's other income will influence the outcome considerably due to the different ways in which this other income is treated for NI purposes. As usual, we will assume the other income does not include interest or dividends, although modest amounts of these types of income will only make a slight difference to the results shown below.

The first table deals with the situation where the trader's other income is made up of rental profits or pensions. (Remember, for residential lettings, it is the rental profit **before interest** that forms the individual's taxable income.)

Annual Trading Profits	Tax Paid Personally	Tax Paid Via Company	Tax Saving
£10,000	£4,204	£1,900	£2,304
£20,000	£9,104	£3,800	£5,304
£30,000	£14,004	£5,700	£8,304
£40,000	£18,904	£7,600	£11,304
£50,000	£23,804	£9,500	£14,304
£60,000	£30,004	£11,400	£18,604
£75,000	£39,304	£14,250	£25,054
£100,000	£49,804	£19,000	£30,804
£125,000	£61,554	£23,750	£37,804
£150,000	£73,304	£28,500	£44,804
£200,000	£96,804	£38,000	£58,804

For the next table, we will assume the trader's other income is employment income:

Annual Trading Profits	Tax Paid Personally	Tax Paid Via Company	Tax Saving
£10,000	£4,204	£1,900	£2,304
£20,000	£8,559	£3,800	£4,759
£30,000	£12,759	£5,700	£7,059
£40,000	£16,959	£7,600	£9,359
£50,000	£21,159	£9,500	£11,659
£60,000	£27,359	£11,400	£15,959
£75,000	£36,659	£14,250	£22,409
£100,000	£47,159	£19,000	£28,159
£125,000	£58,909	£23,750	£35,159
£150,000	£70,659	£28,500	£42,159
£200,000	£94,159	£38,000	£56,159

The savings are slightly reduced here because the self-employed trader would be able to claim a partial repayment of their Class 4 NI. This repayment must be claimed: it is not automatic.

If the trader's other income is other self-employed trading income, the results would be exactly the same as in the table above except that 'Tax Paid Personally' and the saving arising by using a company would both be £159 less at all profit levels, except where trading profit is £10,000, when they would be just £4 less.

This is because the self-employed trader would have already paid Class 2 NI of £159 and would automatically pay Class 4 at just 2% on their additional trading income (there would be no need to claim a repayment in this case).

Conclusions

A property trading company can produce considerable tax savings for a higher rate taxpayer prepared to retain all the after tax profits in the company. (The same level of savings will be maintained where small dividends covered by the dividend allowance are paid.)

10.14 PARTIAL EXTRACTION FOR HIGHER RATE TRADERS

The previous section demonstrated the benefits of a property company for higher rate taxpayers with a property trade who were prepared to retain their after tax profits in the company.

Now let's look at the position where the company owner extracts half the company's after tax profits. As before, we will assume this is done in the most tax efficient manner, as described in Section 9.6, and on the basis that the employment allowance is not available. Other assumptions remain the same as in the previous section.

Firstly, here is the position where the trader's other taxable income consists of £50,000 of taxable rental profits or pensions (see previous comments regarding taxable income from residential lettings):

Annual Trading Profits	Tax Paid Personally	Tax Paid Via Company	Tax Saving
£10,000	£4,204	£2,376	£1,828
£20,000	£9,104	£5,215	£3,888
£30,000	£14,004	£8,259	£5,744
£40,000	£18,904	£11,476	£7,428
£50,000	£23,804	£14,692	£9,112
£60,000	£30,004	£17,908	£12,095
£75,000	£39,304	£22,733	£16,571
£100,000	£49,804	£30,773	£19,030
£125,000	£61,554	£39,106	£22,448
£150,000	£73,304	£49,171	£24,132
£200,000	£96,804	£67,936	£28,868

And here is the position where the other income consists of £50,000 of employment income:

Annual Trading Profits	Tax Paid Personally	Tax Paid Via Company	Tax Saving
£10,000	£4,204	£2,376	£1,828
£20,000	£8,559	£5,215	£3,343
£30,000	£12,759	£8,259	£4,499
£40,000	£16,959	£11,476	£5,483
£50,000	£21,159	£14,692	£6,467
£60,000	£27,359	£17,908	£9,450
£75,000	£36,659	£22,733	£13,926
£100,000	£47,159	£30,773	£16,385
£125,000	£58,909	£39,106	£19,803
£150,000	£70,659	£49,171	£21,487
£200,000	£94,159	£67,936	£26,223

As in the previous section, this is subject to the comments regarding the need to claim a repayment of some of the Class 4 NI suffered as a self-employed individual.

See Section 9.2 regarding potential additional savings in this scenario where the employment allowance is available (the table above is prepared on the basis that it is not).

This table can again be applied equally where the other income is self-employed trading income, subject to the same small differences discussed in the previous section.

Conclusions
A property trading company still produces considerable tax savings for a higher rate taxpayer prepared to retain half the after tax profits in the company.

10.15 OLDER PROPERTY INVESTORS

Individuals over state pension age are exempt from all classes of NI on their income. This makes no difference to individuals running a property investment business, so the tables in Sections 10.3 to 10.10 continue to apply to such investors (subject to the points below regarding salaries).

However, the exemption from NI alters the position on trading income. In effect, investors over state pension age suffer the same effective tax rates on trading income as they do on rental income with no interest or finance costs on residential property.

Hence, the tables in Sections 10.3 to 10.7 show the savings available to property investors over state pension age running a property business classed as a trade for tax purposes: subject to the further points discussed below.

Higher Salaries

There is sometimes an additional advantage to taxpayers over state pension age using a company for any type of property business.

For these individuals, payment of a salary in excess of the primary NI threshold will not attract Class 1 employee's NI; although salaries in excess of the secondary threshold are still subject to employer's NI unless the employment allowance is available (see Section 9.2).

This means, under certain circumstances, paying higher salaries to taxpayers over state pension age will produce a better result than the usual optimum profit extraction strategies outlined in Section 9.6. As usual, the position is dependent on whether the employment allowance is available.

Without Employment Allowance

Where the employment allowance is not available, the optimum profit extraction strategy for an individual over state pension age is generally as follows:

- Firstly pay their maximum tax-free salary and any 'low tax salary' (Section 9.5)
- Secondly pay any dividend covered by the dividend allowance
- Thirdly pay any further salary required to bring their total salary up to the level of the secondary NI threshold (currently £8,788)
- Pay any further amounts required by way of dividend

Salaries paid under the first step will yield an overall saving and could produce additional savings of up to £478 compared with the results for younger investors shown throughout this chapter.

With Employment Allowance

Where the employment allowance **is** available, the optimum profit extraction strategy for an individual over state pension age is generally as follows:

- Firstly pay their maximum tax-free salary and any 'low tax salary' (Section 9.5)
- Secondly pay any dividend covered by the dividend allowance
- Thirdly pay any further salary covered by the employment allowance
- Pay any further amounts required by way of dividend

148

Once again, salaries under the first step will yield an overall saving. However, in this case, they will only produce maximum additional savings of up to £389 compared with younger investors.

Further salaries under the third step will not produce overall savings but could provide substantial savings compared with younger investors.

As we saw in Section 9.2, a salary of up to £37,772 may sometimes be covered by the employment allowance. Such a salary paid to an individual over state pension age represents a 'low cost option' (see Section 9.7) and could yield a further saving of up to £1,387 compared with a younger investor.

In other words, an investor over state pension age following the optimum profit extraction strategy set out above could be up to £1,776 better off in total compared with a younger investor extracting the same net sum after tax using their own optimum profit extraction strategy.

A couple running a property company together could take salaries of up to £23,280 each covered by the employment allowance (see Section 9.2). If the couple are both over state pension age, this would provide the opportunity to make total savings of £1,961 compared with a younger couple extracting the same net sum after tax.

See Section 9.2 for more details regarding the availability of the employment allowance. Note also that higher salaries will only generate additional savings where those salaries can be claimed as an expense for CT purposes: this issue is also examined in Section 9.2.

10.16 INVESTORS WITH CHILDREN

Investors with young children may be able to realise additional benefits by investing in property via a company. By keeping profits in the company and thus ensuring their personal income is kept at a lower level, they may be able to avoid the High Income Child Benefit Charge. This will be a major benefit for many investors where the highest earner in the household faces additional tax charges on personal taxable income between £50,000 and £60,000.

As each investor's position is different, it is not possible to take these extra savings into account in all the calculations in the rest of this guide, but the additional savings available in 2020/21 alone could be as much as those shown in the table below.

No. of Qualifying Children	Maximum Additional Saving
1	£1,095
2	£1,820
3	£2,545
4	£3,271
Each Extra	£725

'No. of Qualifying Children' represents the number of children living in the investor's household for whom Child Benefit is being claimed.

The 'Maximum Additional Saving' is the amount of additional tax saved (on top of any savings calculated elsewhere in this guide) where:

i) Using a property company enables the personal taxable income of the highest earner in the household for the year to be kept to £50,000 or less, and

ii) Without the company, the highest earner in the household for the year would have had taxable income of £60,000 or more.

Smaller savings remain available in other cases where using the company enables less of the taxable income of the highest earner in the household to fall within the £50,000 to £60,000 bracket. For example, reducing taxable income from £60,000 or more to £52,000 would produce additional savings equal to 80% of the figures in the table above; reducing taxable income from £54,000 to £50,000 or less would produce additional savings equal to 40% of the figures in the table.

In considering these potential savings, it should be borne in mind that the High Income Child Benefit Charge is based on the income of the highest earner in the household. Reducing one person's income may result in another adult in the household becoming the highest earner instead and this would limit the savings available: unless their income can also be reduced.

The potential additional savings available by avoiding or reducing the High Income Child Benefit Charge are not taken into account throughout the rest of this guide.

10.17 CAPITAL GAINS

For our final scenario in this chapter, we will take a quick look at the difference in tax on a typical capital gain on a property held by an individual investor or by a property investment company. In this scenario, we will assume the following:

i)   The property is sold producing a total gain before exemptions and reliefs equal to the amount shown in the first column below
ii)   The individual investor is a higher rate taxpayer
iii) The gain does not qualify for business asset disposal relief
iv)   No indexation relief is available (see Section 6.4)
v)   The individual has not made any other capital gains during the same tax year
vi)   The annual CGT exemption remains at £12,300
vii) No other reliefs or exemptions are available to either the individual or the company
viii) Company profits are retained

First, we will look at the position for a residential property:

Capital Gain Before Reliefs	Tax Paid Personally	Tax Paid By Company	Tax Saving/(Cost)
£25,000	£3,556	£4,750	(£1,194)
£50,000	£10,556	£9,500	£1,056
£100,000	£24,556	£19,000	£5,556
£200,000	£52,556	£38,000	£14,556
£300,000	£80,556	£57,000	£23,556
£500,000	£136,556	£95,000	£41,556

The company benefits as it pays CT on all capital gains at just 19% but the individual has the advantage of their annual CGT exemption.

As a result, the individual is better off for smaller capital gains but, as the gains get larger, the lower tax rate paid by the company begins to outweigh the saving produced by the individual's annual exemption.

In this scenario, based on the assumptions set out above, the company produces savings once the gain exceeds £38,266.

For non-residential property, the differential in tax rates is just 1% (20% for a higher rate taxpayer individual; 19% for a company), so it takes a much larger gain before the company becomes beneficial, as illustrated by the following table:

Capital Gain Before Reliefs	Tax Paid Personally	Tax Paid By Company	Tax Saving/(Cost)
£25,000	£2,540	£4,750	(£2,210)
£50,000	£7,540	£9,500	(£1,960)
£100,000	£17,540	£19,000	(£1,460)
£200,000	£37,540	£38,000	(£460)
£300,000	£57,540	£57,000	£540
£500,000	£97,540	£95,000	£2,540

This time, the company does not produce savings until the gain exceeds £246,000.

Basic rate taxpayer individuals pay CGT at lower rates (see Section 7.2). Individual investors can also save CGT through joint ownership (so that two annual CGT exemptions are available).

These factors can mean it takes a greater capital gain before the company is beneficial. Keeping all other assumptions the same, the amount of capital gain required before the company becomes beneficial is as follows:

- Individual owner with income not exceeding the personal allowance: residential property £79,933; non-residential £621,000
- Joint owners, both higher rate taxpayers: residential property £76,533; non-residential £492,000
- Joint owners, both with income not exceeding the personal allowance: residential property £159,866; non-residential £1.242m

As we can see, for large enough capital gains, the company will eventually prove beneficial in all cases: although under some scenarios it does require pretty large gains before this happens.

It is important to remember, however, that no account has been taken here of the additional tax costs involved in extracting the sale proceeds from the company.

We will look at this factor in the next chapter, which includes a far more detailed analysis of the impact of the difference between the company and personal tax regimes for capital gains.

10.18 SUMMARY

I will attempt here to briefly summarise our findings in this chapter. Before I do so, I would like to make a few key points:

i)   As explained in Section 10.1, these findings are based on current tax rates. In practice, what is important is to consider the long-term position. Current rates have only been used as an approximation for the long-term position in this chapter in the absence of any better information about the long-term tax regime for both companies and individuals. In Chapter 17, we will look at some potential pointers towards that long-term tax regime.

ii)   These findings are based on tax considerations only and are subject to the important non-tax considerations examined in Chapter 1

iii)   These findings are also based simply on a 'snapshot' of the position for a single year. In the next chapter we will look at the more detailed factors that should be considered in the long term

iv)   These findings do not take account of a property investment company's ability to set interest and finance costs off against other types of income or capital gains. We will look at the importance of interest relief in more detail in Chapter 12

v)   These findings are subject to any special circumstances that may apply

Rental Income

Property investment companies are of no benefit to basic rate taxpayers. (It must be borne in mind, however, that it is rental profit **before interest** from residential property that is counted as an individual landlord's taxable income, and this makes many more landlords higher rate taxpayers.)

Major savings are available to higher rate taxpayers prepared to retain a significant proportion of their company's rental profits within the company. The more profit retained, the greater the savings.

The savings are reduced where profits are extracted and, indeed, where there are no interest costs relating to residential lettings, a property investment company will be of no benefit when all profits are extracted.

If there are interest costs relating to residential lettings, higher rate taxpayers will enjoy an even greater benefit using a company. Some benefit is likely to remain even with all profits extracted. The benefit is so great it may compensate for higher interest costs paid by the company.

Property Trades

A property trading company is generally of little or no benefit where all the profits are being extracted each year. There are a few exceptions at certain profit levels due to some particular quirks in the UK tax system.

Even when profits are retained, the benefit to basic rate taxpayers remains questionable as the amount of savings involved may not be significant enough to compensate for the higher costs of running a company.

However, major benefits remain for higher rate taxpayers prepared to retain a significant proportion of profits within the company.

Capital Gains

Smaller capital gains may be subject to less tax where property is held by individuals, but larger gains may suffer less tax within a company. The point at which the company becomes beneficial varies as it depends on a number of factors, but if the gain is large enough, the company is always beneficial in the end. This, however, is before considering the additional costs of extracting sale proceeds from the company.

Chapter 11

Making the Big Decision

11.1 THE 'BIG PICTURE'

Before you can decide whether a company is for you or not, you will need to look at what I call the 'Big Picture'.

Many investors concentrate almost exclusively on the taxation treatment of their income. Others are mainly concerned with capital gains.

Neither approach is correct. The only way to carry out effective tax planning is to take every applicable tax into account. In the case of property companies, we are not concerned only with income, nor solely with capital gains, but with both. On top of that, we must also consider the costs of extracting profits and sale proceeds from the company.

VAT, SDLT, and any other tax costs should also be considered and, if one is taking the really long view, it makes sense to give some thought to IHT as well.

Fully effective tax planning is only possible once all potential tax costs have been taken into account, however and whenever they are likely to arise. But, even this is still not truly the 'Big Picture'.

Bayley's Law
'The truly wise investor does not seek merely to minimise the amount of tax paid, but rather to maximise the amount of **wealth** remaining after all taxes have been accounted for.'

Taking the Long Term View
The more favourable regime for tax relief on interest and finance costs may sometimes provide the greatest benefit when using a property company. Undoubtedly, this is an important factor and we will be looking at this issue in detail in Chapter 12.

The most effective tax planning, however, is always based on a long-term view. This is seldom truer than when looking at the issue of whether to use a property company. My aim in this chapter is therefore to show you the likely outcome provided by using a property company in the long-term.

In the long-term, history shows that UK property tends to grow in value at an average annual rate of around 7.5%. Due to the compound effect of this growth, this roughly equates to properties doubling in value every ten years.

In order to take a long-term view, therefore, we will use this growth rate for the models we will explore in this chapter.

Readers will, of course, be acutely aware that actual growth rates fluctuate significantly, and we do not always see these sorts of growth rates in the short term. Furthermore, current market conditions are far from normal due to the impact of the coronavirus crisis.

Nevertheless, our purpose in this chapter is to look at the 'Big Picture' and to plan for the long-term. This necessitates taking a hypothetical approach based on long-term trends. I make no apologies for this, because this is the right approach when considering effective long-term planning.

In reality, the short-term position will, of course, often be very different, especially at present and probably for a while to come. It is therefore imperative that readers form their own opinion on current and likely future market conditions. The models used in this chapter are entirely hypothetical and are in no way intended to be a true indication of the likely performance of the property market over the next few years.

Interest and Finance Costs
Another difficulty in preparing long-term hypothetical forecasts is in deciding what interest rates to apply to borrowings.

Interest rates fluctuate greatly over time. Furthermore, many landlords frequently refinance their portfolios in order to benefit from lower fixed rates, typically for somewhere between two and five years, and seldom actually pay the higher standard variable rates that usually apply thereafter. This reduces the interest cost but adds other finance costs in the form of loan arrangement fees, broker's fees, etc.

All this means that, in practice, an accurate long-term average rate for a landlord's typical interest and finance costs is almost impossible to establish.

But remember, what we are trying to do here is create a long-term forecast of the benefits of using a property company. As with the tax regime, it is the differential between the finance costs for an individual, and for a company, that matters, rather than establishing an accurate rate.

Hence, for the sake of illustration, rather than try to reflect all the complexities of refinancing, fixed rates, standard variable rates, and fluctuations in the base rate, I will simply use the following estimated interest rates to reflect the average, annual interest and finance costs incurred by property investors:

- Individuals: 4%
- Companies: 5%

For the reasons explained in Section 10.9, it is appropriate to reflect the likelihood that finance costs will be higher in a company, and applying a factor of one quarter for the relevant increase seems reasonable.

In reality, your own interest and finance costs will be different. They will be unique to you and they will vary from year to year, and from property to property. You will have to bear that in mind as you study the results of my forecasts. Nonetheless, I am sure you will appreciate the simplification I have applied in those forecasts, as the examples in this chapter will get complex enough!

11.2 TYPES OF PROPERTY BUSINESS REVISITED

Following on from our conclusions in Section 10.18, it is already reasonable to surmise that the current tax regime produces the potential to make significant tax savings by operating most property development, property trading or property management businesses through a company where:

- The company owner is a higher rate taxpayer (or would be if they had not used a company), and
- A significant proportion of after tax profits are retained in the company

This arises mainly because of the preferential CT rate when compared with the combined Income Tax and NI cost of trading on a personal basis.

Add to this the fact that a trading company's shares will usually qualify for business asset disposal relief (see Section 7.3) and the position appears fairly clear-cut in the case of any property trade producing a substantial level of annual profits, of which a significant proportion can be retained in the company. The only dangers lie in potential future changes to the tax regime or, perhaps, with the investor's inability to comply with the more stringent administrative necessities involved in operating a company.

We will return to take a more detailed look at the advantages of property trading companies in Section 11.16.

As far as property investment companies are concerned, our findings in Chapter 10 tell us these are not generally beneficial for basic rate taxpayers. (But readers should bear in mind that many more residential landlords have become higher rate taxpayers due to the restrictions in interest relief that we will be looking at in Section 12.12.)

Property investment companies do appear to be beneficial for higher rate taxpayers under certain circumstances: namely when a significant proportion of profits are retained in the company, or when there are interest costs relating to residential lettings.

But, in most cases, we also need to factor in the costs involved in extracting both rental profits and property sale proceeds. Even if the company owner does not extract all their profits and gains every year, they will usually want to extract them eventually. Hence, this is where we are going to concentrate for most of this chapter.

11.3 THE RENTAL INCOME POSITION

In the preceding chapters, we have looked at the mechanics of how UK resident companies are taxed. We will now begin to look at how this all affects property investment businesses and whether a company becomes beneficial or not.

The best way to illustrate this is by way of an example. We will start with a simple scenario that does not involve any interest or finance costs. As usual, we will use current tax rates as our best approximation of the long-term position. However, in practice, it is important to remember to take the long-term view.

Example 'A', Part 1
Humphrey has decided to begin investing in property with the intention of building up a portfolio over the next few years. He is already a higher rate taxpayer before taking any rental income into consideration.

Although his friend Charlie said, "You'd be daft not to use a company, old boy," Humphrey goes ahead and buys three flats in his own name for £130,000 each and begins to rent them out.

During the following year, Humphrey receives rental income of £10,000 from each flat, but has deductible expenditure totalling £6,000, leaving him with a profit of £24,000. Humphrey's accountant, Edmund, advises him he has an Income Tax liability of £9,600 (£24,000 at 40%), leaving him with net income of £14,400.

Feeling frustrated by his inability to persuade Humphrey to invest through a limited company, Charlie decides to try it himself. He sets up a company, Murrayfield Ltd, and, through this, he too buys three flats for £130,000 each. He incurs the same level of expenses as Humphrey and Murrayfield Ltd therefore also has a profit of £24,000.

Murrayfield Ltd's profits are taxed at 19%, meaning the CT payable by the company is £4,560.

At first glance, Charlie appears to be over £5,000 better off than Humphrey, indicating that a company seems to be highly beneficial.

Now feeling rather pleased with himself, Charlie shows what he has done to Edmund (who happens to be his accountant too). Unfortunately for Charlie, Edmund has two pieces of bad news for him.

Firstly, as using a company has a few extra complications, Edmund's fees to Charlie will be rather more than he charged Humphrey. However, the difference is not a huge sum compared with the tax he has saved, and it is a tax-deductible expense in itself, so Charlie is not too concerned by this. (We will ignore Edmund's additional fees from here onwards, for the sake of illustration.)

Secondly though, Edmund points out that if Charlie wants any of the money Murrayfield Ltd has made, he will have to pay himself a salary or a dividend. Edmund advises the best course of action in this case is to first take a salary of £8,788, since this will attract CT relief; then pay out the remaining after tax profits as a dividend.

The salary reduces the company's taxable profit to £15,212, meaning the company's CT bill will now be £2,890. That leaves a profit after tax of £12,322 which can be paid out as a dividend.

Charlie suffers Income Tax of £3,515 on his salary (at 40%) and £3,355 on his dividend (at 32.5%, except the first £2,000, which is covered by the dividend allowance).

*This leaves Charlie with total net income of £14,240 (£8,788 – £3,515 + £12,322 – £3,355), or **£160 less** than Humphrey!*

For the sake of illustration, I have treated Charlie's salary and dividends as arising in the same year as his company's rental profits. In practice this may not always be the case: especially in view of the 'Wealth Warning' in Section 10.6.

Analysis of Example 'A' so Far
In tax terms alone, Charlie is worse off than Humphrey. Furthermore, after taking account of Edmund's higher fees and other costs associated with running a company, Charlie will be even worse off. This is mainly because Charlie has withdrawn all his rental profits from the company.

In this example, we have examined the position of two higher rate taxpayers with no interest or finance costs who both want to spend all the profits from their property business. The example confirms our findings in Chapter 10 that a company is of no benefit in this situation.

Humphrey and Charlie are typical of the type of property investor who already has a good level of income from other sources and wishes to supplement it through property investment.

Conclusion: Using a property investment company is of no benefit when there are no borrowings relating to residential lettings and all the profits are needed to fund the investor's current lifestyle

11.4   REINVESTING RENTAL PROFITS

In the previous section, we saw that a property investment company was of no benefit when all its profits were being withdrawn by the proprietor and there were no borrowings relating to residential lettings.

However, where a property investment company can really produce significant financial benefits is when the property investor does not need their rental income immediately and reinvests their profits to build up a substantial investment portfolio over a number of years.

To see how a company may benefit these investors, let's return to our friends Humphrey and Charlie.

Example 'A', Part 2
Humphrey and Charlie both continue to accumulate a property portfolio. After a few years, each of them has ten properties, which have cost a total of £1.5m. Each of them now has total annual rental income of £135,000 and annual expenditure of £20,000, leaving rental profits of £115,000. Let us also assume Humphrey and Charlie each have existing taxable income from other sources of £60,000.

Humphrey will therefore face Income Tax on his rental income as follows:

£90,000 (£150,000 - £60,000) x 40%	*£36,000*
£25,000 (£115,000 - £90,000) x 45%	*£11,250*
£12,500 (lost personal allowance) x 40%	*£5,000*
Total	*£52,250*

This will leave him with net income of £62,750 (£115,000 – £52,250).

If Charlie continues to pay himself a salary of £8,788, this will reduce Murrayfield Ltd's taxable profit to £106,212, giving the company a CT bill (at 19%) of £20,180. This would leave a profit after tax of £86,032 and, if this were paid to Charlie as a dividend, he would suffer Income Tax as follows:

Salary - £8,788 x 40%	£3,515
Dividend - £2,000 x 0%	£0
£79,212 x 32.5%	£25,744
£4,820 x 38.1%	£1,836
£12,500 (lost personal allowance) x 40%	£5,000
Total	£36,095

This would leave Charlie with net income of £58,725 (£8,788 + £86,032 – £36,095), or **£4,025 less** than Humphrey!

Let us suppose instead, however, that Humphrey and Charlie each wish to reinvest £60,000 of their rental profits in a new property.

In Humphrey's case, this makes absolutely no difference to his Income Tax bill, which remains £52,250. Similarly, the reinvestment makes no difference to Murrayfield Ltd's CT bill of £20,180. What the reinvestment **_does_** mean, however, is that, since Murrayfield Ltd is reinvesting £60,000 of its rental profits, Charlie will only be taking out a dividend of £26,032, thus reducing his Income Tax bill as follows:

Salary - £8,788 x 40%	£3,515
Dividend - £2,000 x 0%	£0
£24,032 x 32.5%	£7,810
Total	£11,325

Between Charlie and his company, the total tax burden for the year will be reduced to £31,505, which is £20,745 less than Humphrey's Income Tax bill!

Analysis of Example 'A', Part 2

To begin with, the example reinforces the fact that there is no benefit in using a company, even at higher levels of profit, if there are no interest costs relating to residential lettings and all the income continues to be withdrawn.

However, it can also be seen that using a company can save a considerable amount of tax on the investor's rental profits where these are **not** all withdrawn.

A property investment company can prove highly beneficial for income purposes when a substantial proportion of the profits are being reinvested

11.5   CAPITAL GAINS

In Chapter 6, we looked at the basic mechanics of how a company is taxed on its capital gains.

Now, in order to illustrate the impact of the differences between how capital gains are taxed in a company and how individuals are taxed on capital gains, let's turn to another example.

Example 'B', Part 1

Michelle and Yvonne share a lottery win and each decide to invest £250,000 in residential property. Yvonne buys her property personally; Michelle forms a company, Dawson Ltd, to buy her property. Both properties are rented out to provide income. Twelve years later, Michelle and Yvonne both sell their properties for £500,000. They are both higher rate taxpayers at this time and the CGT annual exemption remains £12,300.

Yvonne has made a capital gain of £250,000. After deducting her annual exemption, her taxable gain amounts to £237,700, giving her a CGT liability of £66,556 (£237,700 x 28%).

Dawson Ltd also has a taxable gain of £250,000 because the company can no longer deduct indexation relief (see Section 6.4). This gives rise to a CT bill, at 19%, of £47,500.

Again, at first glance, we see that the corporate investor appears to be better off. However, once again, we must also consider how to extract the after-tax proceeds from the company.

If Michelle removes the net proceeds of £452,500 from Dawson Ltd as a dividend then, as a higher rate taxpayer she would have to pay Income Tax of at least £170,353.

Analysis of Example 'B', Part 1

Clearly, Michelle now appears much worse off than Yvonne, but could she have done something better than simply paying herself this enormous dividend?

The answer is probably yes, but, to a large extent, the position depends on how the company was financed in the first place. For example, if Michelle had simply loaned the original funds of £250,000 to Dawson Ltd, and had not withdrawn any of her loan capital since, then it will be a simple matter for her to repay herself this element of the sale proceeds tax-free.

In other cases, however, it may not be so easy to return the original cost element of the company's property investments to the company owner. We may have to look at winding the company up, and this is something we will cover in the next section. We will also cover the issue of financing the company, and the pros and cons of the various options available, in more detail in Chapter 12.

Another alternative for Michelle might be to leave the proceeds in the company for reinvestment in new property (or some other form of investment). Again, we can see from this example that a property company works best in a reinvestment environment.

In practice, it is unlikely that a property investor like Michelle would have simply taken a dividend of this magnitude out of the company. In many cases, there will be borrowings to be repaid and these will reduce the amount available. Alternatively, as discussed above, the company may owe the owner money that can be repaid tax-free before there is any need to resort to dividends. Furthermore, company law would prevent a company owner from taking a dividend in excess of the company's distributable profits.

For the sake of illustration, therefore, let's consider Michelle's tax position if she only withdraws her after-tax profit, rather than her entire sale proceeds.

Example 'B', Part 2
Michelle takes a dividend of £202,500 out of Dawson Ltd, representing her after-tax profit on the sale of the property. As a higher rate taxpayer, her Income Tax liability on this dividend will be at least £75,103.

Combining this with the CT already suffered in Dawson Ltd (£47,500) gives a total tax cost on the property disposal of at least £122,603.

Analysis of Example 'B', Part 2
Now that we have altered the situation so we are only looking at the profit element of the proceeds, we can clearly see that Michelle, the corporate investor, is still considerably worse off than Yvonne, the private investor. As a higher rate taxpayer, Michelle would, in fact, be at least £56,047 worse off (£122,603 - £66,556).

Michelle could possibly improve the situation by taking her dividends over a few years, so she kept her taxable income under £100,000 each year, retained her personal allowance, and avoided any additional rate tax. Nonetheless, as a higher rate taxpayer, spreading the dividends over, say, five years, she would still suffer a total of at least £62,563 in Income Tax; leaving her at least £43,507 worse off than Yvonne (£62,563 + £47,500 = £110,063 – £66,556 = £43,507).

This clearly demonstrates that a company is not a good investment vehicle if the investor wishes to realise capital gains and extract them from the company for private use, rather than reinvest them within it.

11.6   WINDING UP THE COMPANY TO REDUCE TAX

In Section 11.5 we encountered a situation where an investor was left with funds in a company that had perhaps outlived its usefulness. In such a case, the most tax-efficient procedure may be to wind the company up.

162

Unfortunately, this can be a very expensive process if the company still has assets and liabilities, or has recently been in active business. For the sake of illustration, however, let us return to Example 'B' and ignore the impact of these costs.

Example 'B', Part 3
Rather than pay herself a huge dividend, Michelle decides to wind Dawson Ltd up. First, however, she pays herself a small tax-free dividend of £2,000, which is covered by the dividend allowance (see Section 9.3). The remaining net proceeds left in Dawson Ltd now amount to £450,500 (£452,500 – £2,000).

Ignoring costs, this sum can be distributed to Michelle on the winding up and will be treated in her hands as a capital disposal subject to CGT and not Income Tax (subject to the 'Wealth Warning' below).

Michelle originally invested £250,000 in Dawson Ltd. This may have been by way of loan, which can now simply be repaid (assuming it hasn't been repaid already); or by an investment in share capital. Either way, deducting her original investment means the capital gain on her shares is £200,500. After deducting her annual exemption of £12,300, this leaves a taxable gain of £188,200.

Michelle's CGT liability at 20% (see below) will therefore be £37,640. Combining this with the CT paid by Dawson Ltd (£47,500) gives Michelle a total tax cost on this disposal of £85,140.

Analysis of Example 'B', Part 3
Firstly, it is worth noting that business asset disposal relief is not available on the disposal of Michelle's property company shares. As explained in Section 3.2, this will generally be the case for property investment companies (but see Section 7.4 for a possible way to obtain this relief). The shares do, however, benefit from the lower, 'non-residential', rate of CGT (see Section 7.2) because the shares themselves are not residential property (even though Dawson Ltd invested in residential property).

By winding up the company rather than merely paying herself a huge dividend, Michelle has dramatically improved her position from Part 2 (Section 11.5). In effect, changing the way most of her sale proceeds are treated to a capital gain instead of a dividend has reduced the tax rate on a large part of her profits from 38.1% to just 20%.

It's a big improvement, but still not enough to match the private investor's position. In fact, Michelle still remains £18,584 worse off than Yvonne (£85,140 – £66,556). Hence, it appears quite conclusive that a company is not beneficial when we are looking at fairly static levels of capital growth, without any serious reinvestment activity, which are ultimately being returned into the hands of the individual investor.

Wealth Warning (A *Major* Wealth Warning in Fact!)

As discussed in Section 7.7, there is a risk that sums distributed on a winding up of the company could be treated as dividends if the company owner, or a connected person (see Appendix B), continues to invest in a similar property business within the next two years. This would put an investor like Michelle back in the position shown in Part 2 (Section 11.5), leaving her at least £56,047 worse off than the private investor.

11.7 WHAT IF THE COMPANY STILL HOLDS PROPERTY WHEN WOUND UP?

Generally, this would not be a good idea:

- Firstly, the costs of the winding up would be considerably greater
- Secondly, the company would be treated as having made a disposal of the property at its market value and taxed accordingly
- Thirdly, the shareholder would be taxed on the 'disposal' of the company shares, again based on the market value of the property!

In Michelle's case (Example 'B' in Sections 11.5 and 11.6), tax liabilities of at least £85,540 would be incurred without there being any actual sale proceeds from which to fund them. This demonstrates the fact that, once you have your investments in a company, it can be very difficult (or expensive) to get them out!

11.8 NON-RESIDENTIAL PROPERTY

So far, we have looked at the position on residential property investments. How would things differ if we were investing in non-residential property?

Firstly, any interest and finance costs incurred by the individual investor would be fully relieved, meaning the position described in Example 'A' (Sections 11.3 and 11.4) would remain the same even if there were borrowings against the properties.

Secondly, the individual investor would suffer CGT on a property disposal at the lower, non-residential, rates of 10% for basic rate taxpayers and 20% for higher rate taxpayers. Hence, for example, Yvonne's CGT liability in Example 'B' (Sections 11.5 and 11.6) would be reduced to just £47,540 (£237,700 x 20%), whereas the tax incurred by both Michelle and Dawson Ltd would remain unaltered.

Overall, therefore, the conclusions we have drawn so far would simply be further reinforced if the investor is looking to invest in non-residential property.

11.9   FURNISHED HOLIDAY LETS

The position also differs significantly where the investor is looking to invest in furnished holiday lets.

Once again, any interest and finance costs incurred by the individual investor would be fully relieved, meaning the position described in Example 'A' (Sections 11.3 and 11.4) would remain unaltered where there were borrowings against the properties.

The private investor might be eligible for business asset disposal relief on a disposal of their property: providing they were disposing of an entire furnished holiday letting business (see the Taxcafe.co.uk guide 'How to Save Property Tax' for a detailed examination of the considerations involved).

The corporate investor should definitely be eligible for business asset disposal relief on a disposal of their shares, provided all the conditions described in Section 7.3 are met.

Assuming both investors are eligible for business asset disposal relief, the results in Example 'B' would differ as follows:

Yvonne's CGT liability (see Section 11.5) would be reduced to £23,770 (£237,700 x 10%).

Michelle's final CGT liability in Part 3 (Section 11.6) would be reduced to £18,820 (£188,200 x 10%). However, the total tax incurred by both Michelle and Dawson Ltd would be £66,320 (£47,500 + £18,820), leaving her £42,550 worse off than Yvonne. (The 'Wealth Warning' in Section 11.6 would also remain highly relevant!)

Once again, therefore, the conclusions we have drawn so far would simply be further reinforced if the investor is looking to invest in furnished holiday lets.

11.10   INTEREST RELIEF

What we have not factored in so far in this chapter is the impact of the dreadful interest relief restrictions applying to individual landlords investing in residential property.

Example 'C'
James and Robert have similar residential property portfolios yielding profits before interest of £100,000 each. They both have £60,000 in other taxable income.

James holds his properties personally and has annual interest and finance costs of £40,000. Robert holds his properties through Tipp Holdings Ltd, which has annual interest and finance costs of £50,000 (a quarter more than James).

James suffers Income Tax on his property profits as follows:

£90,000 x 40%	£36,000
£10,000 x 45%	£4,500
£12,500 (lost personal allowance) x 40%	£5,000
Less interest relief	
£40,000 x 20%	(£8,000)
Tax liability	£37,500

This leaves James with net income of £22,500 (£100,000 – £40,000 – £37,500).

Robert takes a salary of £8,788 from Tipp Holdings Ltd, leaving the company with a taxable profit of £41,212 (£100,000 – £50,000 – £8,788). The company therefore pays CT of £7,830 (£41,212 x 19%) leaving it with profits after tax of £33,382, which it pays to Robert as a dividend. Robert then has an Income Tax liability made up as follows:

Salary - £8,788 x 40%	£3,515
Dividend - £2,000 x 0%	£0
£31,382 x 32.5%	£10,199
Lost personal allowance	
£1,085* x 40%	£434
Total	£14,148

* Robert's total income is £102,170 (£60,000 + £8,788 + £33,382) so he loses £1,085 (£2,170 x ½) of his personal allowance (see Section 10.2)

Robert has net income of £28,022 (£8,788 + £33,382 – £14,148), leaving him £5,522 better off than James.

Analysis of Example 'C'
As we can see, using a property investment company can yield savings for a residential property investor even when the company's interest costs are higher than they would have suffered as an individual **and** they are extracting all their company's after tax profits.

11.11 LONG-TERM REINVESTMENT

What we have not yet considered is how the incorporated property business's long-term capital growth might benefit from its ability to reinvest a greater share of its profits owing to the fact its annual tax bill is much reduced under the CT regime.

Reinvesting Profits Over a Number of Years

We now know that a property company can produce a significantly better outcome in the short term, year on year, when either:

a) Its profits are being reinvested, or
b) There are borrowings on residential rental property

In Example 'A', we assumed the investors had built up identical portfolios over a period of time. However, in practice, it is likely that if both investors reinvest all or most of their profits, the company investor will eventually build up a larger portfolio of properties. This is because the lower CT rates will leave the company investor with extra resources to invest in new properties.

The long-term effect of reinvestment through a property company is best illustrated by way of the example that follows (Example 'D'). In this example, we will have to make many assumptions, including rates of return, interest rates and the rate of growth of property values. Here again we will follow the hypothetical long-term trend for the reasons discussed in Section 11.1.

While the real outcome over the coming years will almost certainly be different to that which is predicted here, the example will still serve as a valid illustration because we will apply all our assumptions equally to the company investor and the personal investor, except for their different tax environments, and an assumed higher interest rate for the company investor.

The numbers will get quite messy in this example but please bear with me, as it is worth persevering to see the ultimate result.

Example 'D', Part 1

Lenny and Dawn are both higher rate taxpayers and they each own residential rental properties worth £320,000. They each earn annual rents of £24,000 and, after deducting costs of £4,000, are left with annual profits of £20,000. At present, neither of them is paying any interest.

Lenny's property is owned personally and, because he is a higher rate taxpayer, he is left with after-tax profits of £12,000.

Dawn uses a company, Saunders Ltd, to invest. Saunders Ltd's rental profits will be subject to CT at 19%. On a profit of £20,000 this will give rise to a CT bill of £3,800, leaving the company with £16,200.

Each investor is using their property business to save for retirement, so all after-tax profits are saved and reinvested.

After three years, Lenny will have £36,000 available for reinvestment. With a 70% Buy-to-Let mortgage, this will enable him to buy a new property at a cost of £120,000. This brings in rental income of £9,000, less interest of £3,360 and other costs of £1,100, leaving him with an annual rental profit of £4,540.

Lenny's total annual rental profit for both properties is now £24,540 (£20,000 + £4,540) but he is subject to Income Tax at 40% on his profit before interest of £27,900 and only gets basic rate tax relief at 20% on his interest cost. This gives him an Income Tax liability of £10,488, leaving him with after-tax profits of £14,052.

Dawn, the company investor, also buys a new property after three years, but she has £48,600 available (3 x £16,200). This enables her to buy a property for £162,000, which produces rental income of £12,150. After interest of £5,670 and other costs of £1,310, Dawn's company receives an annual rental profit of £5,170 from this property.

Saunders Ltd's annual profits are now £25,170, giving rise to CT, at 19%, of £4,782, leaving profits after tax of £20,388.

Analysis of Example 'D', Part 1

Already, we can see Dawn is moving ahead of Lenny. Her company's second property is worth £42,000 more and her annual after-tax profits are now over £6,000 greater (assuming she retains them within the company).

For the sake of illustration, I have had to make a number of assumptions here, which are worth explaining:

- Rental income, or yield, is assumed to be 7.5% of the property's value
- Mortgage interest is at 4% for individuals and 5% for a company
- Other annual costs amount to a fixed element of £500 per property, plus a variable element equal to 0.5% of the property's value

We are now going to move forward many more years, assuming Lenny and Dawn continue to reinvest all their available after-tax profits in new property every three years using 70% Buy-to-Let mortgages.

The result in Part 2 will be based on the same assumptions as Part 1, assuming, in turn, these all remain valid throughout that period. Additionally, and purely for the sake of simplicity, we will also assume:

- The rent is never increased on any of the properties
- There is no capital repayment of any of the mortgages (i.e. they are all interest-only)
- Lenny and Dawn's other taxable income amounts to £60,000 each
- Current tax rates continue to apply throughout the relevant period

Example 'D', Part 2

After continuing in the same way for 15 years, Lenny and Dawn each have a portfolio of six properties.

Lenny's properties now produce total annual rental profits of £50,647 but he is taxed on his profit before interest of £72,744 and only gets basic rate tax relief on his interest costs of £22,097. This gives rise to a net Income Tax bill of:

£72,744 x 40%	*£29,098*
£12,500 (lost personal allowance) x 40%	*£5,000*
Less interest relief	
£22,097 x 20%	*(£4,420)*
Tax liability	*£29,678*

This leaves him with just £20,969 of annual after-tax income.

Dawn's property company is now receiving annual rental profits of £65,285, leaving a sum of £52,881 after CT.

Let us suppose, at this point, both Lenny and Dawn wish to stop reinvesting and start spending their rental profits privately. We already know how much net income Lenny will receive.

For Dawn, we now need to take account of the Income Tax she will suffer when she withdraws her after tax profits from the company. First, she takes a salary of £8,788. This reduces the company's taxable profit to £56,497, leaving £45,762 after CT, which is available for her to take as a dividend. Her Income Tax liability will be as follows:

Salary - £8,788 x 40%	*£3,515*
Dividend - £2,000 x 0%	*£0*
£43,762 x 32.5%	*£14,223*
Partial loss of personal allowance	
£7,275* x 40%	*£2,910*
Total	*£20,648*

* Dawn's total income is £114,550 (£60,000 + £8,788 + £45,762) so she loses £7,275 (£14,550 x ½) of her personal allowance (see Section 10.2)

Dawn will therefore be left with net annual income from her property business of £33,902 (£8,788 + £45,762 – £20,648), or £12,933 more than Lenny.

Analysis of Example 'D', Part 2

What this example shows is the ability to reinvest a greater share of annual rental profits over a number of years has ultimately provided Dawn, the corporate investor, with a greatly increased income.

In fact, in this example, **the company investor has an after-tax income almost 62% greater than that enjoyed by the personal investor!**

This example has shown, in a long-term reinvestment scenario, a property investment company can provide enormous tax benefits to those who build up a portfolio of properties and ultimately use it to generate income.

11.12 RETAINING THE WEALTH

So far, so good, but we still haven't tackled the issue of capital gains. Although Lenny and Dawn have now stopped reinvesting, they do still have the pressure of a property-letting business to worry about. To genuinely retire, they may, in fact, wish to sell their properties.

To look at the final outcome on the ultimate sale of the property portfolios, let's move on one final three-year period and assume Lenny and Dawn then sell all their properties. We need to make two more assumptions for this purpose:

i)   Property values have increased at an average compound rate of 7.5% per annum (see Section 11.1)
ii) There have been no changes to the tax system (but see Chapter 17 for some potential alternatives)

Example 'D', Part 3

Eighteen years after we started, Lenny's property portfolio is worth a total of £2,687,731. The total cost of this portfolio was £1,109,206, giving him total capital gains of £1,578,525.

Let's assume Lenny's disposals are spread over two tax years, with annual exemptions of £12,300 in each year. Deducting these two annual exemptions leaves Lenny with total taxable gains of £1,553,925, thus giving rise to total CGT liabilities (at 28%) of £435,099.

After paying his CGT and repaying his mortgages, Lenny will be left with net proceeds of £1,700,188.

The property portfolio in Dawn's company will now be worth a total of £3,654,928. The cost of the portfolio was £1,685,274, producing total capital gains of £1,969,654. Indexation relief will not be available as the properties were purchased after 2017. The CT on the company's capital gains therefore amounts to a total of £374,234 (at 19%).

After paying this CT and repaying its mortgages, the remaining funds in the company will be £2,325,002. Dawn winds up Saunders Ltd to get these proceeds into her own hands. We will assume she originally invested £320,000 in the company (the value of her first property), meaning she will have a capital gain of £2,005,002. (We are again ignoring the costs of the winding up as we did in Section 11.6)

Dawn is entitled to an annual exemption of £12,300, leaving her with a taxable gain of £1,992,702. Her CGT liability at 20% on the winding up of her property investment company will therefore amount to £398,540, leaving her with net proceeds of £1,926,462 (£2,325,002 – £398,540).

Analysis of Example 'D', Part 3

So how much better off is the company investor compared with the private investor?

Ultimately, our corporate investor, Dawn, has emerged £226,274, or over 13.3%, better off than Lenny, our personal investor.

This represents **over 70% of the original amount invested!**

What this means is, over a reasonable period of time, the reinvestment of the additional net income receivable through using a company should eventually produce a sufficiently improved position to more than compensate for the disadvantages of realising capital gains in a company and suffering a second layer of tax when extracting the net sale proceeds.

Readers should, however, bear in mind the 'Wealth Warning' in Section 11.6 and the 'anti-phoenixing' rules described in Section 7.7, which could mean the eventual proceeds received on the winding up of the company may be treated as dividends.

In Dawn's case, this would have led to an Income Tax liability of £763,216, reducing her net proceeds to £1,561,786 and leaving her **over £138,000 worse off** than Lenny.

Readers in this sort of position should seek professional advice regarding the potential application of the rules in Section 7.7.

11.13 AN ALTERNATIVE FUTURE

In Section 11.12 we saw a long term investor could end up over 13.3% better off by using a property investment company. However, we also considered the risk the 'anti-phoenixing' rules described in Section 7.7 might result in a less beneficial outcome.

Alternatively, another option might simply be to reinvest the proceeds of property disposals within the company and thus avoid the risk of the 'anti-phoenixing' rules applying. This could have huge benefits, and we will illustrate these by returning to Example 'D'.

Example 'D', Part 4
Lenny takes his net proceeds of £1,700,188 and invests them in a share portfolio. Let's say this yields an annual return of 5%, or £85,009. Let's also say this is all in the form of dividends. Lenny will suffer tax on this income as follows:

£83,009 (£85,009 – £2,000) x 32.5%	£26,978
£12,500 (lost personal allowance) x 40%	£5,000
Total	£31,978

This leaves him with £53,031 of annual after-tax income (£85,009 – £31,978).

Dawn takes the net proceeds of £2,325,002 held by Saunders Ltd and invests these in a share portfolio held by the company. This yields an annual return at 5% of £116,250. The company is exempt from CT on dividend income so it is able to redistribute all the dividends it receives to Dawn, again in the form of dividends. Her Income Tax liability on this income will be as follows:

£2,000 x 0%	£0
£88,000 x 32.5%	£28,600
£26,250 x 38.1%	£10,001
£12,500 (lost personal allowance) x 40%	£5,000
Total	£43,601

This leaves her with £72,649 of annual after-tax income (£116,250 – £43,601) or £19,618 more than Lenny.

Analysis of Example 'D', Part 4

Reinvesting her ultimate sale proceeds within her company has left our corporate investor, Dawn, with 37% more after tax income than Lenny, our personal investor.

At this stage, Dawn's company would be a 'close investment holding company' (Section 15.2). This should not cause too many problems, although Dawn would cease to qualify for Income Tax relief on any interest on funds borrowed to invest in the company (see Section 12.3).

11.14 LONG-TERM REINVESTMENT CONCLUSIONS

After a long, detailed look at the possible outcomes for two investors (one corporate and one personal) over many years, we can see using a property investment company can be hugely beneficial when building a portfolio over a long period of time.

The benefits come in three possible forms:

- By building the portfolio for an extended period and then beginning to extract income: we saw an increase of almost 62% in after-tax income for the corporate investor (Example 'D', Part 2, Section 11.11)

- By eventually selling the portfolio after an extended period of growth: we saw an increase of over 13.3% in the total net proceeds for the corporate investor (Example 'D', Part 3, Section 11.12)

- By selling the portfolio after an extended period of growth and then reinvesting the funds in other, more 'passive' forms of investments within the company: we saw an increase of 37% in after-tax income for the corporate investor (Example 'D', Part 4, Section 11.13)

11.15   STRESSING THE MODEL

The model we have used in Example 'D' throughout Sections 11.11 to 11.13 incorporates a great many assumptions and, naturally, a change in those assumptions will lead to different results.

Nonetheless, I feel the assumptions are valid as they are based on real life experience and long-term trends.

One point that may concern readers is the assumption the company would be able to obtain the same level of borrowings as an individual investor. This may not always be the case so it is worth considering the outcomes where the company is unable to obtain mortgages at 70% LTV (loan-to-value) and can only obtain 60% LTV mortgages.

This would leave Dawn with net income of £30,060 at the end of Example 'D', Part 2, in Section 11.11: still £9,091, or over 43%, better off than Lenny.

However, it would leave Dawn with net proceeds of just £1,694,870 at the end of Example 'D', Part 3, in Section 11.12: which is £5,318, or 0.3%, **_worse off_** than Lenny.

Nonetheless, it would leave her with net income of £63,689 at the end of Example 'D', Part 4, in Section 11.13: still £10,658, or more than 20%, better off than Lenny.

While these results are less impressive than those shown earlier, they still show the company to be beneficial where properties are still held, or sale proceeds are retained. However, winding up the company could eventually produce less net after tax proceeds overall.

Having said that, it is worth pointing out, even though Dawn would end up with £5,318 less than Lenny at the end of Part 3 of the example, she would have enjoyed £9,091 more net income for three years before that: so she'd still be £21,955 better off overall.

Nonetheless, where you intend to grow your portfolio quickly though a high level of borrowing, and eventually sell everything off and wind your company up, the finance deals available may be a crucial factor in deciding whether a company may be beneficial in the long run.

Where the same level of LTV is available, the company proves beneficial even on a winding up (after a long reinvestment period); where only a lower level of LTV is available, the investor's ability to grow their portfolio within the company is hampered, and this may mean the company produces less total net proceeds in the end.

On the other hand, we must remember we have already reflected 25% higher finance costs for the company within the model used in Example 'D' and one might reasonably expect this would mean the same level of LTV will be available. In reality, you will have to do your own research on this point.

11.16 THE BENEFITS OF REINVESTMENT FOR A TRADING COMPANY

The one thing we have not yet covered is the situation where profits from a property **trade** are reinvested over a long period.

I did suggest in Section 11.2 that this was almost a 'no-brainer', with a property company being the obvious winner in most cases. However, I feel this stance warrants an illustrative example to back up my assertions!

Example 'E' Part 1
Linda and Crispin are both property developers. Each of them acquires a derelict property in Newcastle at a cost of £180,000, which they plan to renovate and convert into flats they will then sell. Crispin is going to carry on his business as a sole trader. Linda, on the other hand, forms a property development company, Sunshine Developments Ltd.

Neither Linda nor Crispin has any other income, so each will need £20,000 out of their net profits to cover modest living expenses.

In their first year of trading, each of them manages to develop their property and sell all the flats. After building costs, interest costs, and other trading expenditure, each makes a total net profit before tax of £100,000, which they plan to reinvest in their business, together with their original capital of £180,000.

Crispin will have a total Income Tax and NI liability of £32,304, leaving him only £67,696 of net, after-tax profit. £20,000 of this goes on living expenses, leaving £47,696 available to reinvest, plus his original capital of £180,000, making a total of £227,696.

Linda, on the other hand, pays herself a salary of £9,500 (the NI primary threshold). This leaves a taxable profit in the company of £90,500. After CT of £17,195 (at 19%), the company is left with a net profit of £73,305. From this, Linda pays herself a dividend of £10,946: of which £3,000 is covered by the remainder of her personal allowance (£12,500 – £9,500), £2,000 by her dividend allowance, and the final £5,946 is taxed at 7.5%. After paying tax of £446, she is left with a final sum of £20,000 to cover living expenses as required (£9,500 + £10,946 – £446 = £20,000).

The company is therefore left with £62,359 (£73,305 – £10,946) to reinvest plus Linda's original capital of £180,000, making a total of £242,359.

Analysis of Example 'E' Part 1

Already we see Sunshine Developments Ltd, the property development company, has an extra £14,663 available for reinvestment. This is because the company has been able to retain over 30% more of its profits than Crispin.

Example 'E' Part 2

The following year, Linda and Crispin both reinvest their available profits and capital in a new development. In each case, they double the amount available by borrowing the same sum as they are investing themselves.

After all relevant expenditure, each development yields a profit of 25% before interest costs at 7.5% (this will be an unsecured loan, so a higher interest rate is appropriate). Throughout the rest of this example, I'm also going to assume Linda and Crispin's requirements for living expenses each increase by £2,000 per annum.

On the basis of the above assumptions, Crispin will make a profit of £96,771 and will have total Income Tax and NI costs of £30,947. After living expenses of £22,000, he will have total profits and capital left for reinvestment next year of £271,520.

In the same year, Sunshine Developments Ltd will make a net profit before tax of £103,003, which is £6,232 more than Crispin, owing to the greater amount of profit available for reinvestment from the previous year.

Sunshine Developments Ltd will then pay Linda a salary of £9,500 and the CT at 19% on the remaining £93,503 profit will be £17,765. Linda will take a dividend of £13,108 to top up her total after tax income to the level required to cover her living expenses.

This will leave the company with net retained profits of £62,629 which, this time, is £18,805 more than Crispin had left for reinvestment.

Sunshine Developments Ltd's total funds available for reinvestment at this point are £304,988. This is £33,468, or over 12.3%, more than Crispin is able to invest.

In fact, by using a company, Linda has experienced 37% more growth (£124,988) than Crispin (£91,520).

Analysis of Example 'E' Part 2
After only two years of trading, the property development company is producing 6.4% more profit before tax and has accumulated 37% more after-tax profit for reinvestment. Through her company, Linda is already seeing the twin benefits of:

- Having greater funds available for reinvestment, while
- Being able to do so within a lower tax environment

Example 'E' Part 3
Linda and Crispin both continue trading for several years in exactly the same vein. After five years, Crispin will be making profits after tax of £97,545 and will have accumulated funds available of £448,451.

*By the same point in time, Sunshine Developments Ltd will be making profits after tax of £162,749, even after paying Linda a salary of £9,500. The total funds generated will be £172,249, which is **77% more** than Crispin's business.*

By this time, Sunshine Developments Ltd will have total accumulated funds available of £638,272, almost £190,000, or over 42%, more than Crispin!

Analysis of Example 'E' Part 3
After five years of trading, the property development company is clearly substantially more successful than the sole trader property developer. All of this simply because of the ability to reinvest a greater proportion of each year's profits.

As with property investment companies however, we must also consider the position on a final dissolution of each business.

Example 'E' Part 4
Linda and Crispin each reinvest their available funds in one last development. By the time he has completed and sold his last development, Crispin will be left with a sum of £531,661 after tax and his usual living expenses.

What about Sunshine Developments Ltd and Linda, though?

*Sunshine Developments Ltd **started** its last development with funds available of £638,272, already almost £190,000 ahead of Crispin.*

176

Let us suppose the company then invests in a new development in the usual way. On completion, the new development will be worth £1,595,680.

After accounting for borrowings, including accumulated interest, the CT on its final development, and Linda's usual salary of £9,500, the net worth of the company will be £850,302. Even if Linda takes out her maximum tax free dividend of £5,000, it will still be worth £845,302.

By this point, a business like Sunshine Developments Ltd's property development trade could have some substantial goodwill value, although we are going to ignore that here for the sake of illustration.

Nevertheless, by selling the company rather than the property development within the company, Linda may be able to avoid the costs of winding it up.

At this stage, therefore, Linda might potentially be able to sell the company for the net value of its assets: £845,302.

After deducting her original investment of £180,000, Linda would have a capital gain of £665,302. Deducting her annual CGT exemption of £12,300 would leave a taxable gain of £653,002. Linda's shares will qualify for business asset disposal relief, so her gain will be subject to CGT at just 10%, giving her a tax bill of a mere £65,300.

This would leave Linda with net proceeds from her company sale of £780,002 (£845,302 − £65,300). Adding her salary of £9,500 and dividends of £5,000, and then deducting £30,000 to cover her usual living expenses, would leave her with a final sum of £764,502.

Analysis of Example 'E' Part 4
After one last development, Linda has been able to sell her company and retain almost £233,000, or 44%, more than Crispin, her sole trader rival. In the final period, she was able to add the benefit of a CGT rate of just 10% (see Section 7.3) to the advantages she had already accumulated over the preceding years.

And The Purchaser Can Save Money Too!
If Sunshine Developments Ltd's final development was a commercial property, then a purchaser who bought the property directly would suffer SDLT of £85,241 (£1,595,680 + VAT at 20% = £1,914,816 taxed at the rates set out in Section 8.4).

If it were one or more residential properties, the SDLT is likely to be between £47,870 and £153,102, depending on the exact circumstances (and assuming the purchase takes place after the current 'holiday' period: see Section 8.4).

By purchasing the company for £845,302 instead, the Stamp Duty charge will be just £4,227 (0.5%), giving the purchaser a saving of somewhere between £43,644 and £148,875.

Wealth Warnings

The VAT position on the final development held by Sunshine Developments Ltd would need to be considered, as there is some risk of a 'claw back' of any VAT claimed by the company on this last project, depending on the purchaser's future intentions for the company. There is also a risk of SDLT anti-avoidance legislation applying under some circumstances. Hence, if you are buying a property development company of this nature, take professional advice!

An Alternative Strategy

Alternatively, Linda could sell off her last development and then wind up the company. This should leave her with the same level of final net proceeds as outlined above, but the 'anti-phoenixing' rules set out in Section 7.7 would need to be considered.

Chapter 12

Financing the Company and Interest Relief

12.1 INTRODUCTION

A property company that borrows to finance property purchases or other aspects of its business obtains CT relief for interest and finance costs.

Relief may follow either the special rules explained in Section 4.9, or the general principles for any trading deduction explained in Chapter 5, depending on the type of business the company has. Either way, as long as the interest or finance costs are incurred for business purposes, the company gets full, unrestricted CT relief on annual costs up to £2m (see Section 4.9).

Investors themselves may obtain Income Tax relief for interest on borrowings invested in the property company, provided it is a 'Close Company', but not a 'Close Investment Holding Company'. These terms are explained in Section 15.2. This relief is subject to some limitations, which we will look at in Section 12.11.

To obtain relief, the investor must also either have a 'material interest' in the company, or must hold some ordinary shares in the company and work for the greater part of their time in the actual conduct or management of the company's business.

A 'material interest' is broadly defined as more than 5% of the company's share capital and shares held by 'connected persons' (see Appendix B) may usually be counted for this purpose, as long as the individual concerned does hold some of the shares personally.

In the case of most private property companies, the investor will usually qualify as having a 'material interest', although, for a large property company, it may be that some new investors come on board who qualify for relief through the second criterion instead.

Where the investor qualifies, they are equally eligible for interest relief on funds borrowed to purchase shares in the company, or to lend to the company.

Top Tax Tip
In most cases, an investor who borrows to invest in their own property company can claim tax relief for their interest by setting it against their other income.

For this purpose it does not matter what form the investor's other income takes and it does not have to be in any way related to the property business.

We will look at the potential benefits of interest relief claimed directly by the investor personally later in this chapter.

This form of interest relief is not subject to the restrictions now applying to residential landlords: **even when the property company is investing in residential property!**

Wealth Warning
While the above 'Tax Tip' is true in most cases, investors may not always be able to obtain full relief for interest on funds borrowed to invest in their property company, especially (but not exclusively) where annual interest costs exceed £50,000. See Section 12.11 for details.

Despite the 'Wealth Warning' above, combining the potential for personal interest relief for the investor with the beneficial regime enjoyed by the company (see Section 4.9) will often make a property investment company very attractive.

12.2   WHO SHOULD BORROW THE FUNDS?

When investing in property through a company, there are three possible approaches to the financing structure:

i)   Borrow the funds personally and invest them in shares in the company
ii) Borrow the funds personally and lend them to the company
iii) Borrow the funds within the company

These three different structures make several important differences to the overall tax situation:

- Tax relief on the interest paid
- Additional tax arising due to the need to extract funds to service personal debt held outside the company
- The CGT position on an ultimate winding up or sale of the company
- Stamp Duty on a sale of the company's shares

180

They do not, however, make any difference to the capital gains position on property disposals made by the company itself.

An additional non-tax issue is the impact on the investor's ability to withdraw the sums invested back out of the company.

Over the next few sections, we will take a look at the implications of each structure in turn. In each case, we will assume the company is a Close Company, but not a Close Investment Holding Company (Section 15.2).

We will also assume the rate of interest charged will be unaffected by the funding method used. In practice, this may not be the case and investors will therefore also need to weigh up the impact of any differences in interest rates.

In Sections 12.3 to 12.9, we will assume the investor is able to obtain full Income Tax relief for interest paid on sums borrowed to invest in the company and is not affected by the limitations discussed in Section 12.11.

Where those limitations do apply, however, it will generally make sense for funds to be borrowed within the company whenever possible and not by the investor personally: or at least for the investor's personal borrowings to be limited to a suitable level so the restrictions in Section 12.11 do not affect them.

Finally, we will assume throughout this chapter that the company's total annual interest cost is less than £2m, so there is no risk of the restrictions discussed in Section 4.9 applying.

12.3   BORROWING TO INVEST IN SHARES

The individual will obtain interest relief on the borrowings. This can be highly advantageous, as relief is being given at a higher rate than the CT paid by the company on its profits.

If the individual is able to service the debt from other resources then this is all well and good and, in Section 12.9, we will look at the significant benefits this can produce. In many cases, however, it will be necessary to extract funds from the company to service the debt.

Example
Sarah, a higher rate taxpayer, borrows £100,000 to invest in her property company. She pays annual interest totalling £5,000, providing her with effective relief of £2,000 (at 40%). However, in order to pay this interest, Sarah takes a dividend of £5,000 out of her company. This costs her an additional £1,625 (32.5%) in Income Tax, meaning her effective relief for the interest is only £375 (7.5%). (I have ignored the dividend allowance here on the assumption Sarah is already using it against other dividends from the company.)

Clearly, if personal debt needs to be serviced through the withdrawal of funds from the company, this will generally eliminate any apparent advantage of obtaining interest relief personally: Sarah's effective rate of relief is only 7.5%; the company would obtain CT relief at 19% if it were paying the interest.

Alternatively, Sarah might take a salary of £5,000 to fund her interest. This would attract Income Tax at 40% leaving Sarah with no effective relief at all. However, the company would obtain CT relief at 19% for the salary (subject to the points in Section 9.2). In effect, this transfers relief for the interest from Sarah to the company, although it is generally only worth pursuing this option if the salary required does not exceed either of the NI thresholds.

We have only considered the payment of interest here and ignored capital repayments. These would, of course, only serve to further increase the Income Tax cost on the withdrawal of the necessary funds from the company.

Hence, corporate borrowings will generally provide better tax relief than individual borrowings invested in property company shares in most circumstances.

On a winding up or sale where borrowings have been invested in company shares, the individual will have a high base cost, thus reducing the potential CGT impact.

A sale of the company's shares may give rise to more Stamp Duty for the purchaser under this structure, as much of its value will be held as non-distributable share capital.

The major drawback to this structure is the difficulty in withdrawing the funds invested. This requires a winding up, corporate restructuring, or company purchase of own shares. We have covered winding up in Section 11.6. While in some cases they can prove worthwhile, the other possible methods are likely to prove costly in terms of the tax charges arising and/or professional fees incurred.

12.4   BORROWING TO LEND TO THE COMPANY

Borrowing to lend funds to the company will produce the same interest relief as in Section 12.3 above as long as the loan to the company is structured properly.

The same issues regarding withdrawal of the necessary funds to service the debt apply here in equal measure except that the investor can, if desired, also charge the company interest on the outstanding loan from them to the company.

Provided the interest charged does not exceed a normal commercial rate, the company will obtain CT relief on interest paid to the investor, although the investor will, of course, be taxed on this income. This is a useful third alternative for 'profit extraction' (Chapter 9), as CT relief is obtained without any NI cost, and we will explore this idea further in Section 12.10.

A slight cashflow disadvantage arises due to the fact the company must deduct 20% Income Tax at source from payments of interest to the individual investor and account for this to HMRC on a quarterly basis. The tax deducted can later be set off against the individual's Income Tax liability under self-assessment, but this can leave investors 'out of pocket' when they have to service personal borrowings while only receiving 80% of the interest due from the company.

The major advantage of this structure (over Section 12.3) is that the funds invested can be withdrawn from the company at any time (with no tax liability), if the cash is available.

On a winding up, the amounts due to the investor can be repaid without any tax implications. This would leave the same level of CGT as in Section 12.3 above.

Sums due to the investor effectively reduce the company's overall net worth, thus reducing the company's price on a sale, and both the CGT payable by the seller and the Stamp Duty payable by the purchaser. This is generally achieved by ensuring the outstanding loan is repaid to the investor prior to the sale. Other methods for taking account of the debt can be used to obtain the same result but these may carry more commercial risk: it's generally better to get repaid first.

All in all, lending funds to the company is generally to be preferred to borrowing to invest in shares and still has the potential to produce the significant benefits we will explore in Section 12.9. The company will, of course, need some share capital, but this can be kept at a minimal level in most private companies (e.g. £100).

12.5   CORPORATE BORROWINGS

Where the company obtains funds through its own direct borrowings, this will mean it is the company that claims relief for the interest costs. Whether this is better than personal borrowings invested into the company depends on whether the investor would have had to withdraw funds from the company to service any private debt.

Borrowings in the company will generally produce a better overall result for interest relief where it would otherwise be necessary to pay out dividends, or salary in excess of the secondary NI threshold, to service personal debt.

Where the company pays either interest, or salary not exceeding the secondary NI threshold, to an investor to enable them to service personal debt, the position regarding interest relief is effectively the same as for corporate borrowings, except (in the case of interest) for the cashflow disadvantage discussed in Section 12.4.

Where the investor is able to service the debt from other resources, however, a better rate of tax relief is usually obtained by borrowing funds personally for investment into the company.

The position on a winding up where corporate borrowings have been used will depend on whether the borrowings are still in place at that time. If there are still loans to be repaid out of property disposals, the total sums to be distributed on the winding up will be reduced.

Hence, if all the borrowings were still in place, the tax position would be much the same as in Example 'B', Part 3 in Section 11.6. However, if the borrowings have been repaid, this means the sum distributed on the winding up is increased.

Example 'B', Part 4
Returning to our earlier example in Sections 11.5 and 11.6, let us now suppose Michelle set Dawson Ltd up with only a small nominal sum in share capital (so small, in fact, we will ignore it for the sake of illustration). She loaned £118,500 to the company and it borrowed a further £131,500 to finance the property purchase. At the time of the property's sale, the external borrowings have been completely repaid out of rent received.

As before (Section 11.6), we will assume Michelle first takes a dividend of £2,000, which is covered by her dividend allowance, leaving net proceeds of £450,500 in Dawson Ltd. Next, the company repays Michelle's loan, leaving a sum of £332,000 to be distributed on the winding up (once more ignoring professional fees, etc).

This represents a capital disposal and, as Michelle has no (or very little) base cost to set off, she will have a capital gain of £332,000. After deducting her annual exemption of £12,300, her taxable gain will be £319,700.

Michelle's CGT bill on this gain, at 20%, will therefore be £63,940, meaning the total tax burden on this property disposal would be £111,440 (including the CT paid by Dawson Ltd, £47,500).

Analysis of Example 'B', Part 4
Clearly, this is a poor result for Michelle. However, we must bear in mind the company has repaid its borrowings from rental profits. To repay £131,500 out of after tax profits will have required pre-tax profits of

184

£162,346 (based on CT at 19%). In achieving this result, it is reasonable to assume the company will have paid interest of around £42,000 in total (based on the same assumptions regarding rental yield and corporate interest rates used in Example 'D' in Chapter 11). Hence, its total profit before interest will have been about £204,000.

If Yvonne, the private investor (see Part 1 of Example 'B' in Section 11.5) received the same profits before interest, she would suffer Income Tax at 40% on them, with only basic rate relief at 20% on her interest costs. Assuming she also borrowed £131,500 to fund the purchase her after tax income would not be sufficient to repay the full sum within twelve years. In fact, even assuming the rate of interest she paid was lower than Dawson Ltd by a factor of a fifth, I estimate around £43,500 of her loan would remain outstanding at the time of the property's sale. In summary, therefore, the final position can be compared as follows:

	Michelle (Corporate)	Yvonne (Private)
Sale proceeds	£500,000	£500,000
Total tax suffered	(£111,440)	(£66,556)
Loan repayment on sale	-	(£43,500)
Net proceeds	£388,560	£389,944

As we can see, in the end, the overall difference is minimal. In this particular scenario, the additional costs arising when the business is wound up are almost exactly balanced by the tax savings on rental income yielded by using a company.

As usual, this is based on the assumption the anti-phoenixing rules do not apply (see Section 7.7 and the 'Wealth Warning' in Section 11.6).

12.6   LOSS-MAKING COMPANIES

Our analysis so far has been based on the assumption the company will obtain CT relief for any interest costs it incurs.

If the company is loss-making, or would make a loss if it incurred the interest costs, then it may be more beneficial for the investor to borrow personally. This, in turn, however, is based on the assumption the investor would obtain Income Tax relief on the interest and would be able to service the debt from other resources without the need to extract funds from the company.

It should also be borne in mind that a property investment company can effectively 'roll up' its interest costs for set off against future capital gains. We will look at the benefits of this in Section 12.8.

On the other hand, where property trading companies or companies engaged in furnished holiday lets are making losses, it may be difficult for them to obtain relief for their interest costs. Personal borrowings by the investor may then be preferable: *if* Income Tax relief is available!

12.7 DEEDS OF TRUST

As explained in Section 1.2, it is sometimes difficult for a company to borrow funds for the purchase of investment property at the same level as a personal investor.

Whereas an 85% LTV may sometimes be possible for an individual, the maximum borrowing afforded to corporate investors is often 70% or less. This, in effect, means having to raise twice as much deposit money when investing via a company.

One way some advisers suggest to resolve this dilemma is for the individual to take legal title to the property in their own name, thus enabling borrowings to be obtained at the desired level. The investor then enters into a 'Deed of Trust' with the company. This is a legal agreement under which the investor agrees the beneficial ownership of the property actually lies with the company and the company agrees to recompense the investor for costs incurred in relation to the property.

The intended effect of the Deed of Trust is therefore to put both the company and the individual investor in the same position they would have been in if the company had purchased the property, while allowing a more favourable level of borrowings to be obtained.

Opinions differ on the effectiveness of this arrangement. Some advisers claim that as long as the Deed of Trust is prepared and executed correctly and its terms adhered to in practice, the position for tax purposes will be just as if the company had legal title to the property.

Others have their doubts and feel the arrangement could be overturned by HMRC or, more importantly, in court, and thus rendered ineffective. In particular, there is a concern that an SDLT charge could arise on a later transfer of the legal title in the property to the company due to the market value rule explained in Section 14.3.

Whatever the position, Deeds of Trust have some important legal implications, so professional advice is essential. In particular, it is important to ensure the arrangement does not invalidate any mortgage agreements relating to the properties involved.

12.8   ROLLING UP INTEREST IN A COMPANY

As explained in Section 4.9, a property investment company can effectively 'roll up' its accumulated interest costs and set them off against the capital gains arising on the sale of its investment properties.

This is clearly much better than the position for individual investors, for whom any surplus interest costs can generally only be relieved against future rental profits: and only at basic rate!

To see what an enormous advantage this provides in practice, let's look at an example.

Example

Brian and Jason are both higher rate taxpayers. They each buy a portfolio of UK residential properties for £1m. They each borrow £750,000 to fund their purchases, on which the interest charge, at 5%, is £37,500 per annum.

Each investor has other allowable costs of £35,000 per annum and each portfolio yields rental income of £60,000. Each portfolio is therefore making an overall profit of £25,000 before interest.

Brian makes his investments through his company, Habana Properties Ltd. The company sets £25,000 of its annual interest cost against its rental profits, leaving it with no CT liability on its rental income. It carries its excess interest costs of £12,500 forward. (If the company had other sources of income it could set this excess against them)

Jason makes his investments personally and therefore has unrelieved surplus interest of £12,500 per year, which he can only carry forward for basic rate tax relief against future rental profits from UK property. He also has an annual Income Tax bill of £5,000: his profit before interest is taxed at 40%; with only basic rate tax relief at 20% for the £25,000 of interest he is able to claim.

After twelve years, Jason and Habana Properties Ltd have each accumulated total unrelieved interest costs of £150,000. We will assume the company has borrowed a further £150,000 to fund the deficit in its rental income, bringing its total borrowings to £900,000. Jason will also have had to borrow a further £60,000 to pay his Income Tax bills, so his total borrowing will now be £960,000. (We will ignore the additional interest costs arising for both investors for the sake of simplicity)

At this point, both investors decide to sell off their portfolio. They each sell their properties for a total of £1.8m, making capital gains of £800,000 before any reliefs.

Jason deducts his annual exemption of £12,300 and is left with taxable gains of £787,700. His CGT liability at 28% amounts to £220,556, leaving him

with net proceeds of £619,444 after repaying his borrowings (£1.8m –
£960,000 – £220,556).

Habana Properties Ltd has a taxable gain of £800,000. The company can set
its unrelieved 'rolled up' interest costs of £150,000 against this gain, leaving
£650,000 chargeable to CT. The company's CT bill, at 19%, therefore amounts
to £123,500.

Factoring in the Income Tax savings already achieved means, **at this stage,**
the company has saved almost £160,000 compared with the
individual investor!

But what if the investor wishes to wind the company up so he can obtain his net
sale proceeds?

Taking account of its borrowings, the company's remaining funds amount to
£776,500 (£1.8m – £900,000 – £123,500). Of this, £250,000 represents the
equity invested by Brian and can be returned to him tax free. Hence, if Brian
takes a small tax-free dividend of £2,000 (his dividend allowance) and then
winds up Habana Properties Ltd, he will have a capital gain of £524,500
(£776,500 – £250,000 – £2,000).

After deducting his annual exemption of £12,300, Brian is left with a taxable
gain of £512,200, giving him a CGT liability, at 20%, of £102,440.

Hence, deducting his CGT bill from his net proceeds of £776,500 (ignoring the
costs of the winding up as usual) we see Brian eventually keeps a net sum of
£674,060, or £54,616 more than Jason.

As we can see from this example, the ability to 'roll up' interest in the
company provides the opportunity to make enormous CT savings. In this
case, the CT bill on a gain of £800,000 was reduced to just over 15%!

Where sale proceeds are being retained in the company for reinvestment,
this will provide a massive advantage over individual investors.

Admittedly, as we can see from the last part of the example, a large part of
the initial savings may effectively be lost if the proceeds are returned to
the individual investor: but, even then, a significant saving may still arise
overall. However, it is important to remember the 'Wealth Warning' in
Section 11.6, which might potentially apply to Brian in this situation.

Note that Jason's unrelieved interest of £150,000 simply goes to waste. In
practice, an investor such as Jason would be well advised to keep at least
part of their portfolio in order to utilise these costs. More advice on
getting value out of unrelieved interest is contained in the Taxcafe.co.uk
guide 'How to Save Property Tax'.

If we reverted to the model used in Chapter 11 and assumed, as an individual, Jason's interest rate would have been a fifth lower than the company's (i.e. 4% instead of 5%), he would still have had an annual Income Tax bill of £5,000 and an eventual CGT bill of £220,556. However, his surplus unrelieved interest costs would have been just £5,000 each year. Combining this yearly loss with his Income Tax bill would mean he had a total annual deficit of £10,000 and borrowings, after twelve years, of £870,000 (£750,000 + 12 x £10,000). His final net proceeds would then have been £709,444 (£1.8m – £870,000 – £220,556) and he would have been £35,384 better off than Brian.

This goes to show that the cost of finance, and the approach to the financing structure used, can make a critical difference to the final outcome: especially when the company is being wound up after the property investments are sold.

12.9   PERSONAL INTEREST RELIEF

At this stage, it is worth taking a look at the benefits of personal Income Tax relief for interest on funds invested in a property company. Before we do that, I must reiterate that the points made in this section are based on the assumption the investor will obtain full Income Tax relief for their interest costs. Everything in this section is therefore subject to the limitations on Income Tax relief that we will examine in Section 12.11.

As we saw in Section 12.4, it will generally be sensible to lend borrowed funds to the company rather than use them to purchase company shares.

In Section 12.3, we saw that borrowing to invest in a property company is not beneficial where the debt has to be serviced by paying dividends to the investor.

Where the personal debt can be serviced by paying interest to the investor, the position is effectively neutral, since the taxable income matches the personal interest relief obtained (subject to the cashflow issue discussed in Section 12.4).

What we have not yet looked at is the position where interest relief is being obtained personally without the need to extract funds from the company to service the debt. Here again, the use of a property investment company will provide enormous advantages over the personal investor due to the more beneficial interest relief regime.

Example
Patrick and Francois both have salaries of £150,000. Each borrows £1m to invest in residential property and incurs annual interest charges, at 5%, of £50,000.

Patrick invests directly in a personal property portfolio. His properties yield a rental profit of £40,000 before interest. This gives rise to an Income Tax charge of £18,000 (at the additional rate of 45%). He claims basic rate relief for £40,000 of his interest costs, reducing his tax bill to £10,000.

The remaining £10,000 of Patrick's interest can only be carried forward for basic rate tax relief against future rental profits.

Francois lends his borrowed funds to his company, Wadyamin Fudpoiznin Ltd, and the company invests in a property portfolio. The company's properties also yield rental profits of £40,000 before interest, giving rise to a CT bill of £7,600 (at 19%).

Meanwhile, Francois claims interest relief for £50,000, providing him with a tax repayment of £25,000 (including an extra £5,000 arising as a result of regaining his personal allowance: see Section 10.2).

*In net terms therefore, Francois and his company receive an overall tax **refund** of £17,400 (£25,000 – £7,600).*

Remarkably, this net refund actually exceeds the overall deficit of £10,000 on Wadyamin Fudpoiznin Ltd's property portfolio (i.e. the deficit that arises after taking Francois' interest costs into account: £50,000 – £40,000).

*In other words, Francois' interest relief has turned an effective **loss** before tax of £10,000 into an effective **profit** after tax of £7,400 (£17,400 – £10,000). The Government is effectively funding Francois' property portfolio and adding a little extra!*

Meanwhile, poor Patrick, who is also making an effective loss before tax of £10,000, has an Income Tax bill of £10,000, giving him a loss after tax of £20,000!

As we can see from this example, where a taxpayer borrows to lend funds to their property company, the tax relief on the interest arising is highly beneficial.

The example also demonstrates that, where rental income is insufficient to cover interest costs, using a company can actually enable the investor to recover their deficit from the Government!

Even when rental profits are being made, the fact that tax relief can be obtained at 40% or even 45% on interest, when company profits are being taxed at only 19%, will continue to provide a significant benefit.

12.10 PROFIT EXTRACTION BENEFITS

Where a director/shareholder lends money to their company, we call this a 'director's loan account'. Director's loan accounts can also be created, or their balance increased, in a number of other ways, including where a director:

- Transfers property into the company for 'cash' left outstanding as a loan account (see Section 14.8)
- Incurs expenses on behalf of the company, including amounts due in respect of business mileage payments or 'use of home' costs
- Takes notional payments, such as salary, dividends, or interest, out of the company and lends them back again (the potential benefits of this were covered in Section 9.7)

Director's loan accounts provide a great deal of scope for additional tax planning. As I have already mentioned a number of times, some or all of the outstanding balance on a director's loan account can be paid to the director tax-free at any time, provided the company has sufficient funds available.

However, as we saw in Section 9.7, it is often preferable to pursue other payment options first, in order to preserve the director's loan account as long as possible. In effect, the sums in the director's loan account have been 'banked' and are available to withdraw tax-free at any time: perhaps when the company owner is suffering higher tax rates on dividends or salary.

A director's loan account also provides the opportunity to pay interest to the shareholder/director, which provides a useful third alternative method of profit extraction.

It is important the rate of interest charged by the director does not exceed a normal commercial rate. Having said that, a typical director's loan account is, in effect, an unsecured loan with no fixed repayment terms: hence, when we come to look at what is a 'normal commercial rate', what we are looking at is more like a business overdraft than a mortgage, and the rate charged can therefore reflect this.

Market rates vary tremendously, and it is important to be aware of these when setting an interest rate for your director's loan account but, at present, a rate of up to 10% would not seem unreasonable for this quasi business overdraft facility. This will, however, depend on your exact circumstances, as there are many other factors to be taken into account. It might therefore make sense to obtain a quote for a business overdraft before you set the interest rate on your director's loan account to provide some evidence that you are using a normal commercial rate.

If you are going to charge interest on your director's loan account, there are some other formalities to be observed. As explained in Section 12.4, you will need to deduct basic rate Income Tax at 20% from your interest charges and account for this to HMRC quarterly, then reclaim any excess tax suffered through your self assessment tax return. Both the level of admin involved and the cashflow disadvantage arising can often be mitigated by making a single annual interest payment shortly before the end of your company's accounting period, but you do need to be careful what tax year the payment falls into in order to ensure you ultimately get the best result for Income Tax purposes.

You will also need some sort of loan agreement between you and the company to give you a legal basis for charging interest; although this document can be kept fairly brief.

Subject to these points, the company will be able to claim CT relief for your interest charges. You, on the other hand, will be subject to Income Tax on the interest receivable. However, interest is not subject to NI, and is tax free if it is covered by your:

i)   Personal allowance (see Appendix A),
ii)   Starting rate band, or
iii)   Personal savings allowance (see Section 9.4)

The starting rate band is currently £5,000. In effect, the starting rate of 0% applies to interest or other savings income that falls into this band, which is currently normally the band of taxable income between £12,500 and £17,500. However, interest and savings income only falls into this band if it is not used up by other taxable income, with the exception of dividends.

Hence, if your other taxable income excluding dividends is no more than £12,500, combining the starting rate band with your personal savings allowance means you can receive up to £6,000 of interest tax-free; although this falls to £5,500 if you then take enough dividends to make you a higher rate taxpayer, or £5,000 if you take enough to make you an additional rate taxpayer.

Even those with other taxable income, excluding dividends, of more than £17,500 can benefit from the personal savings allowance, as we saw in the example in Section 9.7.

Optimum Profit Extraction with Interest
What all this adds up to is the fact that, where you have a director's loan account, interest payments of anything up to a normal commercial rate are a better form of profit extraction than any dividends in excess of the dividend allowance, or any salary that attracts either employer's or employee's NI.

Furthermore, interest payments that are covered by your personal allowance, starting rate band, or personal savings allowance are even better than tax-free dividends covered by your dividend allowance, or any salary that attracts Income Tax, even when it is free from NI. That's because the interest payments are tax-free and also provide CT relief, creating an overall negative tax cost of 19%.

In 2020/21, an individual with no taxable income from outside their company, and a sufficiently large director's loan account balance could take:

- A salary of £8,788 free from Income Tax or NI
- Interest of £3,712 to use up the rest of their personal allowance
- Further interest of £5,000 covered by their starting rate band
- Further interest of £1,000 covered by their personal savings allowance
- A dividend of £2,000 covered by their dividend allowance

That's a total of £20,500 of tax-free income, of which £18,500 attracts CT relief. In other words, not only can you pay yourself £20,500 tax-free, your company will also save £3,515 in the process.

If that's not enough, further interest payments of up to £29,500 will be subject to Income Tax at 20%, but will provide CT relief at 19%, giving you a net cost of just 1%. As we saw in Section 9.7, this may be a better long-term strategy than taking tax-free loan repayments that diminish your ability to charge interest in the future.

Additional interest payments of £29,500 would give rise to Income Tax of £5,900, leaving you with total net, after tax income of £44,100. Meanwhile, the company would now obtain CT relief, at 19%, totalling £9,120. Hence, a net income of £44,100 can be obtained while still achieving an overall net tax saving of £3,220 (£9,120 – £5,900). Assuming an interest rate of 10%, this strategy would require a director's loan account balance of at least £392,120.

(It may, in fact, sometimes be worth paying yet another £2,000 in interest, creating a further CT saving of £380 at an additional Income Tax cost of £500. See Section 9.7 for a detailed analysis.)

Where there is a director's loan account, and the formalities detailed above have been observed, the optimum profit extraction strategy in most cases becomes as set out below. In this case, 'Other Taxable Income' means total taxable income from outside the company, excluding dividends; and we are assuming the employment allowance is not available.

As in Section 9.6, I have worked on the basis that the company owner needs a certain net sum, after tax, in their hands, and looked at the most tax efficient way to achieve this, taking all the relevant factors into account.

Optimum Profit Extraction 2020/21 with Director's Loan Account

Other Taxable Income up to £3,712
- Firstly pay a salary of £8,788 (the secondary NI threshold)
- Secondly pay interest up to the lower of:
  - A normal commercial rate, or
  - The amount required to bring total taxable income, excluding dividends, up to £18,500
- Thirdly pay any dividend covered by the dividend allowance
- Fourthly pay any further interest required to bring the total paid up to a normal commercial rate
- Pay any further amounts required by way of dividend

Other Taxable Income between £3,712 and £12,500
- Firstly pay sufficient salary to bring total taxable income, excluding dividends, up to £12,500
- Secondly pay interest up to the lower of:
  - A normal commercial rate, or
  - £6,000
- Thirdly, pay any dividend covered by the dividend allowance
- Fourthly, pay any further interest required to bring the total paid up to a normal commercial rate
- Pay any further amounts required by way of dividend

Other Taxable Income between £12,500 and £18,500
- Firstly pay interest up to the lower of:
  - A normal commercial rate, or
  - The amount required to bring total taxable income, excluding dividends, up to £18,500
- Secondly pay any dividend covered by the dividend allowance
- Thirdly pay any further interest required to bring the total paid up to a normal commercial rate
- Pay any further amounts required by way of dividend

Other Taxable Income over £18,500
- Firstly pay any dividend covered by the dividend allowance
- Secondly pay a salary of £8,788
- Thirdly pay interest at a normal commercial rate
- Pay any further amounts required by way of dividend

Interaction with Employment Allowance
Where the employment allowance is available (see Section 9.2), salary payments should generally be increased to £9,500, except where other taxable income, excluding dividends, from outside the company is

between £3,000 and £12,500, when they should be limited to the amount required to bring total taxable income, excluding dividends, up to £12,500. As above, no salary should be paid where other taxable income, excluding dividends, from outside the company is between £12,500 and £18,500.

The position will also differ again where the employment allowance is available **and** the investor is over state pension age. In this case, for those with other taxable income, excluding dividends, of less than £12,500, the salary should be the amount required to bring total taxable income, excluding dividends, up to £12,500; no salary should be paid where other taxable income, excluding dividends, is between £12,500 and £18,500; and, in all other cases, interest at a normal commercial rate, and a salary up to the amount that exhausts the employment allowance (see Section 9.2), are equally beneficial.

12.11 LIMITATIONS ON INCOME TAX RELIEF

The total combined amount of Income Tax relief that any individual may claim under a number of reliefs taken together is limited to the greater of £50,000, or 25% of their 'adjusted total income': their taxable income for the year, after deducting gross pension contributions (including tax relief given at source), but before any other reliefs. In effect, for anyone with taxable income of no more £200,000, the limit is £50,000.

The limit applies to individuals only, so it will not directly affect companies; but it will affect investors using a company. Eleven different reliefs are affected. The most important ones for property investors to be aware of are considered below.

Qualifying loan interest: this is precisely the relief we have been talking about throughout this chapter, i.e. relief for interest on personal borrowings used to invest funds in a qualifying company (or partnership: although the relief is now restricted to basic rate only where the partnership invests in residential rental property).

Relief for trading losses against other income: individuals with trading losses can set them off against their other income in the same tax year or the previous one. Additional relief applies in the early years of a trade. (See the taxcafe.co.uk guide *'How to Save Property Tax'* for further details.)

Property loss relief: an individual may set capital allowances within rental losses against their other income for the same tax year. (Again, see *'How to Save Property Tax'* for further details.)

Share loss relief: under certain limited circumstances, owners of some private companies may claim Income Tax relief for losses on their shares. Sadly, this relief is not usually available to property company owners.

Summary for Property Company Investors

In effect, in most cases, individuals with total taxable income of no more than £200,000 have an annual limit of £50,000 on the amount of Income Tax relief they may claim for interest on funds borrowed to invest in property companies (i.e. a maximum deduction from taxable income of £50,000).

Those with total income over £200,000 are subject to a limit equal to the greater of £50,000, or 25% of their income after deducting gross pension contributions.

Further restrictions will apply in cases where the individual is also claiming relief for trading losses, capital allowances within rental losses, or losses on shares in a different (non-property) company.

12.12   INTEREST RELIEF FOR INDIVIDUAL LANDLORDS

Income Tax relief for interest and finance costs relating to residential property lettings made by individuals is now restricted to basic rate only. This restriction does not apply to furnished holiday letting businesses or landlords renting out non-residential property.

Most importantly, it does not apply to companies. Furthermore, it also does **not** apply to individuals claiming relief for interest on funds invested in their own property company (although it does apply to funds invested in a partnership that holds residential rental property).

Relief for interest and finance costs on residential rental property is also restricted to the lower of the landlord's:

i)   Taxable residential rental profits for the year, or
ii)   Total taxable income for the year, excluding dividends, interest, and savings income; after deducting the personal allowance

Any unrelieved excess interest and finance costs eligible for relief at basic rate may be carried forward for relief in future years.

Example

Panashe has both a property investment company and her own private portfolio of residential rental properties. In 2020/21, her private portfolio yields rental profits of £20,000 before deduction of interest and finance costs. She has no other taxable income from outside her company.

Panashe has £12,000 of allowable interest and finance costs. However, the amount eligible for Income Tax relief is restricted to £7,500: the amount by which her taxable income of £20,000 exceeds the personal allowance of £12,500.

As things stand, Panashe has no tax to pay and unrelieved interest and finance costs of £4,500 to carry forward.

This example illustrates the only bit of good news about the interest relief restrictions: landlords like Panashe, whose overall income is quite low, are able to carry forward some of their interest and finance costs rather than set them against income covered by their personal allowance.

The position will alter if Panashe takes a salary out of her company (note, her interest relief will be unaffected if she pays herself a dividend or interest from her company).

Nonetheless, Panashe could take a salary of £4,500 out of her company with no immediate Income Tax cost. The salary would increase her taxable income to £24,500 but she would then get basic rate tax relief on the whole £12,000 of her allowable interest and finance costs, leaving her with no Income Tax to pay.

In a sense, Panashe can be regarded as having a maximum tax-free salary of £4,500. However, while the salary is tax free this year, there are no longer any excess interest and finance costs to be carried forward. This could lead to increased Income Tax in a future year if Panashe starts to make profits *after* interest in excess of the personal allowance from her private portfolio. She may also suffer future Income Tax increases if she begins to receive other taxable income from outside the company.

It is also important to remember, while she has no Income Tax to pay, her taxable income is now £24,500, meaning she has less scope to take dividends or interest from her company taxed at the basic rates of 7.5% or 20% respectively.

None of this means the salary is not a good idea; it is just that these factors need to be taken into account. In fact, if paying the salary is the only way Panashe is ever likely to get relief for her interest and finance costs, it is probably the best thing to do. Remember the salary will attract CT relief (subject to the points discussed in Section 9.2). In effect, this means the company is getting relief for personal interest costs that would otherwise have gone unrelieved.

For further details on the restriction in tax relief for individual landlords' interest and finance costs, see the Taxcafe.co.uk guides *'How to Save Property Tax'* and *'The Big Landlord Tax Increase'*.

Chapter 13

How to Set Up Your Own Property Company

13.1 WHO CAN HELP AND HOW MUCH DOES IT COST?

If you decide to go ahead and form a property company, it is pretty easy to do. There are a number of websites available that enable you to complete the task online at minimal cost.

If you feel you need further assistance, most lawyers can form a company for you, as well as many accountants. Some have so-called 'off-the-shelf' companies available for use at a moment's notice.

If you use a lawyer or accountant to assist with the task, or need to set up a specialised share structure, the costs may be significantly more, perhaps as much as £500 to £2,500 in some cases.

13.2 THE COMPANY'S CONSTITUTION

The company's constitution is embodied in two documents, its Memorandum of Association, and its Articles of Association.

The Memorandum covers what the company is empowered to do and sets out the framework for its share structure. Most modern Memorandums of Association empower the company to do pretty much anything. For a property company, it is important to ensure the company has the power to borrow money, buy or sell land and property, and rent out, or grant leases over, property (as well as anything else you are expecting the company to do).

The Articles of Association govern the rights of holders of each class of shares (there only needs to be one class, but there can be more), as well as the power to appoint or remove directors or auditors (where necessary) and the conduct of general meetings of the company's members.

The company will need a registered office address, which must be occupied and cannot be a mere P.O. box. The company's name should be displayed prominently at the registered address and its statutory books and records should usually be kept there.

A UK company can be registered in Scotland, in Northern Ireland, or in England and Wales, depending on where its registered office is located.

You will need to appoint at least one person to serve as a director. You may also need to appoint a company secretary if required by your company's Articles of Association. (A company secretary is no longer a mandatory requirement but many company's constitutions still require one.)

Directors and company secretaries are referred to as the company's 'officers'. You will need to provide Companies House with a home address for each officer. You can also provide a 'service address' for each officer. The service address will appear on the public record and can therefore be used to keep the officers' home addresses private. If you do not provide a service address, the officer's home address will be made public!

The company's registered office address can be used as the service address for one or more of the company's officers, if desired. A service address must again be occupied and not a mere P.O. Box.

The owners of shares in the company are referred to as 'members'. A company must have at least one member. Until a few years ago, companies had to have at least two members.

A UK company may either be a private company or a public limited company (PLC). Most companies are private companies and there is little point in being a PLC unless you are seeking a stock-market quotation.

The act of forming a company is referred to as 'incorporation'. The day on which the company is formed is known as its 'date of incorporation'. Once you have formed your company, it can go ahead and borrow money or purchase properties. Provided the lenders are willing to co-operate of course!

13.3   OTHER COMPANY FORMATION FORMALITIES

Shortly after you register your company with Companies House, you will receive a letter from them congratulating you on your new company and advising you of some of your responsibilities as a company director.

You will also receive a form CT41G from HMRC. You should complete and return this form in order to get the company into the CT system. It is important to do this within three months of when the company commences any business activities, as penalties will be imposed if you do not return the completed form within this timescale. This process is now generally completed online.

You will often need to register the company as an employer for PAYE purposes. Remember that paying yourself, your spouse, or partner, a small salary may be enough to mean the company must register. You may also need to register the company for VAT, if applicable (see Section 15.1).

In some cases, you will need to submit a 'Form 42' to HMRC by 6th July following the end of the tax year in which the company's shares are issued. This form provides details of shares issued to a company's employees, including directors, and may need to be submitted again following any further share issues. Form 42 is not generally required in the case of a new company incorporation where the company issues a single class of ordinary shares to one or more shareholder/directors with no previous employment relationship with the business.

13.4   YOUR COMPANY'S ACCOUNTING DATE

Initially, the company's accounting date will automatically be set as the date falling twelve months after the end of the month in which the company was incorporated. However, a company's accounting year-end date does not need to permanently remain the same calendar date and can generally be changed.

Generally speaking, in order to change the company's accounting date, you simply need to submit form AA01 to Companies House any time before the earlier of the filing deadline for the accounts based on its original accounting date and the filing deadline based on the revised accounting date you are requesting (see Section 13.6 for details of Companies House filing deadlines).

Subject to a few restrictions, a company may change its accounting date at any time. This generally happens most often at the beginning of a company's life due to the application of the initial rule explained above.

Naturally, where a change is made to the accounting date, for whatever reason, the company will have a short or long accounting period (i.e. a period other than a year). This has some important consequences for the company's CT position and we will look at these in Section 15.4.

13.5   DEALING WITH COMPANIES HOUSE

You will need to advise Companies House of changes in the company's:

- Directors (or their particulars: name, home address, service address)
- Company Secretary (or their particulars)
- Registered Office
- Accounting Date (as explained in Section 13.4)
- Issued share capital
- Charges (i.e. mortgages and other secured loans)

The last point is particularly significant for property companies. It is important to ensure charges over the company's properties are registered with Companies House and the details are kept up to date.

There are also two things Companies House will require from you on an annual basis: statutory accounts (see Section 13.6), and a confirmation statement.

The confirmation statement provides details of the company's share capital and shareholders. A notice to complete the statement will be sent to the company's registered office a few weeks in advance of the filing deadline, which is usually 14 days after the anniversary of the date of incorporation, but can change if you submit details to an earlier date (the deadline has temporarily been extended to 42 days where it would otherwise fall between 27th June 2020 and 6th April 2021). This process now generally takes place online and, in many cases, simply requires you to confirm no changes have taken place.

13.6   STATUTORY ACCOUNTS

Every company must prepare a set of statutory accounts for each accounting period. These accounts must adhere to a standard format specified by Company Law and either UK generally accepted accounting practice (sometimes referred to as 'GAAP') or International Financial Reporting Standards ('IFRS').

The statutory accounts must be filed with Companies House and must also be submitted to HMRC together with the company's Corporation Tax Return, as explained in Section 2.6.

Small companies (see below) may prepare and file abridged accounts, which provide less detail on the company's activities. This is to ensure smaller companies do not need to make too many of their business dealings public. Remember, accounts held at Companies House are part of the public record and can be seen by anyone, so I would generally recommend abridged accounts are prepared whenever possible.

Broadly speaking, a company is 'small' for these purposes if it meets at least two of the following tests:

i)   Turnover (i.e. gross income) does not exceed £6.5m per annum
ii)   Total asset value does not exceed £3.26m
iii)   It has no more than 50 employees

It is important to note test (ii) is based on **gross** asset values (i.e. the total value of the company's properties and other assets, with no deduction in respect of borrowings and other liabilities). Nonetheless, most property companies tend to qualify as 'small' on the basis they meet tests (i) and (iii).

Companies that qualify as 'small' do not usually require an audit, although there is nothing to stop you having an audit if you wish. An audit of the company's accounts **must** be carried out by a firm of qualified accountants registered to carry out audit work. Most other people operating a business through a company usually find they need the services of an accountant, even if they don't need an audit. In this case, there are no legal requirements regarding the type of accountant you must use, although I would generally recommend you use a firm of qualified chartered accountants.

Statutory accounts are usually prepared on an annual basis, although other accounting periods may sometimes be used, generally up to a maximum of 18 months. We will look at the CT consequences of this in Section 15.4.

Where it has been necessary to prepare additional, more detailed, accounts for CT purposes, these should not be filed with Companies House.

Private companies must generally file the appropriate statutory accounts at Companies House within nine months of their accounting date, although this deadline has been temporarily extended to twelve months where it would otherwise fall into the period between 27th June 2020 and 5th April 2021.

The company's **first** set of accounts must, however, be filed by the **earlier** of nine months from the accounting date, or 21 months from the date of incorporation (temporarily extended to twelve and 24 months respectively where the deadline would otherwise fall into the period between 27th June 2020 and 5th April 2021).

As with taxation, there are harsh penalties for late filing. Extensions to the filing deadline are, however, sometimes granted. You must apply to Companies House directly (and in advance), for these.

Wealth Warning
Do not confuse Companies House requirements with HMRC's requirements. Both institutions require a set of accounts from you each year, usually with different deadlines. Complying with one institution's requirements will not satisfy the other, and you will suffer penalties if you make the mistake of thinking it does.

13.7   PROPERTY REVALUATIONS

Investment properties (including most rental properties) must be shown in statutory accounts at their current market value. This creates the need to carry out regular valuations: an additional administrative burden resulting from the use of a property company.

In practice, most companies only carry out formal valuations of their investment properties every few years. This is considered acceptable provided the previous valuation still provides a reasonable reflection of the properties' value during the intervening years.

For accounting purposes, increases in the value of investment properties are included in the company's profit and loss account. This, however, is only a matter of presentation since, where the properties are still held by the company, any increase in value over and above their original cost is not included in the company's taxable profits and is not considered part of the company's distributable profits for the purpose of paying dividends.

It is only when an investment property is sold that the resultant profit is taxed (as a capital gain) and is available for distribution as a dividend (after accounting for the resultant tax liability).

Chapter 14

How to Put Existing Property into a Company

14.1   INTRODUCTION

The basic problem with transferring anything into your company is the fact you and the company will generally be 'connected' (see Section 14.2). As explained in Section 6.2, this means, in principle, transfers of assets between you and the company will be deemed to take place at market value for CGT purposes. Furthermore, as explained in Section 14.3, transfers of property to a 'connected company' may also be deemed to take place at market value for SDLT purposes.

Potentially, therefore, you could face a huge tax bill if you transfer existing properties into a company.

In this chapter, we will look at how and when such huge tax charges can be avoided, or at least mitigated. We will also look at when it may make sense to bear the charges in order to make greater savings in the long term.

In other cases, you may conclude the cost of putting an existing property portfolio into a company is not worthwhile and we will look at some potential alternative strategies in Section 14.21, at the end of the chapter.

Before that, let's look at how the rules work on a transfer of property into a company, so at least you know what you're up against. We will start with SDLT but, first of all, what exactly is a 'connected company'?

14.2   WHAT IS A CONNECTED COMPANY?

You are automatically 'connected' with a company if you, either alone, or together with 'connected persons', control it. Appendix B provides a list of people deemed to be 'connected persons' for this purpose.

Control is usually taken to mean a person, or group of persons, hold over 50% of the company's ordinary share capital. If there is one class of shares, it's as simple as that, but more complex share structures will also make the definition of 'control' more complex.

Hence if you and your spouse, close relatives, any business partners you have, and any trust you've set up, own over 50% of the share capital, you're automatically connected with the company.

Additionally, you are also deemed to be 'connected' with a company if you, acting together with one or more other persons, are able to exercise control over that company. In this case, those 'other persons' do not need to appear on the list in Appendix B, so this would include unmarried partners, nephews, nieces, friends, just about anyone, in fact.

This additional rule requires you to be 'acting together' so, unlike the rule for 'connected persons', it doesn't automatically apply in every case.

Nonetheless, what this does mean is the only way to transfer property to a company you're not connected with is to have no control over it. And who would want to do that?

In short, if you're a private property investor wishing to operate through a company, you can assume you will be connected with it and (subject to the exemptions we will explore in this chapter) transfers of property to the company will generally be deemed to take place at market value for the purposes of both CGT and SDLT.

14.3   STAMP DUTY LAND TAX ON TRANSFERS

The general rule is that transfers of UK property to a connected company (see Section 14.2) give rise to SDLT liabilities based on the greater of:

- The amount of consideration actually paid by the company, or
- The market value of the properties transferred

The higher SDLT charges set out in Section 8.4 apply in the case of residential property.

'Consideration' for this purpose will include not only any amount actually paid, or payable, by the company, but will also include the amount of any mortgages or other loans over the properties the company takes over. 'Consideration' also includes the value of any shares issued in exchange for the properties.

There is a major exception to the above rules in the case of transfers from a partnership. We will look at how this may benefit existing partnerships in Section 14.6, and how others might benefit in Section 14.18.

In the meantime, let's look at what happens where this exception does not apply.

14.4   MULTIPLE TRANSFERS

Where a whole business is transferred (e.g. to obtain incorporation relief or business asset disposal relief: see Sections 14.9 and 7.3), all the property transfers will amount to 'linked transactions' (Section 8.8). Any other simultaneous transfers of more than one property will also be 'linked transactions', as will all the transfers in any pre-arranged series of transfers.

Residential Property
Even taking multiple dwellings relief (see Section 8.8) into account, the SDLT applying to multiple transfers of residential property into a company is likely to be at least 3% of the total value of the properties transferred: more in some cases.

Example 'F'
Finn has a residential property portfolio made up of 20 properties with a total value of £6m. In April 2021, he transfers the properties to his company, Russell Rentals Ltd, and claims multiple dwellings relief. The average value of each property is £300,000, so the SDLT charge is as follows:

First £125,000 @ 3%:	£3,750
Next £125,000 @ 5%:	£6,250
Next £50,000 @ 8%	£4,000
Total per property:	£14,000
x 20 =	£280,000

The overall effective rate of SDLT on the transfer is 4.67%.

Finn could have made a substantial saving by transferring his properties to his company during the current SDLT 'holiday' (Section 8.4). We will revisit this in Section 14.22 to see how much he would have saved.

Transfers of six or more residential dwellings may be treated as non-residential property instead for the purposes of SDLT charges. Whether this is helpful or not depends on the exact circumstances. In Finn's case, this would increase the SDLT charge to £289,500, so it would not be beneficial (but see Section 8.8 for an example where a saving does arise).

Where any residential dwelling within the transfer has a value in excess of £500,000 and is not being used for business purposes, the rate of SDLT applying to that property will be 15% (see Sections 8.6 and 15.6 for further details).

Where a transfer of residential property to a company deemed to be non-UK resident for SDLT purposes takes place after 31st March 2021, the additional 2% non-resident surcharge will apply. Note the definition of a 'non-UK resident company' for this purpose is different to other tax definitions: see Section 8.5 for details.

Non-Residential Property

The rates applying to non-residential property will again be based on the total value of the properties transferred and could therefore be almost 5% in some cases (see Chapter 8).

Example 'G'
Sonia owns a portfolio of commercial property (shops and offices) with a total value of £1.5m. She transfers the portfolio to her company, Pitchside Properties Ltd. The SDLT arising is as follows:

First £150,000 @ 0%:	*£0*
Next £100,000 @ 2%:	*£2,000*
Next £1.25m @ 5%:	*£62,500*
Total:	*£64,500*

The overall effective rate of SDLT on the transfer is thus 4.3%.

Summary

Transfers of property into a company are likely to lead to SDLT charges at effective overall rates of at least 3% for residential property and up to 5% for non-residential property. In many cases, these charges are quite prohibitive and can make it impractical for the property owner to make the transfer. There is one major exception to these rules: which we will examine in Section 14.6.

14.5   TRANSFERRING OTHER ASSETS

SDLT only applies to the transfer of land and property, so the value of other assets can be disregarded for these purposes. When transferring a whole business it will be necessary to make an apportionment.

Example
Chris transfers his property development business, worth £1m, to Paterson Developments Ltd in exchange for shares. The business value is made up of:

	£
Office premises	*100,000*
Work-in-progress & land bank	*300,000*
Building materials in stock	*50,000*
Plant and machinery	*100,000*
Motor vehicles	*50,000*
Debtors	*550,000*
Goodwill	*100,000*
	1,250,000
Less Creditors	*-250,000*
	1,000,000

Of these, only the office premises and work-in-progress would be subject to SDLT. This gives a total value of £400,000 subject to Duty. The exact amount of SDLT payable would depend on the nature of the properties within work-in-progress, but it is likely to be at least £9,500.

Tax Tip
When transferring a property development business to a company, it is worth trying to time the transfer at a point when the business has as little work-in-progress on hand as possible, including its land bank. This will help to reduce the amount of SDLT arising on the transfer.

Alternatively, by using the 'gifts of business assets' route (see Section 14.8), the transferor could refrain from transferring any work-in-progress, thus reducing their exposure to SDLT.

14.6   PARTNERSHIP TRANSFERS

A transfer of properties from a partnership business to a company will often enjoy substantial or complete exemption from SDLT. To obtain the exemption, the company needs to be 'connected' with one or more of the partners (see further below). If it is 'connected' with all/both partners, complete exemption is available.

The good news is a company will generally be 'connected' with all/both partners whenever the same individuals own that company.

Hence, **most transfers of partnership property into the partners' own company will be completely exempt from SDLT!**

We covered the question of when an individual is connected with a company in Section 14.2. However, for the purposes of the SDLT partnership exemption, individuals are not classed as 'connected persons' simply because they are business partners (i.e. heading (vi) in Appendix B is disregarded in this case).

What this means is where a partnership is made up of a married couple, or relatives falling under headings (ii) to (v) in Appendix B (or trusts falling under heading (vii)), a transfer of property into a company owned by the same individuals will usually be completely exempt from SDLT.

For other partnerships, complete exemption remains available provided all/both partners are individuals acting together to control the company. This will usually be the case, but there will be exceptions.

The exemption applies equally to LLPs (although these are not usually a good vehicle through which to invest in property due to some even more restrictive rules on interest relief and loss relief).

208

However, it does not generally apply for corporate partners (i.e. companies or other non-natural persons), unless they are also the company to which the property is being transferred.

Some or all of the exemption may be lost if SDLT has not been properly paid on the partnership's acquisition of all its properties, or if SDLT has not been paid in full on previous changes in partnership profit shares (see the Taxcafe.co.uk guide 'How to Save Property Tax' for details). For transactions that took place before 20th October 2003, the equivalent Stamp Duty requirements (and payments) must have been met. In cases of doubt seek professional advice.

Some people have put forward the view that a property portfolio that is jointly owned by a married couple, or by any two individuals, is effectively a partnership, even if not formally constituted as one. I am afraid I disagree and would regard a formally constituted partnership as being necessary for the exemption to apply. It will also be essential that Partnership Tax Returns have been submitted (see the Taxcafe.co.uk guide 'How to Save Property Tax' for further details).

In Section 14.18, we will look at the process of forming a partnership and the costs and benefits involved. If done carefully, it may be possible for most property investors to ultimately use this to gain complete exemption from SDLT on a subsequent transfer of the partnership business into a company. Even where complete exemption is not possible, the SDLT cost may be reduced significantly.

However, while some people are suggesting it is only necessary to form a partnership for a brief period, I am not comfortable with this idea as there is anti-avoidance legislation that could be used to overturn the exemption in such a case. I will look at this issue further in Section 14.18.

In the meantime, it is clear that a transfer of property from a long-term, well-established, partnership to a company owned by the same individuals will usually be completely exempt from SDLT.

Partial Exemption
Where all/both partners are not deemed to be 'connected' with the company, partial exemption may still be available. Generally speaking, the exemption is then based on the profit shares held by the partner, or partners, who are 'connected' with the company.

A partial exemption might arise in the case of a retiring partner.

Example Part 1
Sheree and Jenny are a married couple. They are in a property investment partnership with their friend Megan. Each of the partners has a one third profit share. Megan would now like to retire, but Sheree and Jenny wish to carry on the business through a new company, Hamilton Holdings Ltd.

The partnership holds 20 residential properties, worth a total of £6m, which are transferred to the company. Sheree and Jenny receive shares in exchange for their partnership shares and the company agrees to pay Megan £2.1m for her share.

Sheree and Jenny are deemed to be 'connected' with the company, but Megan is not. Sheree and Jenny's partnership profit shares total two thirds, so the deemed consideration for the transfer is reduced by two thirds for SDLT purposes. This reduces the deemed consideration from £6m to £2m, or an average of £100,000 per property, giving rise to an SDLT charge of £60,000 (£100,000 x 3% x 20) with multiple dwellings relief (see Section 8.8).

If we compare this with the SDLT paid on the transfer of a similar portfolio from an individual to a company (see Example 'F' in Section 14.4), we see the SDLT charge has been reduced from £280,000 to £60,000. In other words, the two thirds exemption has reduced the SDLT charge by much more than two thirds (by almost 80%, in fact).

(As we will see in Section 14.22, the SDLT arising on the transfer of such a portfolio from an individual to a company during the current SDLT 'holiday' would be reduced to £180,000. However, there is still a substantial saving.)

Practical Pointer

Partial exemption may be worth more than you think as it reduces the deemed consideration rather than the SDLT charge. Where partial exemption applies the deemed consideration will be the appropriate proportion of the properties' total market value. Any actual consideration paid by the company is disregarded.

Example Part 2

Let us now suppose it is Jenny who wishes to retire and Sheree and Megan will continue in business using the new company. Sheree and Megan are not 'connected persons' for the purposes of the SDLT exemption (as heading (vi) in Appendix B is disregarded for this purpose), BUT they are both connected with the company because they are acting together to control it (see Section 14.2). Hence, the two thirds exemption for SDLT purposes continues to apply.

In this second scenario, a small change in the shareholdings might restore full SDLT exemption.

Example Part 3

Let us now suppose that, although Jenny wishes to retire, she still takes a 1% shareholding in Hamilton Holdings Ltd. Sheree has 50% and Megan has 49%. As Sheree and Jenny are 'connected persons', and together hold more than 50% of the company's shares, they are both deemed to be 'connected' with the company. Megan is also deemed to be 'connected' with the company provided she and Sheree are 'acting together' to control it. Hence, complete SDLT exemption can be obtained on the transfer of the partnership's properties: as long as Megan is willing to co-operate!

Another reason partial exemption might arise is where a partner who is otherwise not 'connected' with the other partners does not take an active role in the new company. For example, if it had been Megan who took a 1% shareholding in the new company, it is unlikely she could be regarded as 'connected' with the company, so the SDLT exemption would have remained two thirds. Each case will have to be decided on its facts as it all depends whether the partners are 'acting together' to control the company. This issue is not based on the size of their shareholdings alone.

14.7   CAPITAL GAINS TAX ON TRANSFERS

As far as CGT is concerned, there are two reliefs available that may potentially resolve the problem discussed in Section 14.1 in some cases. Careful use of these reliefs may even create additional tax advantages for those with the 'right kind' of property business.

These important CGT reliefs are relief for 'Gifts of Business Assets', and 'Incorporation Relief'. Whether either or both of these reliefs are available, and the extent to which they may be used to defer, or even reduce, your potential CGT liabilities, will depend on the exact nature of your property business in the past, the present and the future.

Tax Tip
Both of these reliefs are available when the business qualifies for them at the time of the transfer. The business does not need to continue to qualify for any particular period after the transfer. This creates some significant tax-planning opportunities, which we will explore later in this chapter.

I would, however, suggest that the business generally needs to continue for some period after the transfer, or else the qualifying activity might be regarded as no more than an artificial sham.

Where the business qualifies for one of the CGT reliefs discussed above, the relief is available to transferor individuals, partnerships, or trusts.

14.8   GIFTS OF 'BUSINESS ASSETS'

The first of the potential CGT reliefs available is something of a misnomer since the relief will generally only apply to trading assets, rather than what the average person would regard as a business asset. Within tax legislation, 'business' is a much wider term than 'trade' and, as we have discussed already, property investment or property letting is not usually considered to be a 'trade' for tax purposes.

Hence, this relief is unlikely to be available to a property investment or property letting business, although we will return to this subject in Section 14.14.

Relief for 'gifts of business assets' is available to a property development or furnished holiday letting business. It should, in fact, be available to any business classed as a 'trade' (see Chapter 3), although we will return to this point in Section 14.12.

The relief is available where you transfer qualifying 'trading' properties to your company for no consideration, or for a consideration less than market value. For this relief, it is not necessary to transfer the whole business, as the relief can be claimed in respect of any asset used in a qualifying trade.

Hence, for example, an individual who used both an office and a warehouse in their property development business could claim relief on a 'gift' of the warehouse to a company while still retaining personal ownership of the office.

The relief works by allowing the capital gain that arises on the transfer under the normal rules to be 'held over'. This means the individual making the transfer has no CGT liability, but it also means the base cost (see Section 6.3) of the assets transferred to the company is reduced by the amount of gain 'held over'.

Where the asset is only partly used in the qualifying trade, or has been used in the qualifying trade for only part of the transferor's period of ownership, the amount of gain that may be 'held over' is proportionately reduced. This will usually mean some CGT liability still arises on the transfer.

The relief is not automatic and a joint claim must be made by the transferor and the recipient company, using a prescribed form.

Example

Tom runs a property development business from his office in Glasgow. He transfers the whole business, including his office, into a new company, Smith Developments Ltd. Tom bought his office for £100,000 in March 2000 and has used it as his trading premises ever since. Its current market value is £250,000, but Tom 'gifts' the property (i.e. transfers it for no consideration) to Smith Developments Ltd in March 2021.

Under the normal rules, Tom would have a capital gain of £150,000. However, if Tom and his company jointly elect to 'hold over', he will have no chargeable capital gain. Smith Developments Ltd's base cost in the property will be its market value, £250,000, less the 'held over' gain of £150,000, plus the SDLT arising on the transfer (£2,000), i.e. £102,000.

As we can see, in this case, the company ends up with the same base cost as the individual (plus the additional SDLT arising on the transfer).

Tom's actual capital gain (had he not elected to 'hold over') would have qualified for business asset disposal relief and therefore would probably have been subject to CGT at just 10% (see Section 7.3). Hence, assuming his annual exemption of £12,300 was available, his potential CGT bill may have been as low as £13,770.

Against this, we must weigh the fact that a sale of the property by the company after the transfer would give rise to a CT bill of at least £28,120 (at 19%).

It's a case of a small amount of tax now versus a much greater amount of potential tax in the future. This presents us with a bit of a dilemma and we will return to this point in Section 14.11.

Tax Tip

Rather than 'gifting' assets to the company for no consideration, it is often worth selling them for a small sum in order to utilise the transferor individual's available reliefs.

The 'gifts of business assets' relief can still be used to 'hold over' the element of the gain that arises only due to the 'deemed' sale proceeds at market value rule, with the individual's CGT calculation then proceeding on the basis of the actual consideration.

With many new companies, this is often done by agreeing a sale price for the asset and allowing that sum to be left outstanding as a loan from the transferor to the company.

The loan may be paid back to the transferor as the company's funds permit, giving the transferor what is essentially a tax-free income from the company until the loan is paid off.

Example Revisited

In the above example, Tom could have transferred the office property to Smith Developments Ltd for £112,300. After electing to 'hold over' the amount representing the difference between market value and actual consideration (£137,700), this would leave him with a capital gain of £12,300.

This gain would then be covered by his annual CGT exemption, leaving him with no tax to pay and a 'tax-free' sum of £112,300, which he can draw upon as funds permit.

Meanwhile, Smith Developments Ltd's base cost is £12,300 more than it would have been and this will save at least £2,337 in CT on a sale of the property (at 19%).

213

Interaction with Structures and Buildings Allowance ('SBA')

The gain 'held over' on a 'gift of business assets' will be increased by the amount of any SBA claimed by the transferor (see Section 4.6). This will effectively reduce the relevant property's base cost by the amount of SBA claimed. Nonetheless, the SBA claim will remain worthwhile as it will have provided the transferor with Income Tax relief at 20%, 40% or even more, and the resultant future increase in the capital gain arising on the company's sale of the property will only be subject to CT at 19%.

14.9   INCORPORATION RELIEF

Technically, this relief should be available whenever any 'business' is transferred to a company wholly or partly in exchange for shares.

A huge area of difficulty arises in determining exactly what constitutes a 'business' for this purpose. Certainly, anything deemed to be a 'trade' (see Chapter 3) must also qualify as a 'business', as will furnished holiday lets.

Beyond this, matters become unclear. There is no statutory definition of what constitutes a business for the purposes of incorporation relief.

For a long time, there was no relevant case law to fall back on either but the case of 'Elisabeth Moyne Ramsay v Revenue and Customs Commissioners' (the 'Ramsay case') finally shed some light on this issue a few years ago and we will therefore return to the tricky question of what constitutes a qualifying business for the purposes of incorporation relief in Section 14.15.

For now let's concentrate on how the relief works. Incorporation relief works along similar principles to relief for 'gifts of business assets', except:

- The transferor must transfer the whole of their business as a 'going concern'
- The assets transferred only need to be in use in the business at the point of transfer. Unlike the relief for 'gifts of business assets', there is no restriction to the relief if the assets have not been in business use throughout the transferor's ownership (but see the 'Tax Tip' in Section 14.12)
- The transfer must be made wholly or partly in exchange for shares in the transferee company (the relief will only apply to the part of the sale consideration that is satisfied in shares)
- The gain 'held over' is deducted from the transferor individual's base cost in the shares and not from the value of the underlying assets transferred. In effect (where the transfer is made wholly in exchange for shares), this means the transferor's CGT base cost for those shares becomes the same as the base cost they had for the underlying assets.

- It also follows that the new base costs the company has in the assets transferred are the assets' market values at the date of transfer. This provides a unique opportunity to 'step up' the base cost of those assets and thus save a fortune on their ultimate sale. We will look at this further in Section 14.16.
- Any SBA claimed by the transferor (see Section 4.6) must be added to the proceeds received by the company on the ultimate sale of the relevant property (in addition to any SBA claimed by the company itself). While this will increase the gain subject to CT at 19%, the earlier claims remain worthwhile as they will have provided Income Tax relief at 20%, 40%, or more.
- Where the necessary conditions apply, the relief is given automatically. The transferor may, however, elect to disapply the relief. Why would they want to disapply it: see the warning below

Wealth Warning

Incorporation relief will eliminate, or at least reduce, the CGT arising on the transfer of a qualifying business to a company. However, it is essential to remember this will mean any available business asset disposal relief is not claimed.

Usually, of course, where business asset disposal relief was available on the business, then it will also be available on the company shares and, for share disposals after 5th April 2019, there will generally be no need to hold the shares for any particular period (see Section 7.3).

In some cases, however, there may be a risk the company will not qualify as the transferor's 'personal company' (see Section 7.3) and the chance to claim business asset disposal relief will effectively have been lost. In these cases, it may sometimes be better to disapply incorporation relief.

An election to disapply incorporation relief must normally be made by the second anniversary of the 31st January after the tax year in which the transfer took place. For example, for a transfer made during 2020/21, the normal deadline is 31st January 2024.

However, if the transferor has disposed of all the shares received as consideration for the transfer by the end of the next tax year after the transfer, the deadline is accelerated by a year.

14.10   WHICH RELIEF IS BEST?

In some cases, both relief for 'gifts of business assets' and incorporation relief may potentially be available to prevent any CGT liability arising on the transfer of a property business into a company. In such cases, it is generally possible to choose which of the reliefs you wish to use.

215

Actually, when I say it is possible to 'choose' which relief is used, this choice is made by the way you structure the transaction used to transfer your business.

In essence, by making the transfer of your whole business, wholly or partly in exchange for shares, you will effectively be 'choosing' incorporation relief (as it is then automatic). Alternatively, by transferring qualifying trading properties into a company for no consideration, or a consideration less than market value (and which, if you are transferring your whole business, does not consist wholly or partly of shares), you will be able to claim relief for 'gifts of business assets'. All of this assuming your business qualifies for the reliefs of course!

The best choice will depend on your future plans and expectations for the properties and business being transferred. In general, however, the relief for 'gifts of business assets' offers far greater flexibility, both in terms of the assets that are to be transferred and in the choice of the level of CGT to be paid.

Furthermore, the ability to use the relief for 'gifts of business assets' to create what is effectively a source of tax-free income, as we saw in Section 14.8, means this is often the preferred route.

In the second part of the example in Section 14.8, we looked at a situation where the consideration was fixed at the maximum level that still left the transferor with no CGT to pay. In practice, however, where business asset disposal relief is available, many transferors will choose to pay some CGT at just 10%, in order to increase the level of the loan account, which they can later draw upon tax free. For higher rate taxpayers, the 10% CGT bill is far less than the tax arising on withdrawals made by way of salary or dividend (see Chapter 9).

Hence, in effect, by using the relief for 'gifts of business assets' (where available) you can actually choose how much CGT you want to pay on the transfer and effectively 'bank' the sum that has been taxed and withdraw it later with no further tax to pay.

Admittedly, similar results can be achieved with incorporation relief, by using a mixture of shares and cash as consideration for the transfer of the business, but it is much more difficult to judge this correctly in order to achieve the desired result.

Using the relief for 'gifts of business assets' also means you can keep the share capital in your company at a low level; thus enabling you to withdraw your investment far more easily. By contrast, to use incorporation relief, you will generally need to issue large amounts of share capital, making it difficult for you to withdraw your investment from the company.

Incorporation relief also requires you to transfer your whole business. This could mean having to transfer properties and other assets you did not wish to transfer. Unless you are operating as a partnership, it also maximises your SDLT exposure (see Sections 14.3 and 14.6).

By using the relief for 'gifts of business assets' you can effectively 'cherry pick' the properties and other assets you wish to transfer. Note, however, that business asset disposal relief is only available where the assets transferred constitute a distinct part of the business capable of being operated as a going concern in its own right (see the Taxcafe.co.uk guide *'How to Save Property Tax'* for a detailed examination of this point).

Incorporation relief does, however, have two major advantages over relief for 'gifts of business assets'.

Firstly, as explained in Section 14.9, with incorporation relief there is no reduction in the amount of gain that may be 'held over' if the assets have not been used in the business throughout the transferor's ownership. In some cases, this may enable the owner of business property to obtain relief for their whole capital gain, rather than just part of it.

Secondly, of course, there is the ability for the company to get a 'step up' in the base cost of the assets transferred to their current market values.

In some cases, however, the 'step up' in base cost will be of limited value when the business is eligible for business asset disposal relief and the maximum CGT exposure for the transferor is thus only 10%.

Add to this the fact that most property business transfers will attract SDLT (unless the partnership rules apply: see Sections 14.3 and 14.6) and we can see the benefit of the 'step up' may sometimes be quite doubtful when business asset disposal relief is also available.

Nevertheless, there are occasions when the 'step up' in base cost offered by incorporation relief will be valuable, especially when the use of the properties being transferred is expected to change. We will explore some opportunities for tax planning with incorporation relief in Section 14.16.

In general, however, it is fair to say, where both reliefs are available, most people will benefit more from the relief for 'gifts of business assets'.

14.11 PAY NOW, SAVE LATER

As we have already discussed, where a property business is eligible for business asset disposal relief, the CGT rate the owner will suffer on a transfer into a company is just 10% (on the first £1m of capital gains per person; £10m for transfers before 11th March 2020).

There is therefore a strong argument for saying, in these circumstances, it is better not to claim either of the two hold over reliefs discussed in the previous section since, by paying 10% now, the transferor may achieve greater savings in the future.

Furthermore, as we discussed in the previous section, this will allow the transferor to withdraw substantial sums from the company tax free.

Example
Leigh is a higher rate taxpayer with a furnished holiday letting business in Devon. In March 2021, Leigh transfers all his furnished holiday lets into Halfpenny Lettings Ltd, a new property investment company he has just set up.

Leigh bought the properties many years ago for a total of £200,000 and, at the time of the transfer, they are worth a total of £1.2m. If Leigh does not claim to hold over his gain, his CGT liability will be as follows:

		£
Deemed sale proceeds (market value on transfer)		1,200,000
Less:	Original cost	200,000
	Annual exemption for 2020/21	12,300
Gives:	Taxable gain	987,700
CGT payable at 10%:		£98,770

While Leigh is not exactly happy to pay this tax, he nevertheless appreciates that, at less than 10%, it represents a good rate. He therefore decides to transfer his properties for a sum of £1.2m, which he leaves outstanding on loan account, rather than attempt to hold over the gain arising.

Over the next few years, Leigh is able to take £1.2m out of the company tax free (although he has to use the first £98,770 to pay his CGT bill).

If he took this sum out of the company by way of dividends at, say, £50,000 per year, he would have to pay a total of at least £374,400 in Income Tax (assuming he remains a higher rate taxpayer).

By paying £98,770 in CGT up front, Leigh is likely to save more than £275,000 in the long run, possibly much more.

Furthermore, the company will have a base cost of £1.2m for the properties rather than the £200,000 it would have had if Leigh had 'held over' his capital gains. On a sale of the properties, this higher base cost will save the company £190,000 in CT (at 19%).

Hence, the £98,770 'up front' payment of CGT could eventually save Leigh and the company a total of almost £500,000!

Note that, in this example, Halfpenny Lettings Ltd would have a SDLT bill of at least £36,000 on the transfer of Leigh's properties. This would increase the company's base cost in the properties, leading to a further reduction in the CT arising on their sale. However, since the SDLT cost would be exactly the same whether Leigh held over his capital gains or not, it has no effect on the savings described above.

In addition to withdrawing his loan account tax-free, Leigh might also benefit from paying himself interest: see Sections 9.7 and 12.10 for more information.

The 'pay now save later' strategy will be even more beneficial when the availability of business asset disposal relief is about to be lost. So beneficial sometimes, in fact, it can make the transfer of property into a company a tax saving strategy in itself.

Example
Frank is a higher rate taxpayer and has a small villa he purchased many years ago for £50,000, but which is currently worth £250,000. He used the property as a furnished holiday let until 5th April 2018 then changed over to long-term residential lettings. This means the property will cease to qualify for business asset disposal relief after 5th April 2021. In March 2021, however, Frank transfers the property to a new company, Hadden Lettings Ltd.

Frank has a capital gain of £200,000. He deducts his annual exemption of £12,300, leaving £187,700, which is subject to CGT at just 10%, i.e. £18,770. The company has a SDLT liability of £7,500 on the property, bringing its total base cost up to £257,500.

Five years later, in March 2026, Hadden Lettings Ltd sells the property for £350,000, producing a capital gain of £92,500, which is subject to CT at 19%, i.e. £17,575.

Frank then winds up Hadden Lettings Ltd and his net proceeds of £324,925 (£350,000 LESS £17,575 CT and £7,500 SDLT) give him a capital gain of £74,925. As Hadden Lettings Ltd was not a trading company, Frank will not be eligible for business asset disposal relief on this occasion, but the non-residential CGT rate of 20% will apply (subject to the 'Wealth Warning' in Section 11.6).

After deducting Frank's annual exemption of £12,300, his taxable gain is reduced to £62,625, leaving him with a CGT bill, at 20%, of £12,525.

The total tax costs on the property are thus £56,240 (£18,770 CGT + £7,500 SDLT + £17,575 CT + £12,525 CGT)

If Frank still held the property personally at the time of sale, he would have an overall capital gain of £300,000. As the property had been used for long-term lettings for the previous eight years, no business asset disposal relief would have been available. After deducting his annual exemption, Frank would therefore have had a taxable gain of £287,700 and a CGT liability at 28% of £80,556.

*Hence, by transferring the property into a company in 2021, Frank has ultimately reduced his overall tax bill by £24,316, or **over 30%!***

This example shows an incorporation of a business that qualifies for business asset disposal relief on the transfer may ultimately be beneficial when a change in use of the property (or properties) has occurred, or is anticipated in the future.

This will, however, depend on the relative length of time and growth in value of the property in private ownership and qualifying business use, as compared with the length of time and growth in value of the property in company ownership and non-qualifying use. In practice, it will be necessary to prepare forecasts of the expected final sale position in order to decide if this route is beneficial.

14.12 TRADING BUSINESSES

If your business is classed as 'trading' for tax purposes (see Chapter 3), then both the relief for 'gifts of business assets' and incorporation relief should be available to deal with the problem of capital gains arising on the transfer of assets into your company. However, when considering the transfer of a property trade, it is important to remember there will also be other tax issues involved.

Such a transfer will be regarded as a cessation of trade for Income Tax purposes. It may be necessary to make appropriate elections relating to trading stock, development work-in-progress, and capital allowances, in order to prevent unwanted and unnecessary tax liabilities arising (see Section 14.19 for further advice regarding capital allowances).

The transfer will give rise to SDLT liabilities, as explained in Sections 14.3 and 14.5, unless the business is operating as a partnership (Section 14.6). Transfers of trades will also mean a change in the 'taxable person' for VAT purposes and this will lead to a few formalities that need to be observed (see Section 14.20).

Each of the two key CGT reliefs should readily be available to a property development or property management business, although, in the latter case, there may not be many assets to transfer.

As for a property dealing, or property trading, business (see Section 3.4), the CGT reliefs are theoretically available but will be of little benefit, as the properties held by the business represent trading stock, not capital assets. Furthermore, relief could potentially be denied by HMRC, who may argue the business is actually one of property investment. In most cases, it will make more sense to simply start up a new property dealing business within a company, rather than attempt to transfer the existing business.

14.13 FURNISHED HOLIDAY LETS

As usual, furnished holiday lets (see Section 4.8) have a special status and transfers of such businesses are eligible both for the relief for 'gifts of business assets' and for incorporation relief.

As explained in Section 14.10, where both reliefs are available, the best choice will depend on future plans and expectations and the choice will generally be made through the structure used for the transfer transactions. As also explained in Section 14.10, relief for 'gifts of business assets' is usually preferable where business asset disposal relief is available.

While furnished holiday lets enjoy a number of advantages for CGT and Income Tax purposes, they are still classed as residential properties for SDLT purposes and are subject to charges in the usual way on a transfer into a company, unless being run through a partnership (see Sections 14.3 and 14.6).

Where a furnished holiday letting business is registered for VAT (see Section 15.1), the transfer of the business to a company will again mean a change in the 'taxable person' for VAT purposes. We will look at some of the formalities that need to be dealt with in this situation in Section 14.20.

When transferring furnished holiday lets, it may be necessary to make appropriate capital allowances elections to prevent balancing charges arising. See Section 14.19 for further details.

14.14 TURNING INVESTMENT PROPERTY INTO 'TRADING' PROPERTY

In previous sections, we have seen the benefits of the two CGT 'hold over' reliefs when transferring properties into a company.

Unfortunately, the relief for 'gifts of business assets' is restricted to businesses that qualify as 'trading' for business asset disposal relief purposes (see Chapter 3 and Section 7.3). On the face of it, therefore, it would appear that, apart from furnished holiday lets, a property investment business can never be eligible for relief for 'gifts of business assets'.

Partial relief may, however, be available where the business qualifies as a 'trade' at the point of transfer. One way to qualify as a 'trade' for this purpose would be to use the property as a furnished holiday let (see Section 4.8).

Example
Anne has a house in Edinburgh that she has held as an investment property since buying it for £500,000 in April 2018. In April 2021, she starts to rent the house out as a furnished holiday let.

In April 2024, Anne transfers the property into her company, Patron SRU Ltd. The property's value at this point is £700,000.

Anne is deemed to have made a capital gain of £200,000. However, as she has used the property for a qualifying purpose for three years out of a total ownership period of six years, she may claim to 'hold over' 3/6ths of her capital gain, i.e. £100,000.

As can be seen from the example, changing an existing property's use provides some scope to reduce the CGT liability arising on a transfer into a company by claiming relief for 'gifts of business assets', but the relief is only partial.

Incorporation relief may provide a better solution under these circumstances since (as explained in Section 14.9) there is no reduction in the amount of gain that may be 'held over' when the property has not always been used in a qualifying business. All that is required in order to claim incorporation relief without restriction is that the property is used in a qualifying business at the point of transfer. (Although, in practice, qualification for a reasonable period both before and after the transfer is probably necessary, for the reasons explained in Section 14.7.)

In the next section, we will examine when a property investment business will qualify for incorporation relief. However, where the size of the business is fairly modest, the position may still remain doubtful.

Hence, in many cases, the only way to be sure of obtaining any form of 'hold over' relief on investment property is to change the use of the property so it qualifies as a furnished holiday let (as defined in Section 4.8) or as qualifying trading property.

Unfortunately, not every property is suitable for the 'commercial letting of furnished holiday accommodation': a term that must be met in order for it to qualify as a furnished holiday let. So, can other investment properties ever become trading assets?

To achieve this will require the landlord to provide a significant level of additional services to tenants. Generally speaking, merely ancillary services, such as cleaning the common stairwell in a block of flats, will not usually be regarded as sufficient to give the landlord trading status.

What is usually required is some form of services to individual rooms or tenants, such as the provision of meals, cleaning bedrooms, or making up beds. Where a range of services are provided to individual tenants or their rooms, trading status should be assured and, in these cases, the landlord need not carry out the work personally, but may employ others to do it.

In the middle ground, there are those who provide an intermediate level of services to their tenants, such as window-cleaning and small property repairs. Where the landlord is engaged virtually full-time in managing properties and is providing many of these services personally, HMRC may sometimes accept he or she is trading, although the position is far from certain.

Another useful indicator of trading status is the average length of a tenant's stay in the premises. The shorter the better from this point of view and average stays measured in days are more likely to indicate a trade than those measured in months.

In short, to achieve trading status generally requires the landlord to be running their property more like a guest house or hostel than a normal letting business.

If this can be achieved, then either incorporation relief or partial relief for 'gifts of business assets' should be available on a transfer of property into a company. At a later date (say a year or two after the transfer), the company could then cease providing the additional services and revert to a pure property investment business.

Wealth Warning
It must be remembered that running the business as a trade prior to the transfer will lead to NI liabilities (see Sections 10.2 and 10.11).

Significant levels of ancillary services may also lead to a requirement for the business to be registered for VAT (see Section 15.1). Holiday accommodation businesses will also need to be registered for VAT if total annual sales exceed the VAT registration threshold.

14.15 PROPERTY INVESTMENT BUSINESSES & INCORPORATION RELIEF

Theoretically, the requirements for incorporation relief are not as strict as relief for 'gifts of business assets' and only require a 'business' rather than a 'trade'. However, some of the case law on the subject states 'the mere passive holding of investments and collection of rent does not amount to a business'.

We all know most modern landlords' businesses are not exactly 'passive' but, when it comes to tax law, I am afraid we are not always operating in the real world and archaic notions of landlords as purely passive investors sadly still persist.

The Ramsay Case

Thankfully, the case of 'Elisabeth Moyne Ramsay v Revenue and Customs Commissioners', which was decided in favour of the taxpayer (Mrs Ramsay), has finally given us some legal authority for when a property investment business qualifies as a 'business' for the purposes of incorporation relief.

The judge in this case stated, "It is the degree of activity as a whole which is material to the question whether there is a business, and not the extent of that activity when compared to the number of properties or lettings."

In other words, the judge felt it is the overall scale of activities undertaken by the property investor that determines whether they have a qualifying business for the purposes of incorporation relief.

In Mrs Ramsay's case, she and her husband jointly owned a property divided into ten self-contained flats and they each spent approximately 20 hours per week on activities related to the property.

The Twenty Hours a Week Test

Following the Ramsay case, HMRC now accepts incorporation relief is available where an individual spends 20 hours or more a week personally undertaking activities that are indicative of a business (the question of what type of activities are indicative of a business is examined further below).

In other words, a property investor who spends an average of at least 20 hours per week on their business should qualify for incorporation relief.

> **Tax Tip**
>
> In some cases, it will be obvious a property investor is spending well over 20 hours per week on their business.
>
> In more borderline cases, it may make sense to keep a timesheet and record the hours you spend on your business. Remember to

include all business activities, including: travel time (when on business: but see further below); business meetings; time spent on research (looking for new properties, searching for mortgage deals, etc); admin, such as renewing your property insurance, preparing your accounts, or completing your tax return; attending courses; and even time spent reading this book!

Wealth Warning

Travelling from home to a permanent business base (such as your own office premises) does not count as business travel. HMRC sometimes interprets this as also meaning travel from home to a rental property. I strongly disagree with this view, but it may be wise to anticipate some difficulty in getting HMRC to accept that time spent on this type of travel should be included.

What if You Don't Meet the Test?

While HMRC has decided to go along with the idea that 20 hours a week spent on a business means it qualifies for incorporation relief, this is not what the judge in the Ramsay case actually said. Furthermore, even HMRC does not say an investor spending less than 20 hours per week does **not** qualify, they only say such cases should be 'considered carefully'.

What the judge in the Ramsay case actually said was he accepted Mrs Ramsay had a qualifying business based on all the facts 'taken overall' rather than because of any single factor alone.

Hence, where many of the same factors are present, it is possible the business may still qualify for incorporation relief, even if the owner spends less than 20 hours per week on the business. It is therefore worth us looking at some of the factors that may have acted in Mrs Ramsay's favour:

- Her property business consisted of a joint interest in a property divided into ten self-contained flats
- The property had extensive communal areas, as well as a garden, a car park and some garages
- Substantial repairs and maintenance work was carried out on the communal areas, garden, car park and garages
- Mrs Ramsay carried out some of this work personally
- Additional assistance was provided to one elderly tenant
- Prior to the transfer of the property to a company, Mr and Mrs Ramsay carried out some preparatory work regarding a proposed project to refurbish and redevelop the property
- Neither of them had any other occupation during the relevant period

Based on these facts, the judge concluded, "that the activity undertaken in respect of the property, again taken overall, was sufficient in nature and extent to amount to a business for the purpose of [incorporation relief]. Although each of the activities could equally well have been undertaken by someone who was a mere property investor, where the degree of activity outweighs what might normally be expected to be carried out by a mere passive investor, even a diligent and conscientious one, that will in my judgment amount to a business."

So, Mrs Ramsay qualified but the judge also made the point that other owners of investment property might only be a 'passive investor' who would not qualify and there was no single factor that determined this distinction: it was down to the degree of activity undertaken by the investor.

Hence, the danger for smaller landlords spending less than 20 hours per week on their business is that the business could be regarded as a 'passive investment'. Historically, HMRC has always taken the stance that 'the mere holding of investment property and collection of rent does not constitute a business' (while happily continuing to collect tax on income generated from this 'non-business' activity!)

But the helpful judge in the Ramsay case also gave us some factors that indicate when a business exists. He said one should consider whether there was/were:

i)   A serious undertaking earnestly pursued, or a serious occupation
ii)   An occupation or function actively pursued with reasonable or recognisable continuity
iii) A certain amount of substance in terms of turnover
iv)   Activities conducted in a regular manner and on sound and recognised business principles
v)   Activities of a kind which, subject to differences of detail, are commonly made by those who seek to profit by them

Many smaller landlords would appear to meet most, if not all, of these tests and the idea that it is necessary to spend 20 hours per week on the business is not something either the legislation or the judge ever actually said.

Nonetheless, attempting an incorporation relief claim if you spend less than 20 hours per week on your business could be risky. Sadly, HMRC will not give advance rulings on 'matters of fact, such as if certain activities constitute a business', so you will have no choice but to go ahead and then claim the relief on the basis you believe your business qualifies.

One of the major problems is to get the relief you must transfer your entire business. If relief is not forthcoming, there could be a substantial CGT bill. Furthermore, whether relief is obtained or not, SDLT will usually be payable on the total value of the properties transferred (subject to the partnership exemption examined in Section 14.6). So, the stakes are high and the outcome may be uncertain!

The Ramsay case is helpful, but it will be pretty rare for the property owner's circumstances to be exactly the same as Mrs Ramsay's. Hence, the question remains: how much more than passive investment does the business need to be in order to qualify? Some of the key points to be considered after the Ramsay case are whether it is necessary for:

- The property to contain substantial communal areas
- The owner to carry out repairs and maintenance work personally
- The property business to be the owner's only occupation
- The owner to be actively looking at ways to improve the capital value or rental yield of their property

Mrs Ramsay satisfied all these points. The position where only some of these points are satisfied remains uncertain.

Nonetheless, there will be many cases where a property owner spending less than 20 hours per week on their business meets the standards set by the judge in the Ramsay case and qualifies for incorporation relief.

In Summary
Following the Ramsay case, and HMRC's response, we can conclude the following property investment businesses should generally qualify for incorporation relief:

- Those where the owner spends at least 20 hours per week on the business
- Those where the additional services provided are sufficient to achieve trading status in the manner described in Section 14.14
- Furnished holiday lets (as defined in Section 4.8)

For those not meeting any of these criteria, it will be essential to take a detailed look at the particular circumstances and establish whether the property business would amount to more than 'the mere passive holding of investments' in the eyes of HMRC and the courts. The Ramsay case provides some useful guidance, but the position for many property investment businesses remains uncertain.

In the next section, however, we will take a look at the substantial benefits for property investors who do succeed in obtaining incorporation relief.

14.16 THE BENEFITS OF INCORPORATION RELIEF

A property investor who successfully obtains incorporation relief will achieve a tax-free uplift in the base cost of their properties to current market value.

Well, not exactly 'tax-free', there is SDLT to worry about, and this can be pretty substantial, as we saw in Section 14.4 (unless the partnership exemption applies: see Section 14.6). Nonetheless, this could be a price worth paying in some cases.

As investment properties would be subject to CGT at up to 28% in the transferor's hands, the uplift in base costs could provide the potential to make massive savings.

Once in the company, properties could generally be sold with a CT exposure of just 19% of their future increase in value. The company could then reinvest the vast majority of the sales proceeds, having suffered only a minimal level of tax exposure.

Example
Jim has a residential property investment business with a total current market value of £2.5m. Jim has built his portfolio up over many years and several of the older properties stand at significant capital gains. Jim works full-time in his property business, and certainly spends more than 20 hours per week on it, so he qualifies for incorporation relief.

Jim's portfolio consists of 20 residential properties, including ten houses in Leeds purchased for just £15,000 each many years ago, and currently worth £100,000 each.

Jim would like to sell off the old houses in Leeds and reinvest the money in new properties that, he anticipates, will yield higher rental returns. However, since each property stands at a gain of £85,000 and he is a higher rate taxpayer who has already used his annual CGT exemption, a sale of the houses would leave him with a CGT bill of £238,000 (10 x £85,000 x 28%).

Jim is not happy with the prospect of losing almost £240,000 in CGT so, instead of selling the houses, he transfers his entire property investment business to a new company, Telfer Ltd, in exchange for shares, and holds over his capital gains under incorporation relief.

While Telfer Ltd will have to pay SDLT on the transfer, it will be able to claim multiple dwellings relief (see Section 8.8) to reduce the applicable rate to 3%, thus giving rise to a charge of £75,000.

The houses in Leeds can now be sold with no CT liability arising, leaving a net sum of £925,000 available for Jim to reinvest, or £163,000 more than he would have had if he had simply sold the houses himself.

Furthermore, the company will have capital losses of around £30,000 to carry forward (equivalent to the SDLT paid on the houses that have been sold) and all of Jim's remaining properties will have a base cost equal to 103% of their current market value, thus significantly reducing any exposure to tax on future sales.

14.17 OTHER INVESTMENT PROPERTIES

So, what happens if we transfer investment properties to a company and cannot claim any of the CGT reliefs we have explored so far?

Without the availability of any special CGT relief, the owner of investment properties faces the problem of separate capital gains calculations on the transfer of each individual property and a CGT bill based on a 'deemed' sale at market value. SDLT liabilities will also arise in the usual way, unless the partnership exemption is available.

Sometimes, however, with careful timing and the use of annual exemptions, it is still possible to make the transfers at little or no CGT cost, especially where a couple, or two or more other individuals, own the properties jointly. For example, at 2020/21 rates, two individuals with taxable income of no more than £32,300 each could transfer a jointly owned residential property standing at a gain of £60,000 for a total CGT cost of just £6,372.

This is arguably an acceptable cost when one considers the potential benefits of corporate ownership, although SDLT charges at the higher rates given in Section 8.4 (based on the property's market value) would also need to be taken into account, unless the owners are operating as a partnership (see Section 14.6).

If the joint owners have a portfolio of similar properties, they could make one transfer into their company each year, thus progressively moving the whole portfolio at a reasonable overall cost. Properties with high market values or larger capital gains could be left in personal ownership to avoid higher SDLT and CGT costs.

Principal Private Residences (Former Homes)
The possible availability of principal private residence relief on some properties should also be borne in mind when considering this type of strategy. (But see Section 15.3 regarding the pitfalls of private use after putting property into a company.)

Tax Tip
A former principal private residence may currently be transferred into a property investment company any time up to nine months after it ceases to be your main residence without incurring any CGT liability.

Be careful, however: if the property was not always your main residence throughout the period from purchase until you finally moved out of it, there might be some exposure to CGT. Remember also that SDLT will be payable as usual (including the additional 3% charge) based on the property's market value.

See the Taxcafe.co.uk guide *How to Save Property Tax* for full details on the availability of principal private residence relief.

14.18 FORMING A PARTNERSHIP

As we saw in Section 14.6, a transfer of partnership property to a company owned by the same individuals that make up the partnership will often be exempt from SDLT.

This gives partnerships a tremendous advantage over individual property investors or joint owners (joint ownership does not constitute a partnership), but what does it take to form a partnership?

Many long-established partnerships have been set up without following some of the formalities set out below. However, if you wish to be certain of partnership treatment for tax purposes, it is recommended that you:

- Prepare and sign a written partnership agreement (Note 1)
- Set up a partnership bank account (or accounts, if required)
- Prepare partnership accounts, including a balance sheet with partners' capital accounts
- Prepare tenants' leases in the name of the partnership
- Register your properties in the name of the partnership (Note 2)
- Register the partnership for self-assessment with HMRC (Note 3)
- Submit partnership tax returns each year (Note 3)
- Register for VAT in the name of the partnership, if applicable (Section 15.1) (Note 4)
- Register the partnership as an employer, if applicable (Section 9.2) (Note 4)

Notes
1. This is a legal requirement in Scotland
2. Generally you will need to register the properties in the name of two or more partners 'as nominees for' the partnership; as a partnership is not recognised as a legal person in its own right in England, Wales or Northern Ireland
3. These steps are essential, even for a long-established partnership, since otherwise HMRC will not accept you have a partnership business
4. Missing these steps will also lead to (potentially costly) difficulties with HMRC!

On top of these formalities, it is essential the partners are actually carrying on a business together. In the case of a property investment partnership, this means the partners must be actively involved in the letting of properties.

How Long Do You Need To Be in Partnership?
The question everyone always asks is 'how long do you need to operate as a partnership to get the SDLT exemption?'

As with many other tax issues, there is no statutory minimum period a partnership needs to exist in order to qualify for the SDLT exemption. However, there are anti-avoidance rules that effectively allow HMRC to ignore the existence of a partnership if it has simply been created to avoid SDLT charges.

Hence, what is more important than how long you operate the partnership is making sure it has genuine substance and there is a good commercial rationale for its existence.

Having said that, I would have strong doubts over the viability of any partnership that has operated for less than two years and would continue to have concerns where the partnership exists for less than three years, unless there really is a very good reason why these changes in business structure have taken place so quickly.

Treatment of Partnership Property
For both CGT and SDLT purposes, each partner is effectively treated as if they individually own a share of the partnership properties. This means tax may be charged whenever:

- Property is introduced into a partnership (see below)
- There are changes in partnership shares (see the Taxcafe.co.uk guide *'How to Save Property Tax'* for details)
- Property leaves a partnership (subject to the exemptions detailed throughout this chapter)

For CGT purposes, a partner's share in partnership properties is determined according to the first item on this list the partners have entered into:

i)   An agreement as to how capital assets are allocated
ii)   An agreement as to how capital profits are shared
iii)   An agreement as to how income profits are shared

If there is no agreement falling under any of (i) to (iii) above, the partners' shares are deemed to be equal.

For SDLT purposes, a partner's share in the partnership properties is based on their share of income profits. This makes changes in profit shares a potentially costly exercise. This issue is examined in further detail in the Taxcafe.co.uk guide *'How to Save Property Tax'*.

The treatment of partnership property for LBTT and LTT purposes is broadly the same as for SDLT, but professional advice should be taken locally in respect of property located in Scotland or Wales.

Getting Property into the Partnership

The easiest way to get property into a partnership is to buy it through the partnership in the first place. The partnership will pay SDLT in the normal way and each partner will have a base cost for CGT purposes equal to their share of the purchase cost, as determined above.

Introducing existing property into the partnership is rather more complex. In effect, the person owning the property is treated for CGT purposes as having disposed of the proportion of the property passing to the other partners, based on their shares, as determined above.

The disposal value to be used is based on the actual consideration paid (see below), unless the partners are 'connected persons' (see Appendix B, but disregarding heading (vi)), or the transaction is not taking place at arms' length (see Section 6.2).

In these cases, the appropriate proportion of the property's market value is generally substituted instead. However, market value is not used, even where the partners are 'connected persons', if the transaction is taking place on genuine commercial terms. An example of when this might apply is given in Example 'H' below.

Given the way that partnership shares are determined for CGT purposes, existing joint owners should be able to transfer properties into a partnership free from CGT by ensuring the same proportionate interests are maintained.

An existing sole owner can also avoid CGT by retaining a 100% interest in the partnership property (see Example 'I', Part 1 for an example of how this might apply in practice).

Other cases where properties may be transferred into a partnership free from CGT include where:

- The partners are spouses: the usual rule that exempts transfers between spouses applies (see the Taxcafe.co.uk guide *'How to Save Property Tax'* for details)
- The property qualifies as a 'trading asset' for the purposes of relief for 'gifts of business assets': some or all of the gain may be held over, depending on whether any actual consideration is paid (see Section 14.8)

Gains qualifying for business asset disposal relief will also be eligible for the usual 10% CGT rate (see Section 7.3).

Consideration
The actual consideration for the transfer of property into a partnership is made up of:
- Any amount paid directly from other partners to the partner introducing the property, and
- The appropriate proportion of any amount credited to the partnership capital account of the partner introducing the property

Any capital introduced into the partnership by other partners is ignored for these purposes.

Example 'H'
Tywin owns a residential property portfolio with a total current market value of £10m and total original costs of £2.5m. He is well past normal retirement age and beginning to find his business difficult to manage on his own. He therefore takes his grandson Joffrey into partnership with him and Joffrey takes over the day-to-day running of the business.

Tywin gives Joffrey a 20% share in partnership income; but only a 10% share in the partnership property. Joffrey pays £100,000 directly to Tywin and also pays £100,000 into the partnership, which is credited to his capital account. Tywin's capital account in the partnership is credited by £7m.

Although Tywin and Joffrey are 'connected persons' (see Appendix B), the arrangements between them have genuine commercial substance, as Joffrey has taken on responsibility for the day-to-day running of the business. Hence, we will assume for the sake of illustration that actual consideration may be used to calculate Tywin's capital gain, rather than market value (this point is considered further below).

For CGT purposes, Joffrey has acquired a 10% share in the partnership (see above). Hence, Tywin is deemed to have disposed of a 10% share of his property portfolio for a consideration of £800,000, made up as follows:

Direct payment from Joffrey	*£100,000*
Capital introduced by Joffrey: ignored	*-*
Appropriate proportion of capital account (£7m x 10%)	*£700,000*
Total consideration:	*£800,000*

This will give Tywin a capital gain of £550,000 (£800,000 – £2.5m x 10%).

Note that Tywin's base cost for this capital gain is equal to the same proportion of his base cost in the properties as the partnership share deemed to be passing to Joffrey for CGT purposes. The usual 'part disposal' rules (examined in the Taxcafe.co.uk guide *'How to Save Property Tax'*) do not apply to transactions between business partners.

I assumed actual consideration could be used in this case as the arrangements between Tywin and Joffrey had genuine commercial substance. In practice, this is an issue that may cause some difficulty and HMRC may look closely at the arrangements. Their own guidance in section CG27800 of their manuals (available online) may assist in understanding how they view such matters.

If market value had to be used, this would be calculated as £10m x 10% (Joffrey's partnership share for CGT purposes), which amounts to £1m: thus giving Tywin a capital gain of £750,000 (£1m – £2.5m x 10%).

SDLT on Introduction of Property into a Partnership

For SDLT purposes, partnership shares are based purely on the partners' income profit shares. Furthermore, the deemed consideration for SDLT purposes in the case of transactions between business partners and the partnership is always based on market value.

However, the proportion of the property deemed to be transferred for SDLT purposes is reduced not only by the partnership share held by the transferor, but also by any partnership shares held by 'connected persons' (as per Appendix B, but with heading (vi) disregarded as usual).

Hence, a transfer of property into a partnership made up of yourself and your spouse, or other close relatives (as per headings (ii) to (v) in Appendix B), will be completely exempt from SDLT. (The exemption also covers trusts falling under heading (vii) in Appendix B.)

Other existing joint owners will be able to transfer property to a partnership free from SDLT provided their partnership income profit shares are in the same proportions as their ownership of the property being transferred. Where there is any mismatch in these proportions, some charges will usually arise.

Unconnected Partners

As explained above, it is possible to get property into a partnership free from SDLT by going into partnership with your spouse or a handy relative (under headings (ii) to (v) in Appendix B). It may even be possible to go into partnership with a trust for the benefit of your own minor child.

If there are no handy relatives available, you might be able to go into partnership with another individual at a reasonably modest cost in SDLT. Under the right circumstances, it will also be possible to avoid any CGT.

Example 'I' Part 1

Jon has a portfolio of 50 residential properties with a total value of £25m. He is approaching normal retirement age and is finding it difficult to manage the business on his own. He transfers the properties into a partnership with his friend Danny and she takes over responsibility for the day-to-day running of the business in exchange for a 10% income profit share. However, the partnership agreement stipulates she has no entitlement to any share in the partnership property. Hence no CGT arises on the property transfer.

The deemed consideration for the transfer for SDLT purposes is £2.5m (£25m x 10%), or an average of £50,000 per property. Hence, the SDLT payable on the transfer using multiple dwellings relief (see Section 8.8) is £75,000 (£50,000 x 3% x 50).

As many readers will realise, Jon could have saved a lot if he had married Danny. Perhaps this was not possible for some reason in this case. Nonetheless, let's look at how much more he might save in the future.

Example 'I' Part 2

Some years later, Jon decides he wishes to retire completely. He and Danny therefore agree to transfer the partnership business to a company, Westeros Ltd. Jon will remain as chairman of the company and Danny will become managing director.

Both partners transfer their interest in the business to the company in exchange for shares. Given the substantial size of the business, the transfer qualifies for incorporation relief (see Section 14.15) and no CGT is payable.

As both partners will be acting together to exercise control over the company, they are both 'connected' to the company (see Section 14.2) and full SDLT exemption is available (see Section 14.6). Hence, the ultimate transfer of the properties to the company is completely tax free.

If Jon had transferred his portfolio directly to the company in the first place, he would probably still have qualified for incorporation relief and avoided any CGT. However, the SDLT cost would have been based on an average value per property of £500,000 (£25m/50) and, assuming the transfer was done outside the current SDLT 'holiday' period (see Section 8.4), would have been calculated as follows:

First £125,000 @ 3%	£3,750
Next £125,000 @ 5%	£6,250
Next £250,000 @ 8%	£20,000
Total per property	£30,000

The total charge for 50 properties would thus be £1.5m (£30,000 x 50). By operating as a partnership for a few years before forming a company, **the investor in this case has saved £1.425m** (£1.5m - £75,000) in SDLT!

(This saving is actually less at the moment, as Jon could transfer the portfolio to a company at a much lower cost during the current SDLT 'holiday': we will therefore revisit this example in Section 14.22 to examine Jon's best course of action further.)

In the case of spouses, close relatives, or other existing joint owners, it will often be possible to form the partnership free from SDLT and, in many cases, free from CGT too.

If, in Example 'H' above, Tywin had transferred his business to a company in the first place, the SDLT cost would have been at least £300,000 (£10m x 3%), but this cost will be completely avoided if he and Joffrey eventually transfer their business to a company.

> **Wealth Warning**
> The tax-saving potential of operating as a partnership for a few years before eventually transferring the business to a company is enormous.
>
> BUT, these savings can only be achieved if the arrangements entered into by the partners are genuine commercial arrangements and there is a good commercial rationale for the formation of the partnership in the first place and the eventual decision to transfer the business to a company instead.

14.19 CAPITAL ALLOWANCES AND BUSINESS TRANSFERS

When transferring a business to a company or partnership, there are four areas to consider for capital allowances purposes:

- SBA claims
- Fixtures, fittings and 'integral features'
- Cars
- Other assets on which plant and machinery allowances have been claimed

See Sections 4.5 and 4.6 for full details regarding plant and machinery allowances and SBA claims respectively. A company cannot claim the annual investment allowance on assets transferred from a 'connected person' (see Section 14.2); a partnership cannot claim the annual investment allowance on assets transferred from one of its partners. However, in both cases, the transferee will be able to claim writing down allowances where appropriate.

SBA Claims
No balancing charges or allowances arise on the transfer and the SBA claim should continue afterwards (see Section 4.6). The CGT impact of an SBA claim on property transfers into a company was considered in Sections 14.8 and 14.9. Transfers into a partnership may be similarly affected where CGT arises on the transfer.

Fixtures, Fittings and Integral Features

A Section 198 Election (see Section 4.5) will generally be required to maintain eligibility for capital allowances on fixtures, including 'integral features'. The transferee company or partnership may sometimes also be able to claim extra allowances on items the transferor was unable to claim (see Section 4.5).

The total amounts claimed by the transferee for plant and machinery allowances cannot be more than the actual consideration paid for the transfer of the property, or the original costs incurred by the transferor, if less. Hence, it will often be sensible to ensure actual consideration is paid if there are allowances still to be claimed. See Section 14.3 regarding what counts as 'consideration', which applies equally here.

Anti-avoidance rules apply to prevent a Section 198 Election being used to artificially create a balancing allowance on the transfer of property to a connected company or partnership by fixing a lower value for fixtures, fittings and integral features. However, a lower value can be used if it is a genuine reflection of the items' market value.

Subject to the points made above, there is no restriction on using a higher value to create a balancing charge.

Example

Ned is planning to transfer his property, Winterfell, to his company in exchange for shares. The property contains integral features and other qualifying fixtures on which Ned has incurred total qualifying expenditure of £250,000. The balance on both his main and special rate pools is nil (due to previous annual investment allowance claims) and he has £60,000 of rental losses brought forward.

Ned enters a Section 198 Election with his company fixing the deemed consideration for the integral features and other qualifying fixtures in Winterfell at £60,000. This gives him a £60,000 balancing charge but this is covered by his brought forward rental losses leaving him with no taxable income. Meanwhile, the company will be able to claim writing down allowances on qualifying expenditure of £60,000.

Ned has turned useless rental losses into capital allowances for his company.

Cars

It is generally unwise to transfer your own car into a company due to the substantial Income Tax and NI charges on company cars. Keeping your own car out of the company should not affect your eligibility for incorporation relief. Cars provided to employees should generally be transferred into a company or partnership that is taking over your business and the same points as for 'other assets' below will then apply.

Other Assets

Other assets on which plant and machinery allowances have been claimed will be deemed to transfer to a company or partnership (that is taking over your business) at market value for capital allowances purposes: unless you elect for their 'tax written down value' to be used instead.

Generally, if market value exceeds the balance on your main or special rate pools, you will want to make the election in order to avoid balancing charges. However, if the balancing charge will be covered by brought forward losses, you might prefer to use market value so that the transferee can claim higher allowances in future (like Ned in our example above).

Conversely, if market value is less than the balance on your main or special rate pools, you may not want to make the election: so you can get a balancing allowance on the transfer.

Electing for 'tax written down value' to be used means the assets are deemed to transfer for an amount equal to the remaining balance on your main or special rate pools, resulting in no balancing allowance or charge.

14.20   VAT AND BUSINESS TRANSFERS

Whole Businesses

If the whole business is transferred and is registered for VAT, this will mean there is a change in the 'taxable person' for VAT purposes. The transferor will need to cancel their VAT registration or apply to transfer it to the company (or partnership). The transferee will need to register for VAT.

It is important the business is transferred as a going concern or there may be VAT charges arising on the assets transferred.

Where some assets are retained, VAT charges may also arise on these. VAT charges may also arise if the transferee does not register for VAT.

Partial Transfers

If only part of the business is transferred, the transferor may need to charge VAT on the assets transferred if any of the transfers amounts to a taxable supply (see Section 15.1).

The transfer will not represent a taxable supply, however, if the part of the business transferred amounts to a 'going concern' in its own right (e.g. ten furnished holiday lets, together with an office and staff, out of a total portfolio of twelve properties) **and** the transferee registers for VAT.

If the transferor is not left with a taxable business after the transfer then they will need to cancel their VAT registration and this may lead to VAT charges on the assets retained.

Commercial Properties

If a commercial property on which the option to tax has been exercised (see Section 15.1) is transferred, a VAT charge will arise unless:

i) The transfer is part of the transfer of a business as a 'going concern', and

ii) The transferee notifies HMRC **on or before the date of the transfer** that it also opts to tax the property.

14.21 ALTERNATIVE STRATEGIES

Throughout this chapter, we have considered the potential benefits and costs of transferring property into a company. We have looked at the applicable reliefs for both CGT and SDLT; as well as other potential costs and savings.

Nonetheless, in some cases, it will remain difficult to get an existing property investment business into a company without running the risk of incurring a large tax bill. For example, transferring a residential property portfolio worth £2m, with existing capital gains of £1m, could cost over £340,000 in combined CGT and SDLT if none of the reliefs described in this chapter are available (and often more after the end of the current SDLT 'holiday' period on 31st March 2021).

In many cases, it may therefore be wiser to look to the company as a vehicle for your future investments, while keeping your existing properties in your own hands.

The 'Backdoor Route'

Borrowings secured on your existing personal property portfolio could be invested in the company to enable it to acquire new property. You would be eligible for Income Tax relief on the interest on such borrowings, as the funds are being invested in a 'close company' (see Section 15.2). This would minimise your personal tax exposure on your existing portfolio while enabling you to build up a new portfolio within your company.

Income Tax relief on your interest costs would be subject to the limitations discussed in Section 12.11 (but not the much harsher restrictions applying to individual landlords discussed in Section 12.12).

Other Possibilities

Some other ideas that might be worth exploring in these circumstances are examined in Chapter 16.

14.22   WINDOW OF OPPORTUNITY

As we saw in Section 8.4, the current SDLT 'holiday', ending on 31st March 2021, can provide significant savings on purchases or transfers of residential property during this period; with a maximum saving of £15,000 per property; or per 'dwelling' to be more precise (see Section 8.8 for an explanation of the difference between a property and a dwelling). This maximum saving of £15,000 is available on dwellings worth £500,000 or more, with some saving on any dwelling worth more than £125,000.

These potential savings create a fabulous window of opportunity for property investors wishing to transfer their residential property portfolio into a company.

Example 'F' Revisited
Finn has a residential property portfolio consisting of 20 properties with a total value of £6m, or an average of £300,000 each. As we saw in Section 14.4, outside the current SDLT 'holiday' period, it would cost Finn £280,000 in SDLT to transfer this portfolio to a company.

If Finn makes the transfer by 31st March 2021, however, his SDLT cost will be reduced to £180,000 (£300,000 x 3% x 20), giving him a saving of £100,000.

Example 'I' Part 3
*In Section 14.18, we saw it would have cost Jon £1.5m in SDLT to transfer his portfolio of 50 residential properties with a total value of £25m (an average of £500,000 per property) directly into a company outside the current 'holiday' period. If Jon makes such a transfer by 31st March 2021, however, his SDLT would be reduced to just £750,000 (£500,000 x 3% x 50), **half the cost he would face outside the 'holiday' period**, or a saving of £750,000!*

This gives Jon a bit of a dilemma. He can make a certain saving of £750,000 by acting now, or he could follow the partnership route described in Section 14.18 and make an eventual saving of £1.425m: *if* everything works out as planned *and* there are no changes in the tax legislation in the meantime that alter the position to his detriment. Is a bird in the hand worth two in the bush?

The Impact of Temporarily Depressed Values
This may also be a good time to transfer properties into a company if the market value of your property portfolio is temporarily depressed as a result of the coronavirus crisis. The reduction in your property's market value will give rise to further SDLT savings on top of those already generated by the SDLT 'holiday'.

Furthermore, if you are unable to benefit from either of the two key CGT reliefs described in this chapter, you may also save CGT by making the transfer while your property's market values are depressed.

Example 'F' Revisited Again

Let us now suppose that Finn has built up his portfolio over many years and the total cost of his properties was just £2.5m. Let us also suppose the portfolio was worth £6m before the coronavirus crisis, but is now worth just £5m, or an average of £250,000 per property. Finally, let us assume Finn is not eligible for incorporation relief (see Sections 14.9 and 14.15) and would thus be subject to CGT on the transfer.

If Finn had transferred his portfolio to a company before the coronavirus crisis, it would have cost him £280,000 in SDLT (see Section 14.4) and £980,000 in CGT (£6m – £2.5m = £3.5m x 28% = £980,000; ignoring the annual exemption for the sake of illustration). That's a total tax cost of £1.26m.

If Finn transfers his portfolio now, during the SDLT 'holiday' and while the value of his portfolio is temporarily depressed, his tax costs will be as follows:

SDLT: £250,000 x 3% x 20	*£150,000*
CGT: £5m – £2.5m = £2.5m x 28%	*£700,000*
Total:	*£850,000*

While this is still a hefty cost, it represents a very impressive saving of £410,000 (£1.26m – £850,000).

Many people would baulk at a cost of £850,000, but the key point to remember is this is a massive saving compared with making the transfer at another time in the future when property values have recovered and the SDLT 'holiday' has ended (and I would throw in the possibility that CGT rates may have increased: see Section 17.3).

Furthermore, the cost with a smaller portfolio is likely to be considerably less while, in proportionate terms, the same level of saving could still be available.

The question you need to ask yourself is whether the cost of the transfer is worth it in order to get all the benefits of company ownership we have looked at in this guide. If the answer to that question is 'yes' then this could be the best time to make the transfer.

To put it another way: the sun may not be shining at the moment, but this could be best time to make hay!

Chapter 15

Other Important Tax Issues

15.1 VAT FOR PROPERTY COMPANIES

For VAT purposes, property businesses (all businesses in fact) are treated the same whatever type of business entity is used. Hence, the VAT treatment of a property company is generally the same as an individual, or any other entity, carrying on the same type of business.

The company is, however, a separate legal entity to its owner, so this carries the advantage that, if the company has to register for VAT, the owner, and all the activities they carry out personally, is unaffected. This might be helpful with issues such as whether to use the flat rate scheme, where applicable; although it can also cause difficulties, such as problems over the recovery of VAT on expenses incurred by the owner personally on behalf of the company.

The VAT treatment of property businesses can be summarised as follows:

- Residential property letting: exempt (except as noted below)
- Letting of holiday accommodation: normally standard-rated (see below)
- Provision of ancillary services (e.g. cleaning or gardening): standard-rated
- Hotels, guest houses, etc: normally standard-rated (see below)
- Commercial property letting: option to tax (see further below)
- Commercial property services (e.g. cleaning, security, or maintenance provided under separate contract): standard-rated
- Sales of newly constructed residential property: zero-rated
- Sales of property newly converted from non-residential to residential: usually zero-rated
- Other residential property sales: exempt
- Sales of newly constructed commercial property: standard-rated
- Other commercial property sales: option to tax (see further below)
- Property management services: standard-rated

The most important point to note is that normal residential property letting, and most sales of residential property (except as noted above), are exempt from VAT. Hence, a property investment company that only rents out normal residential property, and does not provide any ancillary services, or holiday accommodation, does not generally need to be concerned with VAT; and simply claims its VAT-inclusive business expenses for CT purposes.

Where a company makes annual taxable supplies (anything that isn't exempt) in excess of the VAT registration threshold (currently £85,000) it must register for VAT and charge it to its customers or tenants at the appropriate rate. Companies making taxable supplies below the VAT registration threshold may register for VAT voluntarily if they wish (this would be beneficial if the company is making zero-rated supplies).

VAT is charged at 20% on standard-rated supplies. Hotels, guest houses, and other supplies of holiday accommodation are temporarily subject to the reduced rate of 5% for the period from 15th July 2020 to 31st March 2021.

Commercial property is subject to an 'option to tax'. This means the landlord may choose, for each property (on a property-by-property basis), whether or not the rent should be an exempt supply for VAT purposes. If the 'option to tax' is exercised, the rent becomes standard-rated and a sale of the property will then also be standard-rated.

VAT-registered companies can generally recover the VAT on purchases of goods or services used in their business: although there are exceptions and restrictions, such as purchases of motor cars, or the provision of private fuel for directors or staff. The position will also be altered significantly if the flat rate scheme is used or the company is making a mixture of taxable and exempt supplies (known as 'partial exemption').

For a detailed review of the VAT treatment of property businesses, including the flat rate scheme, and other issues mentioned in this section, see the Taxcafe.co.uk guide 'How to Save Property Tax'.

Interaction with Corporation Tax
A company that is registered for VAT should generally include only the net (excluding VAT) amounts of income and expenditure in its accounts. Where VAT recovery is barred or restricted, however, the additional cost arising may generally be claimed as an expense for CT purposes (or for capital allowances in some cases).

A non-registered company should include the VAT in its business expenditure for CT purposes.

A company using the flat rate scheme should also include the VAT in its business expenditure for CT purposes, except in the case of capital expenditure of £2,000 or more (including VAT), where the VAT can still be recovered. Sales income should be shown as the total gross, VAT-inclusive amount, less the amount of VAT paid over to HMRC at the applicable rate under the scheme.

15.2 CLOSE COMPANIES AND CLOSE INVESTMENT HOLDING COMPANIES

Broadly speaking, a company is a 'close company' if it is under the control of five people or less. The vast majority of private property companies will therefore be close companies.

This is good news since additional reliefs are available in respect of shares and other investments in close companies: including interest relief, as discussed in Chapter 12.

However, any close company that does not exist wholly or mainly for a 'qualifying purpose' is a 'close investment holding company'. Fortunately, 'qualifying purposes' include carrying on a trade and renting property to unconnected persons.

Hence, a property business will generally represent a qualifying purpose and a property company will not usually be a 'close investment holding company'. This is very important because investors are not eligible for interest relief on investments in close investment holding companies.

15.3 THE DANGERS OF PRIVATE USE

It is generally not advisable to hold properties through a company where there is some private use. For these purposes, 'private use' would include:

- Using it as your own private residence (whether or not your main residence)
- Allowing your spouse, partner or any other member of your family to use it as a private residence
- Letting the property to any 'connected' person (see Appendix B)

Private use of a property held through a company could result in:

- The company becoming a close investment holding company and therefore losing many important tax reliefs
- Loss of interest relief on sums invested in the company
- Loss of business asset disposal relief on company shares (where they might otherwise qualify)
- Income Tax benefit-in-kind charges on the company's directors
- Class 1A NI liabilities for the company
- Deemed distributions of income taxable on the shareholders as if they were dividends
- SDLT at 15% on purchases or transfers (see Section 8.6)
- The Annual Tax on Enveloped Dwellings (see Section 15.6)

Furthermore, where a property with private use is owned personally, there is scope to make use of principal private residence relief and rent-a-room relief. The scope to use these reliefs is lost if the property is held in a company.

Certainly therefore, as far as UK property is concerned, any private use of property held by a company is best avoided.

The position for foreign property is somewhat different since there are often good reasons for holding a second home abroad through a company.

HMRC has confirmed that owners of a company that exists solely to hold a private residence overseas will be exempt from benefit-in-kind charges in the UK in respect of their personal use of the property. The exemption only applies if the company exists solely to hold foreign property. If the company has any other activities, the benefit-in-kind charge for personal use by the company owners will continue to apply under normal principles. The company must also be held directly by individuals. The exemption is not available, for example, where a company is held by a trust or another company.

Hence, it will generally make sense to ensure any company formed to hold a second home abroad is kept entirely separate from any other company owned by the same individuals.

15.4   SHORT AND LONG ACCOUNTING PERIODS

For a variety of reasons, companies sometimes prepare accounts covering periods other than a year. This often occurs at the beginning or end of a company's life, although it will also occur in the event of a change of accounting date. (We saw one reason you might wish to change your company's accounting date in Section 2.5.)

As shorter or longer accounting periods often occur at the beginning of a company's life, it is worth us spending a little time on the CT implications.

Longer Accounting Periods
For CT purposes, periods over a year must be divided into two periods: the first twelve months, and the remainder.

Trading profits may be divided between the two periods on a pro-rata basis, although a strict 'actual' basis may be used if there is reasonable justification for doing so. Rental income should strictly be allocated on an 'actual' basis, although a pro-rata basis will often be acceptable. Other investment income and capital gains should be allocated to the period in which they arose.

Each of the two periods is then taxed separately in its own right. The first period is taxed under the normal principles applying to a period of a year. The second period is dealt with as a short accounting period.

Short Accounting Periods

Where a company has a short accounting period, some key tax reliefs and limits must be reduced accordingly, on a pro rata basis. These include:

- The amount of annual investment allowance available (see Section 4.5)
- The rate of writing down allowances (see Section 4.5)
- The £2m threshold for interest relief restrictions (see Section 4.9)
- The £5m limit for loss relief restrictions (see Section 4.10)

In the case of a very short period, some of these restrictions may affect quite small companies.

Starting Business

For CT purposes, a new accounting period starts when the company starts business. This will often be some time after the date of incorporation.

Example

Webster Ltd is a property investment company. The company was incorporated on 12th May 2020 but does not rent out its first property until 15th September 2020.

Webster Ltd changes its accounting date to 30th June and prepares its first set of accounts for the period from 12th May 2020 to 30th June 2021.

For CT purposes, the company is regarded as having one accounting period as a dormant company, from 12th May to 14th September 2020, and then a second accounting period, as a property investment company, from 15th September 2020 to 30th June 2021.

If Webster Ltd prepared its first set of accounts to a date more than twelve months after it commenced business, it would have three accounting periods for CT purposes.

Ceasing Business

For CT purposes, an accounting period is also deemed to come to an end when the company ceases business.

Tax Returns & Tax Payments

Where a company's accounting period must be divided into more than one period for CT purposes, each period will require its own Corporation Tax Return.

The filing deadline for each return will usually remain twelve months from the company's accounting date, except in the case of periods in excess of 18 months, when returns are due within 30 months of the beginning of the accounting period.

The due date for payment of CT (except large companies under the instalment system: see Section 2.4) remains nine months and a day after the end of each period.

Example

Hastings Ltd draws up accounts for the fifteen months ending 31st December 2020. The company will need to prepare a tax return for the year ending 30th September 2020 and pay the CT due for that period by 1st July 2021. It will also need to prepare a tax return for the three-month period ending 31st December 2020 and pay the CT due for that period by 1st October 2021.

The filing deadline for both tax returns will be 31st December 2021.

It is important to keep HMRC informed of any changes that affect your company's tax return periods, including changes of accounting date, setting up new companies, and commencement of business. Most important of all is to advise HMRC if the company ceases business activity and becomes dormant.

Failure to keep HMRC informed may mean they issue notices requiring the company to deliver a Corporation Tax Return for the wrong period. This can lead to unnecessary complications and even penalties: do not ignore a notice to deliver a Corporation Tax Return just because it has been issued for the wrong period!

15.5   NON-RESIDENT INVESTORS

Throughout this guide, we have been looking at the implications for UK resident property investors of using a UK resident property company. Space does not permit a detailed examination of the position for non-residents, but it is worth making a few brief observations.

Tax Residence for Companies

Subject to any applicable Double Tax Treaty, a company is treated as UK resident if it is UK registered, or has its place of central management and control in the UK. A detailed examination of the concept of 'place of central management and control' would take too long to fit in here, but it is fair to say, if you are UK resident, it is difficult for any property company you run not to be regarded as UK resident also.

The position is different for the purposes of the proposed non-resident SDLT surcharge on residential property (see below and Section 8.5).

Emigration for Companies

Generally speaking, a UK registered company cannot 'emigrate', i.e. it cannot cease to be UK resident. This may, however, be overridden by the terms of a Double Tax Treaty between the UK and another country in some cases.

If a UK resident company does succeed in 'emigrating', i.e. becoming non-UK resident, then, unless it does so with the specific consent of Her Majesty's Treasury, it must pay an 'exit charge' equal to the CT that would arise if it were to sell all its assets at market value.

In view of these points, any UK resident individual who ultimately intends to emigrate should think carefully before using a property company.

Non-Residents and UK Property

Both non-UK resident individuals and non-UK resident companies are now liable for UK tax on all trading profits, income, and capital gains derived from UK land and property.

However, the historic element of gains on UK property arising before 6th April 2015 (for residential property) or 6th April 2019 (for non-residential property) is exempt. These exemptions do not apply if the property is connected with trading activities in the UK.

Non-UK resident individuals or companies buying residential property in England or Northern Ireland after 31st March 2021 are expected to be subject to a 2% SDLT surcharge. The definition of a non-UK resident for this purpose is different to the general rules that normally apply, including those set out above for companies. See Section 8.5 for further details.

Non-Resident Companies

For larger non-UK resident companies that are not 'close companies' (see Section 15.2), the exemption for the historic element of gains on UK residential property extends to 5th April 2019.

If a non-UK resident company is under the control of a UK resident individual, then the individual is personally liable for CGT on any element of capital gains made by that company that are exempt in the company's hands.

A non-UK resident company generally pays CT at normal rates on all income, profits and gains subject to UK tax (including indexation relief up to December 2017 where gains arising prior to that date are taxable).

However, rental profits from UK property arising before 6th April 2020 are subject to Income Tax at basic rate.

Technically, non-UK resident companies paid CGT on gains on UK residential property arising between 6th April 2015 and 5th April 2019, but it was generally computed at normal CT rates. In some cases, however, this was overridden by the higher charge discussed in Section 15.6.

In summary, following a number of recent changes, there is no real benefit for a UK resident individual in holding UK property through an overseas (non-resident) company.

Non-UK Resident Individuals
For new investments in UK property, non-UK residents are now in a similar position to UK residents, as they are subject to both UK Income Tax and UK CGT. From April 2021, they will suffer an additional surcharge on purchases of residential property in England or Northern Ireland, but this will generally be unaffected by whether they use a company or not.

For UK tax purposes, the use of a UK company to hold UK investment property will therefore be subject to the same benefits and pitfalls for these individuals as for UK resident individuals. This, however, is subject to the terms of any applicable Double Tax Treaty. Furthermore, the tax issues arising in the individual's own country of residence must also be considered. Detailed professional advice in both the UK and the individual's own country is therefore essential.

Investment in Overseas Property
From a UK tax point of view, it would not make any sense for a non-UK resident individual to put overseas property into a UK resident company, as this would be bringing the property into the UK tax net.

Trading (or Potential Trading) in UK Property
Non-UK resident individuals are subject to UK Income Tax on trading profits derived from UK land and property. This includes any 'deemed' trading profits under the principles discussed in Section 3.7.

A UK property company may be useful in such a case, as there is little difference in the amount of tax payable within a company on a property 'trading' business or a property 'investment' business: especially since both activities are now fully taxable in the UK in any case.

Indirect Disposals
Non-UK residents are subject to CGT on a sale of an interest (e.g. a shareholding) in any entity (e.g. a company) where UK property held by that entity accounts for 75% or more of its gross asset value. The charge applies where the disposing taxpayer/entity has held at least a 25% interest in the underlying entity at any time in the previous five years. The charge only applies to the increase in value arising after 5th April 2019.

What this means is that a non-UK resident individual investing in UK property via a company will be subject to CGT on a sale of that company. It would, however, appear the charge can be avoided by ensuring the company invests more than 25% of its total asset value in overseas property (or other assets). Naturally this will have foreign tax implications that should be considered.

When selling a property company, one might also reasonably expect the purchaser to take the potential tax liabilities on capital gains within the company into account when negotiating a purchase price!

15.6   THE ANNUAL TAX ON ENVELOPED DWELLINGS

The Annual Tax on Enveloped Dwellings ('ATED') applies to UK residential property owned by companies and other 'non-natural' persons, such as collective investment schemes, unit trusts, and partnerships in which any 'non-natural' person is a partner. The charge applies regardless of where the 'non-natural person' is resident for tax purposes. Most commonly, the charge applies to companies. However, it only applies to single dwellings worth in excess of £500,000. It does not apply by reference to the total value of the company's property portfolio.

Where ATED applies, the purchase of the property is also subject to the 15% rate of SDLT discussed in Section 8.6. Sales and other disposals of property subject to ATED that took place before 6th April 2019 were also subject to CGT at 28% on some or all of the gain arising (see the previous edition of this guide for details).

Business Exemption
The good news for most property investors operating through a company (or any other 'non-natural person') is properties are exempt from ATED if they are being used in a business: including a property rental business.

Hence, in most cases, property investment companies should be exempt from ATED; although it will be essential to ensure that properties are being acquired for use in the business, and continue to be held for business purposes thereafter. Where the property is occupied by a close relative (headings (i) to (v) in Appendix B), or is not being let out at a normal, commercial market rent, this will not count as 'business use' for this purpose.

The bad news is any company or other 'non-natural person' eligible for this exemption will need to claim it: whenever they buy property worth more than £500,000 for SDLT purposes; and on an annual basis when they own any property worth more than £500,000 for the purposes of ATED. Hence, even if there is no extra tax, there will still be plenty of extra administration to deal with!

ATED charges are increased annually in line with the Consumer Prices Index ('CPI'). The charges for 2020/21 are:

Property Value	Charge
Over £500,000, but not more than £1m	£3,700
Over £1m, but not more than £2m	£7,500
Over £2m, but not more than £5m	£25,200
Over £5m, but not more than £10m	£58,850
Over £10m, but not more than £20m	£118,050
Over £20m	£236,250

15.7 THE UPLIFT ON DEATH

For CGT purposes, the base cost of all assets held by an individual at the time of their death is 'uplifted' to their market value on that date. This includes property held directly by the individual, as well as shares in any property company they own.

However, there is no uplift in a company's base cost in the properties it owns at the date of the owner's death. Hence, increases in value that would have escaped CGT in the owner's hands may be subject to CT at 19%.

This point is worth bearing in mind where a property owner has a short life expectancy, although a similar result can be achieved where incorporation relief (see Section 14.9) is available on a transfer of property into a company.

For advice on turning the 'uplift on death' to your advantage, see the Taxcafe.co.uk guide 'How to Save Inheritance Tax'.

15.8 SCOTTISH TAXPAYERS

The Scottish Parliament sets separate Income Tax rates and thresholds for Scottish taxpayers. Generally, you will be a Scottish taxpayer if you live in Scotland (but see the Taxcafe.co.uk guide 'How to Save Property Tax' for further details).

The Scottish Parliament cannot, however, alter:

* The personal allowance (although it could effectively extend it by introducing a zero-rate tax band if it wished)
* The High Income Child Benefit Charge
* The withdrawal of the personal allowance (income over £100,000)
* UK tax rates on dividends, interest, savings income, etc. (see below)
* Capital allowances

Similarly, it has no power over other taxes, such as NI, VAT, CGT, CT and IHT.

The amount of income on which a Scottish taxpayer is liable for tax continues to be computed in exactly the same way as other UK resident taxpayers: it is only the rates of tax that differ. Hence, the vast majority of the advice in this guide remains equally valid for Scottish taxpayers: it is only the amount of tax that might be saved by using a company that will vary.

Scottish Income Tax rates apply to all of a Scottish taxpayer's income except dividends, interest, and other savings income (including income from real estate investment trusts or property authorised investment funds).

Hence, Scottish Income Tax rates apply to all of a Scottish taxpayer's property rental or trading income, regardless of where their properties are located.

In other words, a Scottish taxpayer pays Scottish Income Tax rates on income derived from property both within and outwith Scotland. Other UK resident taxpayers continue to pay Income Tax at normal UK rates on all their income, even if it is derived from property in Scotland.

Scottish Tax Rates
The Scottish Income Tax rates for 2020/21 are as follows:

Up to £12,500	0%	(Personal allowance)
£12,500 to £14,585	19%	(Starter rate)
£14,585 to £25,158	20%	(Basic rate)
£25,158 to £43,430	21%	(Intermediate rate)
£43,430 to £100,000	41%	(Higher rate)
£100,000 to £125,000	61.5%	(Personal allowance withdrawal)
£125,000 to £150,000	41%	(Higher rate)
Over £150,000	46%	(Top rate)

(This table combines the rates set by the Scottish Parliament with the relevant UK provisions regarding the personal allowance)

As the table shows, the current Scottish higher rate threshold of £43,430 is much lower than the UK equivalent (£50,000). This pushes many more Scottish taxpayers into higher rate tax, including those forced into it by the atrocious restrictions on interest relief examined in Section 12.12.

Impact for Scottish Property Investors
Given that Scottish Income Tax rates apply to rental or trading income received by a Scottish taxpayer, but UK Income Tax rates continue to apply to dividend or interest income, and CT rates are the same for

Scottish companies, the potential savings available to a Scottish taxpayer by using a property company are greater.

The maximum **additional** savings available to Scottish taxpayers using a property company, based on current rates for 2020/21, are set out below.

Taxable Income	Additional Saving
£40,000	£128
£50,000	£1,542
£60,000	£1,642
£75,000	£1,792
£100,000	£2,042
£125,000	£2,417
£150,000	£2,667
£200,000	£3,167

Remember that, for residential lettings, taxable income now means rental profits before interest.

The additional savings shown above should be added to the figures in the tables in Chapter 10 for scenarios where the individual has no taxable income from outside the company. For scenarios where the individual has taxable income from outside the company of £50,000 or more, the additional saving is equal to 1% of taxable income, plus a further 0.5% of any taxable income falling into the £100,000 to £125,000 bracket. The position in Section 10.17 (capital gains) will be unaltered, as Scottish taxpayers pay CGT at the same rates as other UK residents.

While the additional savings shown above are based on current rates, it is the differential between the Scottish and UK rates that leads to the extra saving, so it is reasonable to suppose similar levels of additional savings will be available in future years. In fact, if anything, the differential that creates these extra savings is likely to increase, leading to even greater savings for Scottish property investors using a company in future.

Profit Extraction for Scottish Property Company Owners
Generally, in most cases, the optimum profit extraction strategy for Scottish property company owners will be the same as anyone else.

However, the position will be different in a few cases because any salary falling into the income bracket between £43,430 and £50,000 will suffer Income Tax at 41%, whereas interest falling into this bracket would only suffer 20%, and dividends would only suffer 7.5%.

This means it will sometimes be more beneficial to restrict salary payments to a Scottish company owner to a lower level than the amounts recommended elsewhere in this guide (Sections 9.6, 10.15, and 12.10).

The position depends on the level of the company owner's other taxable income from outside the company, excluding dividends, interest, and other savings income. Where this income is:

- Less than the Scottish higher rate tax threshold of £43,430 any salary should generally be restricted to no more than the amount that brings the company owner's total taxable income excluding dividends, interest, and other savings income up to that amount
- Between £43,430 and £48,356 it will not usually be worth paying any salary
- Between £48,356 and £50,000 the position will depend on how much cash the company owner wishes to extract and whether the employment allowance is available: so you will have to do your sums
- £50,000 or more, the optimum profit extraction strategy will be the same as for other company owners.

The position may differ if the company owner is over state pension age and the employment allowance is available. Again, you will have to do your sums.

Chapter 16

Specialised Property Companies

16.1 PROPERTY MANAGEMENT COMPANIES

We have looked at the taxation status of property management companies a few times throughout this guide and it is now worth taking a look at how these companies might be used as a planning tool.

The objective of this type of planning is to reduce the tax burden on the income from your properties without having the problems inherent in putting the properties themselves into a company.

Example
Jonah has a large property portfolio generating annual gross rents of £500,000 and a taxable profit before interest of £350,000. He is therefore an additional rate taxpayer paying Income Tax at 45%.

He decides to sub-contract the management of his properties to a new property management company, Lomu Property Services Ltd.

The company charges Jonah 15% of the gross annual rents on the properties (£75,000) as a service charge for managing the portfolio. Naturally, the company also bears some of the expenses in running the portfolio, and these amount to £10,000.

Jonah will now have £65,000 less taxable income, thus reducing his annual Income Tax bill by £29,250. Meanwhile, Lomu Property Services Ltd will have an annual profit of £65,000 (the £75,000 service charge less £10,000 expenses), giving it a CT bill, at 19%, of £12,350. The overall net saving for Jonah and the company taken together is thus £16,900 (£29,250 – £12,350).

*As usual, it doesn't work so well if the company's profits are extracted. If Jonah follows the usual optimum profit extraction strategy (Section 9.6) and pays himself a salary of £8,788, the company's CT bill will be reduced to £10,680, leaving it with after-tax profits of £45,532 (£65,000 – £8,788 – £10,680), which he can take as a dividend. His salary and dividend together will give him additional Income Tax of £20,540 to pay. This means using the company will now have led to an overall net tax **cost** of £1,970 (£10,680 + £20,540 – £29,250).*

As we can see, this arrangement is generally only worthwhile if profits are retained within the company, perhaps for investment in its own portfolio at a later stage.

Wealth Warning 1

This type of arrangement is likely to attract close HMRC scrutiny and it is essential to ensure the commercial reality of the situation matches up to the tax planning.

Firstly, the amount of service charge levied by the company must not exceed a normal commercial rate for those services.

Secondly, for Jonah to claim a valid Income Tax deduction for these charges, he must be able to show they were incurred wholly and exclusively for the benefit of his property rental business. In other words, there must be a genuine provision of services by the company.

Wealth Warning 2

If the total level of service charges (and other fees, commission, or sales), being charged by the company exceeds the VAT registration threshold, it will need to register for and charge VAT at the standard rate of 20%.

If, as will often be the case, the individual landlord is unable to recover this VAT, it will completely undo the whole purpose of the exercise and could turn it into a costly mess!

The arrangement works best if there is a full-blown property management business, managing properties for a number of unconnected landlords on a fully commercial arm's length basis. The charges levied on the owner's property business should ideally be on the same terms as for other landlords using the same services, or perhaps at a discounted rate, if preferred, but certainly not at a higher rate.

Despite this, the company's total gross income will need to be kept below the VAT registration threshold unless the individual landlord who owns the company is fully taxable for VAT purposes. Generally, this would mean they only hold commercial property they have opted to tax, or holiday accommodation.

Tax Tip

Subject to the points set out above, greater tax savings may be possible if the property management company is owned by and/or employs the investor's spouse, partner, or other family members.

16.2   SUB-LETTING COMPANIES

You can reduce the amount of tax you pay personally by leasing property to your own company, which will then rent the property to your tenants.

This could be a useful way to reduce exposure to higher rate tax.

Example
Sarah has a salary of £35,000 and a small portfolio of residential property yielding total gross annual rental income of £30,000. She pays mortgage interest on her rental properties totalling £15,000 and other annual costs of £5,000, giving her a true rental profit of £10,000.

Due to the restrictions discussed (or should that be 'disgusting restrictions'?) in Section 12.12, Sarah's taxable rental profit is £25,000 (£30,000 – £5,000). At current rates (Appendix A), £15,000 of this falls into her basic rate band to be taxed at 20% and £10,000 will be taxed at 40%. She can then claim basic rate tax relief of £3,000 (£15,000 x 20%) in respect of her mortgage interest, leaving her with a net tax bill of £4,000 and after tax income from her property business of £6,000.

Instead of this, however, Sarah leases her properties to her company for £16,000 per year. She still pays the same amount of mortgage interest but her other annual costs fall to just £1,000, leaving her in a 'true' position of break even. Her taxable rental profit will now be £15,000 (£16,000 – £1,000), which will all be taxed at basic rate, meaning the tax relief on her mortgage interest will leave her with no tax to pay overall.

The company makes a rental profit of £10,000 (£30,000 rent received less lease payments of £16,000 and the remaining £4,000 of annual costs). After paying CT at 19%, it is left with an after tax profit of £8,100.

Sarah can take up to £2,000 of the company's after tax profit as a tax-free dividend but would suffer Income Tax at 32.5% on any excess. Alternatively, if she restricts her dividend to £2,000 and takes a salary of £7,531, the company's CT bill will be reduced to just £469 and her after tax income will total £6,519 (£2,000 + £7,531 – 40%).

Hence, depending on how much profit she extracts from the company, Sarah will end up somewhere between £519 and £2,100 better off overall.

This arrangement has some potential drawbacks. It may be necessary to get the mortgage lender's permission and this will not always be forthcoming. Legal advice is essential, meaning there could be significant professional costs involved that may outweigh the relatively small savings seen in the example (but could be worthwhile on a bigger scale).

Charges under the lease must not exceed a normal commercial 'arm's length' rate. It appears there is no problem with them being lower, however, which is good news since, where the lease has a 'net present value' in excess of £125,000, SDLT would normally be payable at 1% on the excess; although this threshold has been temporarily increased to £500,000 during the current SDLT 'holiday' ending on 31st March 2021 (see Section 8.9).

Chapter 17

Future Tax Changes

17.1 THE STORY SO FAR

In the seventeen years since I wrote the first edition of this guide, we have seen enormous changes to the UK tax system. In fact, if there is one thing the last seventeen years have taught us, it must surely be to take nothing for granted!

One might expect that the changes we have seen over the last seventeen years would have made an enormous difference to the question of whether it is beneficial to use a property company or not.

Not so! My main conclusion seventeen years ago was that a property investment company was of only marginal benefit unless the investor was prepared to reinvest their profits within the company over a long period of time. Seventeen years later, we still see that a property company is at its most beneficial when profits are reinvested within the company.

Admittedly, there is now little or no benefit for basic rate taxpayers in using a company: but there never was much benefit for them anyway. On the other hand, the interest relief restrictions now applying to individual landlords mean some benefit often remains for higher rate taxpayers even when all profits are being extracted from the company.

Nevertheless, despite all the changes over the last seventeen years, higher rate taxpayers remain in the same fundamental position: there are massive savings to be made by using a company as a long-term investment vehicle.

The question for us now is this: if the tax changes made over the last seventeen years have not altered the basic rationale behind using a property company, what is the likelihood that future changes will?

The Government always seems unhappy with the tax advantages enjoyed by private 'owner-managed' companies and appears to be constantly looking for ways to curtail those advantages. But they are hampered in this pursuit by their need to keep the UK's corporate tax regime competitive at an international level. Not to mention the need to stimulate the UK economy!

As a result, many previous proposals and rumoured 'crackdowns' have often come to nothing.

Nonetheless, with the country's finances now in a perilous state, it is highly likely that significant tax changes will take place in the years ahead. In this chapter, I am going to look at some of the potential changes, their probable impact on property companies, and the issue of whether using a property company will continue to save tax.

17.2   WHAT DOES THE FUTURE HOLD?

Future tax changes we already know about have been included throughout this guide, where appropriate. In his November 2020 autumn spending review, Chancellor Rishi Sunak also announced there will be modest increases in the main tax allowances, bands, and thresholds for 2021/22, based on the increase in the CPI for the year to September 2020 of 0.7%. Appendix A includes the relevant estimated figures, but these will make only a miniscule difference to the calculations we have seen throughout this guide, and will certainly not alter any of our conclusions.

Beyond these points, I can't see into the future any better than anyone else. Hence, what follows is mostly just speculation. However, when it comes to property tax, I can at least make a few educated guesses based on over thirty years experience of observing, and analysing, Government behaviour, and some knowledge of tax systems in other countries. Furthermore, it is clear there will be three key objectives driving Government decisions on tax in the years ahead:

i) The need to stimulate economic recovery in the short to medium term,
ii) The need to tackle the massive deficit created by the coronavirus crisis in the medium to long term, and
iii) The desire to win the next General Election

Two of these are essential; the third is purely political, although it will undoubtedly influence their behaviour, even if they dare not admit it (they never do). If Boris was writing a one-line memo to Rishi, it would read like this, "I want you stimulate the economy, raise revenues, and win the next election." It's a tall order, but I'm sure Rishi will try his best. Over the next few sections, I will look at some of the things he might do to try to achieve these partly contradictory goals.

Across the Board Increases

Election manifesto promises can now be safely abandoned due to 'exceptional circumstances', so we are likely to see 'across the board' tax increases in the years ahead. The first objective above means most of these are likely to be delayed a while, and the third means they will be as subtle as the Government can make them. All taxes are potential candidates for increases; I don't think any of them can be ruled out. The Government will no doubt spout comments about 'fairness' and the need for 'those with the broadest shoulders to bear the greatest burden', so increases in the higher and additional rates of Income Tax seem highly likely.

However, the simple fact is an increase in the basic rate of Income Tax is the simplest, quickest and best way for the Government to raise large amounts of extra revenue. I don't think we'll see it for a couple of years (objective (i)) and it will probably not be more than one or two percentage points (objective (iii)), but it must be a strong possibility.

Taken in isolation, increases in Income Tax rates would make a property company more attractive but, as we will see in Section 17.5, these are likely to be accompanied by increases in the CT rate which, in effect, will restore the position to where we are now: remember it is the **differential** between the corporate and personal tax regimes that determines whether a property company is beneficial.

17.3   CAPITAL GAINS TAX CHANGES

For those who've never heard of the Office for Tax Simplification ('OTS'), it really is an actual Government department, not something out of George Orwell's '1984'.

In a report published in November 2020, the OTS made a number of recommendations in response to a request from the Chancellor asking them to review CGT and, in particular, what according to him, are the 'historically low rates' (he has a short memory: until 2008, higher rate taxpayers often paid an effective rate of 10% on non-residential property and 24% on other long-term investments).

It is worth examining the OTS's main recommendations and their potential impact on the issue of whether using a property company will save tax. However, it is important to stress the Government is not committed to following the OTS recommendations and indeed has chosen not to implement many other measures they have recommended in the past. In essence, therefore, these recommendations are only an indicator of what might happen and are far from certain of being implemented. Furthermore, many commentators believe any changes to CGT are unlikely to take place until at least 2023 at the earliest.

The OTS's first main recommendation was that CGT rates should be aligned nearer to Income Tax rates, but with some relief for the effects of inflation, OR there should be a clearer definition of the boundary between what is income, and therefore subject to Income Tax; and what is a capital gain subject to CGT.

Many people see this as a clear signal that CGT rates will be increased to the same level as Income Tax. However, that is not what the OTS actually said. Nonetheless, an increase in CGT rates does seem probable. The OTS also recommended the annual CGT exemption should be reduced, perhaps to something more like £5,000 (instead of the current £12,300).

If the Government were to follow these recommendations, this would mean an increase in the tax burden on individual investors selling property they hold directly, and also on company owners selling shares in their property company.

Increases in CGT would not directly affect capital gains arising within companies, although the OTS has suggested it would also be necessary to look at introducing anti-avoidance legislation to prevent people avoiding CGT by holding assets through companies. Hopefully, any such legislation would include an exemption for 'business use' that covers rental properties in the same way as the ATED exemption (Section 15.6).

Hence, overall, these recommendations would make a property company more beneficial throughout its life, but would increase the tax burden on the investor's eventual exit from the company via a winding up or sale.

The OTS also recommends there should be fewer CGT rates (see Section 7.2), although they appear to be talking about eliminating the lower rates for basic rate taxpayers rather than the higher rates for residential property.

Another recommendation is the abolition of the 'uplift on death', especially in cases where property is exempt from IHT (e.g. a transfer to a spouse). This would eliminate the potential drawback to using a property company discussed in Section 15.7.

The OTS recommends business asset disposal relief (Section 7.3) should be either abolished or linked to retirement. This will only affect those with trading businesses or furnished holiday lets and, if no other changes are made to the relief, will probably have a broadly neutral impact on the issue of whether using a property company is beneficial.

In summary, we are likely to see increases in CGT. Taken in isolation, without corresponding increases in CT on capital gains, these will probably only serve to make property companies more beneficial, although the cost of winding up or selling the company will also increase.

If CGT rates are to increase, it may make sense to 'crystallise' capital gains by triggering a CGT liability now, at current rates. One way to do that is to transfer properties into a company, which makes the 'window of opportunity' discussed in Section 14.22 even more valuable.

Better still, where incorporation relief is available, you may be able to get a 'step up' in the base cost of your properties, thus eliminating the existing capital gains on them, without incurring any CGT liability (see Sections 14.9 and 14.16 for details).

17.4   NATIONAL INSURANCE FOR TRADERS

NI is a prime candidate for increases for a number of reasons. Firstly, it's got form. When Gordon Brown was Chancellor, he needed to raise extra money for the NHS. Rather than increase Income Tax, he put an extra percentage point on all the main NI rates. The parallel with the current situation is obvious.

Secondly, NI is not paid by millions of people over state pension age, many of whom are Conservative voters. Need I say more?

Thirdly, when announcing the SEISS grant (see Section 10.2), the Chancellor made it clear that, if the self-employed were to get the same level of support as employees, they would be expected to contribute at the same level in the future.

The implication is clear: we can expect to see increases in the rate of Class 4 NI. How far it will go is debatable. Philip Hammond tried to get it to 11%. He failed, but Rishi faces very different circumstances now. It could be aligned with employee's Class 1 NI at 12% (or whatever rate Class 1 might be increased to in the future); or the Chancellor might go even further: remember employment income effectively suffers an overall combined rate of 25.8% (see Section 9.2).

Any increase in Class 4 NI will make a property company more attractive to anyone with a property trade, but will have no impact on landlords with property rental income.

17.5   CORPORATE TAX INCREASES

I have seen it suggested that the CT rate will be increased to 24% at some stage in the medium term future. However, this is probably no more than speculation.

Modest increases of a few percentage points seem more likely to me. Beyond that, the Government will watch what other countries are doing, as they will not wish to make the UK uncompetitive. This need to remain competitive is what generally keeps the CT rate in check, although a form of 'regressive' taxation with a higher rate on, say, the first £250,000 of profit, cannot be ruled out. This wouldn't bother the multinationals and hence wouldn't affect the UK's competitive position, but would raise extra tax on small companies operating in the UK.

Increases in Income Tax rates on dividends are also probable, especially as the Government will wish to maintain some sort of balance between the tax burden on self-employed sole traders or business partners, and small private company owners, when it increases the rate of Class 4 NI (see Section 17.4).

Naturally any increases in the CT rate or Income Tax rates on dividends will make a property company less attractive and reduce the potential savings available. However, as stated in the Foreword, it is the differential between the corporate and personal tax regimes that determines whether a property company is beneficial.

Hence, if increases in CT or dividend taxes are accompanied by similar increases in the main Income Tax rates, which I think is likely (see Section 17.2), then the overall tax-saving potential of a property company will be broadly unaltered.

17.6   WEALTH AND PROPERTY TAXES

Many commentators expect to see increases in wealth and property taxes. Could SDLT go any higher than the prohibitive rates we already expect to be reintroduced after the current 'holiday' period? Personally, I find the idea of even higher rates preposterous, but it can't be ruled out.

Could ATED (Section 15.6) be extended to all residential property; or all property; or all assets? Not impossible, other countries have wealth taxes along these lines.

These measures will not affect the tax-saving potential of property companies if they are applied equally to all property (or all residential property), whether held by an individual or by a company.

17.7   TARGETED TAX INCREASES

One way for the Government to balance the second and third (rather contradictory) objectives in Section 17.2 is to apply targeted tax increases to 'unpopular' business sectors. In this way, they can raise tax without losing too many votes. Sadly, as every reader will know, one of their favourite targets over recent years has been residential landlords. I'd hate to see any of this but here are some of the things we might see:

- Income Tax or CGT surcharges (there is *effectively* already an 8% CGT surcharge on residential property)
- Complete abolition of relief for interest and finance costs for residential landlords
- Extension of NI to rental income. However, this would be a complex issue for the Government to tackle, as it would mean reclassifying the nature of rental income and rental businesses, and could cost them as much in other tax reliefs as it raises in NI. For this reason, such a change seems unlikely in the foreseeable future
- Extension of VAT to residential property letting and sales (if that sounds ridiculous, it's worth noting VAT applies to residential property in many European countries)

These measures would all serve to make a property company more attractive (except for VAT on residential property, which would apply to individual landlords and property investment companies equally). However, it is also possible we could see measures specifically targeted at residential landlords operating through companies, such as abolishing:

- Relief for qualifying loan interest on funds borrowed to invest in a company engaged in residential property letting
- Incorporation relief on the transfer of a residential property business into a company
- The partnership exemption for SDLT on residential property

Beyond these points, the question of whether any further attacks might occur really depends on whether the UK Government genuinely believes the terrible damage it is doing to the private rented sector is somehow justified, or unimportant, or whether their peculiar stance on the issue is just political rhetoric. They seem unable to understand the modern private rented sector is a professional business sector providing a valuable service to the general public: a home!

You could manufacture weapons that kill people and get full interest relief, but provide them with a home and you do not!

If the Government genuinely cannot see further attacks on the private rented sector will lead to big increases in homelessness, bankruptcies, and many other problems, they could go further. Who knows what other evil plans they might have in store for the private rented sector?

However, when it comes to corporate residential letting businesses, the Government seems to have a desire to favour large, institutional investors, in the mistaken belief that bigger somehow means better (ignoring the many lessons throughout history that tell us, quite emphatically, this is not always the case!)

So, any further action they might take would probably be targeted at smaller, privately owned companies. This, I think, is where they have struggled to figure out how to target their attacks in the way they desire. But, if they can resolve that problem, they might consider:

- A CT supplement on residential letting profits and capital gains, and/or
- Withdrawal of interest relief for CT purposes on residential letting businesses

Such measures would dramatically reduce the benefit of using a company for a residential property letting business and, unfortunately, under current circumstances, anything is possible.

17.8   IN CONCLUSION

Most of the potential tax changes examined in this chapter would either make a property company more beneficial, have no effect, or be counterbalanced by corresponding changes to the personal tax regime.

Hence, despite the possibility of targeted tax increases, it is worth remembering what I said at the start of this chapter: if the tax changes made over the last seventeen years have not altered the basic rationale behind using a property company, what is the likelihood that future changes will?

Generally speaking, what the Government seems most intent on attacking is not small companies themselves, but rather small company owners who simply use their company as a means to save tax on what, in reality, is effectively just personal income.

Hence, while we have no idea what future tax changes lie ahead, it nevertheless seems probable that any changes we may see are likely to simply reinforce the conclusion that a property company is only really beneficial when a significant proportion of its profits are being retained and reinvested each year.

While the Treasury can be expected to eat into your savings to some extent, my feeling is, whatever changes we may see, property companies are likely to remain beneficial to higher rate taxpayers who wish to make long-term property investments and build up a property business over a number of years.

And long may it continue!

Appendix A

UK Tax Rates and Allowances: 2019/20 to 2021/22

	Rates	2019/20 £	2020/21 £	2021/22(1) £
Income Tax (2)				
Personal allowance		12,500	12,500	12,590
Basic rate band	20%	37,500	37,500	37,760
Higher rate/Threshold	40%	50,000	50,000	50,350
Personal allowance withdrawal				
Effective rate/From	60%	100,000	100,000	100,000
To		125,000	125,000	125,180
Additional rate/Threshold	45%	150,000	150,000	150,000
Starting rate band (3)	0%	5,000	5,000	5,000
Personal savings allowance(4)		1,000	1,000	1,000
Dividend allowance		2,000	2,000	2,000
Marriage allowance (5)		1,250	1,250	1,259
National Insurance				
Primary Threshold	9%/12%	8,632	9,500	9,550
Secondary Threshold	13.8%	8,632	8,788	8,840
Upper earnings limit	2%	50,000	50,000	50,350
Employment allowance		3,000	4,000	4,000
Class 2 per week		3.00	3.05	3.05
Small profits threshold		6,365	6,475	6,525
Pension Contributions				
Annual allowance		40,000	40,000	40,000
Lifetime allowance		1.055m	1.0731m	1.0806m
Capital Gains Tax				
Annual exemption		12,000	12,300	12,400
Corporation Tax Rate		19%	19%	19%
VAT Threshold		85,000	85,000	85,000

Notes
1. Estimated, based on CPI inflation of 0.7%
2. Different rates and thresholds apply to Scottish taxpayers (except on interest, savings, and dividend income, and on capital gains)
3. Applies to interest and savings income only
4. Halved for higher rate taxpayers; not available to additional rate taxpayers
5. Available where neither spouse/civil partner pays higher rate tax

Appendix B

Connected Persons

The definition of 'connected persons' differs slightly from one area of UK tax law to another. Generally, however, for the purposes of the issues discussed in this guide, an individual's connected persons include the following:

i)   Their husband, wife or civil partner
ii) The following relatives:
   o   Mother, father or remoter ancestor
   o   Son, daughter or remoter descendant
   o   Brother or sister

iii) Relatives under (ii) above of the individual's spouse or civil partner
iv) Spouses or civil partners of the individual's relatives under (ii) above
v)   Spouses or civil partners of an individual under (iii) above
vi) The individual's business partners and their:
   o   Spouses or civil partners
   o   Relatives (as defined under (ii) above)

vii) Trusts where the individual is:
   o   The settlor (the person who set up the trust or transferred property, other assets, or funds into it), or
   o   A person 'connected' (as defined in this appendix) with the settlor

viii) Companies under the control of the individual, either alone, or together with persons under (i) to (vii) above

ix) Companies under the control of the individual acting together with one or more other persons

Retail Prices Index 1982 to 2017

	1982	1983	1984	1985	1986	1987	1988	1989
Jan		82.61	86.84	91.20	96.25	100.0	103.3	111.0
Feb		82.97	87.20	91.94	96.60	100.4	103.7	111.8
Mar	79.44	83.12	87.48	92.80	96.73	100.6	104.1	112.3
Apr	81.04	84.28	88.64	94.78	97.67	101.8	105.8	114.3
May	81.62	84.64	88.97	95.21	97.85	101.9	106.2	115.0
Jun	81.85	84.84	89.20	95.41	97.79	101.9	106.6	115.4
Jul	81.88	85.30	89.10	95.23	97.52	101.8	106.7	115.5
Aug	81.90	85.68	89.94	95.49	97.82	102.1	107.9	115.8
Sep	81.85	86.06	90.11	95.44	98.30	102.4	108.4	116.6
Oct	82.26	86.36	90.67	95.59	98.45	102.9	109.5	117.5
Nov	82.66	86.67	90.95	95.92	99.29	103.4	110.0	118.5
Dec	82.51	86.89	90.87	96.05	99.62	103.3	110.3	118.8

	1990	1991	1992	1993	1994	1995	1996	1997
Jan	119.5	130.2	135.6	137.9	141.3	146.0	150.2	154.4
Feb	120.2	130.9	136.3	138.8	142.1	146.9	150.9	155.0
Mar	121.4	131.4	136.7	139.3	142.5	147.5	151.5	155.4
Apr	125.1	133.1	138.8	140.6	144.2	149.0	152.6	156.3
May	126.2	133.5	139.3	141.1	144.7	149.6	152.9	156.9
Jun	126.7	134.1	139.3	141.0	144.7	149.8	153.0	157.5
Jul	126.8	133.8	138.8	140.7	144.0	149.1	152.4	157.5
Aug	128.1	134.1	138.9	141.3	144.7	149.9	153.1	158.5
Sep	129.3	134.6	139.4	141.9	145.0	150.6	153.8	159.3
Oct	130.3	135.1	139.9	141.8	145.2	149.8	153.8	159.5
Nov	130.0	135.6	139.7	141.6	145.3	149.8	153.9	159.6
Dec	129.9	135.7	139.2	141.9	146.0	150.7	154.4	160.0

	1998	1999	2000	2001	2002	2003	2004	2005
Jan	159.5	163.4	166.6	171.1	173.3	178.4	183.1	188.9
Feb	160.3	163.7	167.5	172.0	173.8	179.3	183.8	189.6
Mar	160.8	164.1	168.4	172.2	174.5	179.9	184.6	190.5
Apr	162.6	165.2	170.1	173.1	175.7	181.2	185.7	191.6
May	163.5	165.6	170.7	174.2	176.2	181.5	186.5	192.0
Jun	163.4	165.6	171.1	174.4	176.2	181.3	186.8	192.2
Jul	163.0	165.1	170.5	173.3	175.9	181.3	186.8	192.2
Aug	163.7	165.5	170.5	174.0	176.4	181.6	187.4	192.6
Sep	164.4	166.2	171.7	174.6	177.6	182.5	188.1	193.1
Oct	164.5	166.5	171.6	174.3	177.9	182.6	188.6	193.3
Nov	164.4	166.7	172.1	173.6	178.2	182.7	189.0	193.6
Dec	164.4	167.3	172.2	173.4	178.5	183.5	189.9	194.1

	2006	2007	2008	2009	2010	2011	2012	2013
Jan	193.4	201.6	209.8	210.1	217.9	229.0	238.0	245.8
Feb	194.2	203.1	211.4	211.4	219.2	231.3	239.9	247.6
Mar	195.0	204.4	212.1	211.3	220.7	232.5	240.8	248.7
Apr	196.5	205.4	214.0	211.5	222.8	234.4	242.5	249.5
May	197.7	206.2	215.1	212.8	223.6	235.2	242.4	250.0
Jun	198.5	207.3	216.8	213.4	224.1	235.2	241.8	249.7
Jul	198.5	206.1	216.5	213.4	223.6	234.7	242.1	249.7
Aug	199.2	207.3	217.2	214.4	224.5	236.1	243.0	251.0
Sep	200.1	208.0	218.4	215.3	225.3	237.9	244.2	251.9
Oct	200.4	208.9	217.7	216.0	225.8	238.0	245.6	251.9
Nov	201.1	209.7	216.0	216.6	226.8	238.5	245.6	252.1
Dec	202.7	210.9	212.9	218.0	228.4	239.4	246.8	253.4

	2014	2015	2016	2017
Jan	252.6	255.4	258.8	265.5
Feb	254.2	256.7	260.0	268.4
Mar	254.8	257.1	261.1	269.3
Apr	255.7	258.0	261.4	270.6
May	255.9	258.5	262.1	271.7
Jun	256.3	258.9	263.1	272.3
Jul	256.0	258.6	263.4	272.9
Aug	257.0	259.8	264.4	274.7
Sep	257.6	259.6	264.9	275.1
Oct	257.7	259.5	264.8	275.3
Nov	257.1	259.8	265.5	275.8
Dec	257.5	260.6	267.1	278.1

Abbreviations Used in this Guide

ADS	Additional Dwelling Supplement
ATED	Annual Tax on Enveloped Dwellings
CGT	Capital Gains Tax
CPI	Consumer Prices Index
CT	Corporation Tax
CTSA	Corporation Tax Self Assessment
EBITDA	Earnings before Interest, Tax, Depreciation and Amortisation
GAAP	Generally Accepted Accounting Principles
HMRC	HM Revenue and Customs
ICAEW	Institute of Chartered Accountants in England and Wales
IFRS	International Financial Reporting Standards
IHT	Inheritance Tax
LBTT	Land and Buildings Transaction Tax
LLP	Limited Liability Partnership
Ltd	Limited
LTT	Land Transaction Tax
LTV	Loan-to-value
MTD	Making Tax Digital
NI	National Insurance
OTS	Office for Tax Simplification
PAYE	Pay As You Earn
PLC	Public Limited Company
SBA	Structures and Buildings Allowance
SDLT	Stamp Duty Land Tax
SEISS	Self-Employed Income Support Scheme
UK	United Kingdom
VAT	Value Added Tax